Georges Bernage

The Red Berets in Normandy

5 - 6 June 1944

HEIMDAL

– Conceived and written by Georges Bernage.

– Edited by Georges Bernage.

– Translated by William Jordan.

– Maps by Bernard Paich.

– Design by Erik Groult and Francine Gautier.

– Composition and layout by Christel Lebret.

– Photoengraving by Christian Caira, Philippe Gazagne.

– Computer graphics by Philippe Gazagne.

– Archive material from Bundesarchiv Koblenz,
   Imperial War Museum, London.

Acknowledgements :

– Louis Adelin.
– Ludovic Louis.
– Louis Jaquinot.
– Bertrand Paris.
– Philippe Wirton.
– Mark Worthington.

IWM

Editions Heimdal
Château de Damigny - BP 61350 - 14406 BAYEUX Cedex
Tél. : 02.31.51.68.68 - Fax : 02.31.51.68.60 - E-mail : Editions.Heimdal@wanadoo.fr

ISBN 2 84048 159 6

Contents

Preface

April 2002

It is a privilege for me to write a foreword to a book such as this. When I open thte pages it brings back memories to me of days now far away and long ago when the British, Canadian and American troops landed on the coast of France, aided by the French Resistance, to restore the liberty, not only of France but the world as a whole.

I am told I am now the only Brigade Commander, British, Canadian or American who commanded a Brigade on D-Day who is still alive. In consequence I know many of those mentioned in the book, many of whom have now passed on to higher things, but the memory of their indomitable spirit still lives.

This spirit is responsible for the close links that now exist between members of the 6th Airborne Division and the people of Normandy who suffered so grievously as a result of the invasion.

Anyone wishing to learn about that operation carried out on 6th June 1944 and the problems involved, and inhale the atmosphere, will do well to read the book and enjoy the excellent photographs. I congratulate the author, Georges Bernage on producing such a graphic and accurate picture of the whole scene.

Brigadier James Hill
Commander *3rd Parachute Brigade*
6th Airborne Division
D-Day 1944

1944

2001

Préface

Ce remarquable ouvrage est dédié à la 6ᵉ Airborne Division Britannique. L'historique de sa création, le détail de son organisation et de sa composition, le récit des préparatifs d'« Overlord » et le déroulement des premières heures en Normandie le 6 juin 1944… tout est passionnant et parfaitement documenté.

Premier commandant en 1941 des troupes aéroportées britanniques le Général Browning va insuffler le style de ces troupes d'élite. Son épouse, Lady Browning, la célèbre romancière Daphnée du Maurier choisit l'emblème « le cheval Pegase » et le célèbre béret rouge… le « Parachute Regiment » est né…

Les chefs qui mènent au combat la 6ᵉ Airborne Division sont tous de grande qualité et leurs noms sont devenus familiers aux Normands… auprès desquels ils ont toujours trouvé, et encore aujourd'hui, reconnaissance et chaleureuse amitié.

C'est avec une grande émotion que nous revivons les heures de la nuit du 5 au 6 juin 1944 lorsque les « éclaireurs » repèrent les terrains de posé des planeurs et que les hommes des « coups de main » sur les ponts et sur la batterie de Merville se répandent entre Caen et la mer, écrivant ainsi l'une des pages les plus glorieuses de la Deuxième Guerre mondiale.

Monsieur le Ministre Triboulet a été l'intigateur du musée de Bénouville puis de son héritage le Mémorial Pégasus de Ranville dont la mission principale est de rendre hommage aux « diables rouges » et de conserver précieusement le souvenir de leurs exploits et de leurs sacrifices pour que triomphe la liberté !

Amiral Christian Brac de la Perrière
Président du Comité
du Département

Prologue

The present work is a summary of the organisation and commitment to battle of 6th Airborne Division during its critical role in the Battle of Normandy. It is based on the works listed below as well as on eyewitness accounts of veterans who have spoken to the author : Bill Millin, John Howard, Geoffrey Sneezum, Hans von Luck, Gerhardt Bandomir and others.

In June 1940 the United Kingdom was still without a paratroop force. Churchill ordered one to be formed without delay, and after a difficult start, its first, limited action was launched on 10th February 1941. 1st Parachute Brigade was formed in September 1941 . An early raid into Normandy took place against the radar station at Bruneval on 27th February 1942, led by Major J.C.A.Frost. Then there would be large scale engagements by British paratroops in North Africa and in Sicily. On 6th June 1944, 6th Airborne Division was entrusted with a crucial mission for the D-Day Landings, and there would be heavy casualties to realise it. On the opposite page and at the end of the book all those killed in the Division, and their last resting place are listed. We wish to acknowledge the many years of research which Ludovic Louis has put into establishing this list of the fallen : this work is written in their memory.

Georges Bernage

Bibliography

- Peter Harclerode, « *Go to it* », *The Illustrated History of the 6th Airborne Division*, Caxton Editions, London, 1990. This is the most thorough and detailed work on the engagements of the division in Normandy. The present work is deeply endebted to this book, particularly its second part.

- Major-General Julian Thompson, *Ready for anything, the Parachute Regiment at war*, London, 1990. Full of interesting eyewitness accounts.

- Hilary St George Saunders, *The Red Beret*, The Battery Press, Nashville, 1985. One chapter is devoted to Normandy, with interesting eyewitness accounts.

- Georges Bernage et Jean-Pierre Benamou, *Pegasus Bridge*, Heimdal, Bayeux, 1993. A good source for eyewitness accounts, in part reused·in this work..

- Bill Millin, *La Cornemuse du D-Day*, Heimdal, Bayeux, 1994. An eyewitness account of his crossing of Pegasus Bridge.

- Allan Jefferson, *Assault on the guns of Merville,* John Murray, London, 1987. Highly detailed account of the Merville battery.

- Stephen E. Ambrose, *Pegasus Bridge 6 June 1944,* Allen & Unwin, London, 1984.

- George Chatterton, *The Wings of Pegasus*, The Battery Press, Nashville, 1982. Very interesting eyewitness account by Brigadier Chatterton of his Glider Pilot Regiment.

- Howard P. Davies, *British Parachute Forces*, Arms & Armour Press, London, 1974. Useful information on the paratroopers' equipment.

- Le roy Thompson, *British Paratroops in action*, Squadron/Signal Publications, Carrollton, Texas, 1989. A good follow-up to the preceding work.

- Brian L. Davis, *British Army Uniforms & Insignia of World War Two,* Arms & Armour Press, London, 1983.

6th ARMOURED RECCE CORPS RAC

Date	Matricule	Grade	Nom	Cimetiere
06/06/44	258144	Lieut.	BELCHER R C	Ranville, VIA-C-1.25
06/06/44	7947393	Tpr.	DONE M P	Ranville, VIA-C-1.25
06/06/44	420192	Cpl.	EARWICKER P T	Ranville, VIA-C-1.25
06/06/44	7903897	Tpr.	LAMONT G W	Ranville, VIA-C-1.25
06/06/44	7961412	Tpr.	WILSON A H	Ranville, VIA-C-1.25
15/06/44	14337734	Tpr.	FRIEND A J	Ranville, IIA-J-12
15/06/44	7920336	Tpr.	MUSGRAVE J E	Ranville, IIA-H-12
16/07/44	14200484	L/Cpl.	HARRINGTON E R	Ranville, IVA-N-19
10/08/44	7901228	Cpl.	ELSEY A J W	Ranville, VA-F-9
10/08/44	320940	Tpr.	HUNT W G	Ranville, VA-E-9
20/08/44	14431538	Tpr.	DAVEY F H	La Délivrande, 1-C-2
20/08/44	4622746	Tpr.	MARTIN A C	Putot En Auge, A-7
20/08/44	14525700	Tpr.	TONKS C	Putot En Auge, A-8
26/08/44	14429230	Tpr.	GREENWOOD R C	Saint Desir, III-D-3
21/12/44	7899663	Tpr.	HENDERSON J S	Wallasey, England 20-C-361

2nd AIR LANDING ANTI TANK BATTERY RA

Date	Matricule	Grade	Nom	Cimetiere
10/06/44	271123	Lieut.	BLOWER J W H,	Ranville Church, 2

3rd AIR LANDING ANTI TANK BATTERY RA

Date	Matricule	Grade	Nom	Cimetiere
06/06/44	14207549	Gnr.	NEWHAM F.	Saint Vaast En Auge, 4
06/06/44	5059287	Gnr.	STANLEY D.	Saint Vaast En Auge, 6
06/06/44	4924410	Bdr.	WHITNEY W.	Saint Vaast En Auge, 2
07/06/44	5059289	Gnr.	SHERRATT A.	Ranville, IVA-P-21
08/06/44	828195	Sgt.	HALL W.	Ranville, IA-L-7
09/06/44	1078297	Bdr.	BRADLEY W.	Ranville, IA-F-14
09/06/44	4927123	Sgt.	WEST W S L.	Ranville, IA-G-14
10/06/44	14200279	Gnr.	WALKER, M W R	Ranville, IVA-P-15
16/06/44	4924734	Gnr.	MILLWARD C	Ranville, IIA-B-11
07/08/44	14207891	Gnr.	PERKS G E	Ranville, IIA-D-11
07/08/44	4924673	Gnr.	HEWITT H C	Ranville, IA-P-1
19/08/44	14369541	Gnr.	SYKES J	Ranville, IIA-B-14
20/08/44	4928102	Gnr.	DYCHE A	La Délivrande, I-C-3
20/08/44	3532386	Gnr.	DUBOVITCH M	Ranville, IIA-F-9
20/08/44	554872	Sgt.	WOODWARD C	Ranville, IIA-F-4

4th AIRLANDING ANTI TANK BATTERY RA

Date	Matricule	Grade	Nom	Cimetiere
06/06/44	4924666	Bdr.	HILL J A	M.I.A. Bayeux, P.12C21
06/06/44	138059	Captain	KILBEY F A	Brucourt, 6
06/06/44	4924736	Bdr.	LANE A J	Brucourt, 3
06/06/44	14207469	Lieut.	LAZAROPOULO P	Brucourt, 5
06/06/44	247205	Gnr.	LYONS S A	Fecamp, R.2G.5
06/06/44	4914399	Bdr.	MACHIN J H	Banneville La Campagne, XVII-C-6
06/06/44	5126153	L/Sgt.	SIDNEY W	Ranville, VA-E-5
06/06/44	4928347	Sgt.	TAYLOR R K	Ranville, IX-C-15
06/06/44	4924404	Gnr.	WOODCOCK F L	Saint Desir, III-A-9
07/06/44	4924510	L/Sgt.	BYARD J H	Ranville, IA-D-22
07/06/44	4924643	L/Bdr.	GUEST A J	Ranville Church, 38
07/06/44	14375372	Gnr.	WAINWRIGHT J C	Ranville Church, 16
07/06/44	4924911	Bdr.	WILLIAMS W H	Ranville Church, 9
13/06/44	4924306	Gnr.	YATES J H	Ranville Church, 23
06/07/44	1086255	Gnr.	CRADDOCKR C	Ranville, IA-J-1
06/07/44	4923236	L/Sgt.	JAMES W	Ranville, IIIA-M-3
07/08/44	13068493	Gnr.	PORTMAN C E	Ranville, IIIA-N-3
07/08/44	14208580	Gnr.	RUSSELL A	Ranville, IVA-M-1
07/08/44		Gnr.	THOMAS F	Ranville, IVA-P-13

2nd LIGHT ANTI AIRCRAFT BATTERY RA

Date	Matricule	Grade	Nom	Cimetiere
06/06/44	14622085	Gnr.	DAVENPORT, A	Hermanville, 3-D-12
06/06/44	11055877	Gnr.	DIX, G R	M.I.A. Bayeux, P.11C.2
06/06/44	14503901	Pte.	GRANT W	Hermanville, 3-D-6
06/06/44	1639019	Gnr.	NUTLAND F	M.I.A. Bayeux, P.11C.2
06/06/44	1807362	Gnr.	SIMMONS D	Tilly Sur Seulles, I-D-5
06/06/44	1829314	Gnr.	SMITH A	M.I.A. Bayeux, P.11C.2

53rd (THE WORCESTERSHIRE YEOMANRY) AIR LANDING LIGHT REGIMENT RA

Date	Matricule	Grade	Nom	Cimetiere
05/06/44	949424	Bdr.	HALL H	Ranville Church, 19
06/06/44	828108	Gnr.	DENNISON R T	Bayeux, II-D-18
06/06/44	913299	L/Bdr.	RODWELL K S	M.I.A. Bayeux, P.11C.2
06/06/44	907192	Gnr.	RUSSELL J	M.I.A. Bayeux, P.11C.2
10/06/44	302589	Lieut.	BARRAS A M	Hermanville, 1-H-4
12/06/44	204182	Captain	WARD H W	Breville
17/06/44	2694102	Sgt.	PATERSON A	La Delivrande, I-A-1
30/06/44	137894	Captain	STONE C E	Ranville, IIIA-E-9
05/07/44	1136505	Gnr.	BOWERS D W	Ranville, IIIA-C-7
07/07/44	145786	Gnr.	THOMPSON A	Codington, England
12/07/44	1458677	L/Bdr.	BRYANT C H	Ranville, IVA-M-19
11/08/44	14567585	Gnr.	ANDERSON D J T	Ranville, VA-P-9
11/08/44	984546	L/Bdr.	FOSTER W R	Ranville, VA-G-9
11/08/44	14292566	Gnr.	McWILLIAMS J	Ranville, IA-G-4
11/08/44	1082638	Bdr.	PEERS F L	Ranville, VA-H-9
11/08/44	889214	L/Bdr.	SNOWDEN B	Ranville, VA-J-9
12/08/44	7583798	W.O.1	PIRKIS S H B	Ranville, IA-K-4

3rd PARACHUTE SQUADRON RE

Date	Matricule	Grade	Nom	Cimetiere
06/06/44	1876755	Spr.	MATHESON J A	Ranville, IA-D-6
06/06/44	14317166	Spr.	ROBINSON P	Ranville Church, 37
07/06/44	2008277	Sgt.	JONES G L	Ranville, IA-H-21
10/06/44	2058281	L/Cpl.	GILLOTT L E W	Ranville, IA-K-3
10/06/44	14592382	Spr.	WHYBROW E H	Ranville, IA-J-3
11/06/44	5437032	Spr.	PERRY L R	Ranville, IA-F-3
13/06/44	14531450	L/Cpl.	GILL W R	Ranville, IA-B-20
22/06/44	2078134	Cpl.	GREEN A F	Ranville, IIA-E-6
28/06/44	100294	Captain	JUCKES T R	Ranville, IIIA-H-9
29/07/44	1871964	Cpl.	ROWBOTHAM H.	Ranville, IA-A-16
10/08/44	14356345	Spr.	BENSON J	Ranville, IA-E-6
10/08/44	14534163	Spr.	CROSS S J	Ranville, VA-L-9
10/08/44	2129806	Spr.	DIXON J A	Ranville, VA-K-9
10/08/44	956218	Dvr.	KERRY H R	Ranville, VA-M-9
14/08/44	14647568	Pte.	HICKS A P	Ranville, VA-N-9

591st PARACHUTE SQUADRON RE

Date	Matricule	Grade	Nom	Cimetiere
06/06/44	14404888	Spr.	AUSTIN A E	Bayeux, XXVIII-H-21
06/06/44	1878189	L/Cpl.	BRANSTON K W	Ranville, IVA-D-20
06/06/44	2116526	Spr.	EVANS J J	Ranville, IIIA-D-3.8
06/06/44	882124	L/Cpl.	FRASER T A	Ranville, IIIA-F-2
06/06/44	1944972	Cpl.	KELLY W A	Ranville, IVA-C-20
06/06/44	14283438	Dvr.	THOMPSON G L	Ranville, IIIA-E-2
06/06/44	14537569	Spr.	WHEELER D H	Ranville, IIIA-C-2
06/06/44	14422902	Spr.	WOLFE F	Ranville, VA-D-3.8
06/06/44	1877562	Spr.	YOUELL J	M.I.A. Bayeux, P.12C. 1
07/06/44	1902204	Dvr.	HANDLEY A	Ranville, VA-D-2
07/06/44	14550031	L/Cpl.	REARDON-PARKER J	Ranville, IA-A-21
09/06/44	1906629	Spr.	HART L J W	Ranville, IA-A-17
09/06/44	1896838	L/Cpl.	WHALE F T	Ranville, IA-E-14
10/06/44	5958958	Spr.	KERRY G E	Ranville, IA-E-22
10/06/44	1953107	Dvr.	PALIN G I	M.I.A Bayeux, P.12C.1
11/06/44	6982922	Spr.	COYLE P	Ranville, IIA-G-11
17/06/44	261519	Lieut.	WHARTON G	Ranville, IVA-O-15
24/07/44	278782	Lieut.	SHAND L P	Ranville, IVA-C-14
21/08/44	271173	Lieut.	McCRIRICK P R H	

249th FIELD COMPANY RE

Date	Matricule	Grade	Nom	Cimetiere
09/06/44	2127012	Spr.	GILES F	Ranville, IVA-P-11
09/06/44	1878171	Spr.	McCULLOUGH C J	Ranville, IA-C-18
10/06/44	14663366	W.O.II (CSM)	ALEXANDER A W	Ranville, IVA-O-11
	2025851		ISAAC R	Hermanville, I-H-13

286th FIELD PARK COMPANY RE

Date	Matricule	Grade	Nom	Cimetiere
06/06/44	214389	Lieut.	REID N W	Ranville Church, 8
07/06/44	2090505	Dvr.	GIBBONS E J	M.I.A. Bayeux, P.12C.1
07/06/44	3915974	Spr.	POWELL R	M.I.A. Bayeux, P.12C.1
20/06/44	2003759	Dvr.	ALDOUS W T	Ranville, II-A-J-2
20/06/44	2003215	Cpl.	CUTTING C T	Ranville, II-A-H-2
21/06/44	2193605	Cpl.	McDONALD K A G	Bayeux, IIIA-H-2
02/09/44	14389512	Spr.	GARNER L	Bayeux, VIII-B-20

ATTACHED TO HQ RE 6th AIRBORNE DIVISION

Date	Matricule	Grade	Nom	Cimetiere
06/06/44	1876309	Spr.	GUARD P	Ranville, IVA-B-20

Date	Number	Name	Rank	Location
09/06/44	14301206	KARSTON F J	L/Cpl.	Ranville, IVA-M-8
09/06/44	14575087	SCOTT P W	Pte.	Ranville, IIIA-B-14
08/08/44	14566139	MORRIS D J	Pte.	Ranville, IA-J-10
25/08/44	6202041	KAITS H	Pte.	Beuzeville, 1

RAMC ATTACHED TO THE AIRBORNE FORCES

Date	Number	Name	Rank	Location
06/06/44	7263936	HARRIS G	Sgt.	La Delivrande, IX-A-9
19/08/44	246603	HOLTAN R S	Captain	Villeneuve Saint Georges, 144
07/06/44	167788	MAITLAND R R	Major	Ranville Church, 48
07/06/44	97002801	VENTHAM T C J	Pte.	Ranville, VA-M-2

ROYAL ARMY ORDNANCE CORPS RAOC

Date	Number	Name	Rank	Location
30/06/44	14425232	ALLEN R G	Pte.	Bootle Cemetery, England, 7E-3541

6th AIRBORNE DIVISION RASC

Date	Number	Name	Rank	Location
07/06/44	S/107821	CANE W T	Sgt.	Southampton (Hollybrook), England, M12-129A
07/06/44	S/6403808	PIPER W P	Pte.	Ranville, IVA-E-20
12/06/44	S/221620	REDDALL A L	Cpl.	Herouvillette, 21
19/06/44	T/132867	WADE B	Cpl.	Ranville, IA-M-8
23/06/44	T/138083	NAYLOR R S	Cpl.	Ranville, IIA-L-1

63rd DIVISIONAL COMPOSITE COMPANY RASC

Date	Number	Name	Rank	Location
06/06/44	T/766783	STANNARD A	Cpl.	M.I.A. Bayeux, P.18-C.2
07/06/44	T/155690	BUTCHER, A L	Cpl.	Hermanville, 1-P-9
07/06/44	T/14389025	CORDELL A	Dvr.	Tilly Sur Seulles, III-A-7
07/06/44	T/14520895	DALBY J A	Dvr.	Hermanville, 1-D-4
07/06/44	T/14432248	McNALLY P	Dvr.	M.I.A. Bayeux, P.18-C.2
07/06/44	T/143830	O'LOUGHNANE B T	Dvr.	M.I.A. Bayeux, P.18-C.2
07/06/44	T/13095766	ROE D E	Dvr.	M.I.A. Bayeux, P.18-C.3
07/06/44	T/269383	SMITH D J	Dvr.	Hermanville, 1-W-7
07/06/44	T/497423	TURNER R	Dvr.	Hermanville, 1-P-6
07/06/44	T/5781266	WILLIAMS A G O	L/Cpl.	Hermanville, 3-F-12
07/06/44	T/221303	WOOLLARD S	Cpl.	M.I.A. Bayeux, P.18-C.2

398th COMPOSITE COMPANY RASC

Date	Number	Name	Rank	Location
06/06/44	T/10707464	PARKER F W	Dvr.	M.I.A. Bayeux, P.18-C.2
06/06/44	T/14637268	SMURTHWAITE W T	Dvr.	M.I.A. Bayeux, P.18-C.3
07/06/44	T/14664227	EDDINGTON B H	Dvr.	M.I.A. Bayeux, P.18-C.2
13/06/44	T/14306001	APPLETON R J	Dvr.	Ranville, IIIA-J-5
13/06/44	T/10688761	MASON J C	Dvr.	Ranville, IIIA-K-5
13/06/44	T/4623236	ORTON J W	Dvr.	Ranville, IA-E-6
13/06/44	T/144705	SPROSON J	Dvr.	Ranville, IIIA-M-5
13/06/44	T/153979	VAUGHAN W H T	Dvr.	Ranville, IA-E-1
13/06/44	T/272064	WELLS J	Cpl.	Ranville, IIIA-L-5

716th LIGHT COMPOSITE COMPANY RASC

Date	Number	Name	Rank	Location
06/06/44	T/14425057	CANNING W	Dvr.	Ranville, IIA-H-10
06/06/44	S/14384200	FIELDER R E	Pte.	Ranville, VA-C-6
06/06/44	T/14310775	HARPER I R	Dvr.	Ranville, VA-E-3
06/06/44	T/14525058	HOSEGOOD B S	Cpl.	M.I.A. Bayeux, P.18-C.2
06/06/44	T/14427546	LUNN J W	Dvr.	Ranville, IX-A-34
06/06/44	T/273322	RIPO F	Dvr.	M.I.A. Bayeux, P.18-C.3
06/06/44	276553	SILVERT P	Lieut.	Ranville, IIA-A-18
07/06/44	T/207715	CRAWFORD F J	Cpl.	Bayeux, XI-C-1
07/06/44	T/14312052	McKEE, J E	Cpl.	Bayeux, X-L-2
08/06/44	T/14367919	COATES D W S	Dvr.	Herouvillette, 6
10/06/44	T/2050563	CURTIS S	Dvr.	Ranville, IA-J-14
22/06/44	T/2878789	DOCHERTY C	Dvr.	Hermanville, 1-E-6
22/06/44	T/10688121	SPARK R L L	Cpl.	Ranville, IIA-B-6
22/06/44	284108	BLAND F J	Captain	Ranville, IIA-C-6
23/06/44	T/10671017	FITZPATRICK L L	Cpl.	Ranville, IIA-C-1
23/06/44	T/191650	McGRATH J L	Cpl.	Ranville, II-K-1
06/07/44	T/14636978	MARTIN G F	Dvr.	Ranville, IIIA-H-3
06/07/44	T/14420582	SMITH F	Dvr.	Ranville, IIIA-K-3
07/07/44	T/160298	WILSON J S	Cpl.	Ranville, IIIA-J-3

6th AIRBORNE DIVISION WORKSHOPS REME

Date	Number	Name	Rank	Location
06/06/44	5837460	JACOBS A G	Cfn.	M.I.A. Bayeux, P.18
10/06/44	5960988	STASULEVICH G E	Cfn.	Ranville, IIA-H-6
10/06/44	14504926	THOUMINE, T A	Cfn.	Ranville, IA-C-12
20/06/44	791957	HALL H C	Cpl.	Ranville, IA-K-13
12/08/44	3318126	COCHRANE R V	L/Cpl.	Ranville, IA-J-4

22nd INDEPENDENT PARACHUTE COMPANY (THE PATHFINDERS) AAC

Date	Number	Name	Rank	Location
06/06/44	3663154	HOWARTH L	L/Cpl.	Ranville, IVA-K-4
06/06/44	57305	LENNOX-BOYD F G	Major	Ranville, IIIA-G-5
06/06/44	1435732	O'SULLIVAN E D	L/Cpl.	Touffreville
07/06/44	833785	GLEN E	L/Cpl.	Ranville Church, 39
09/06/44	14401144	GILLUM K S	Pte.	Ranville, IVA-B-6
09/06/44	2818145	SCOGING F	Sgt.	Ranville, IA-A-14
09/06/44	153407	TAIT I A	Captain	Ranville, IVA-L-11
20/06/44	149121	DE LAUTOUR R E V	Captain	Ranville, IIA-E-2
21/06/44	14408455	ALLOCK H	Pte.	Ranville, IIA-F-6
26/08/44	4801227	HARRIS C T G	Cpl.	St Germain Village, 10

6th AIRBORNE DIVISION SIGNALS COMPANY

Date	Number	Name	Rank	Location
06/06/44	2376806	BICKERTON R H	Cpl.	M.I.A. Bayeux, P12-C1
06/06/44	3248522	COLQUHOUN D	Sigmn.	Ranville Church, 11
06/06/44	6144046	DAVIS D I	Sigmn.	Saint Vaast En Auge, 9
06/06/44	14609550	FREEMAN B G	Sigmn.	Ranville, IA-D-1
06/06/44	3253450	MACKIE W S	Sgt.	Ranville Church, 1
06/06/44	2577625	MILNE D	Sigmn.	M.I.A. Bayeux, P.12C.2
06/06/44	281285	ROYLE G	Lieut.	Ranville, IIA-D-2
07/06/44	14407056	FONE R J	Sigmn.	Ranville Church, 21
08/06/44	2344343	HURST A	Sigmn.	M.I.A. Bayeux, P.12C.2
08/06/44	14249454	WALKLEY W S	Sigmn.	M.I.A. Bayeux, P.12C.2
09/06/44	14623371	CONNOLLY B C	Sigmn.	Ranville, IA-A-20
09/06/44	2329499	MOORE J F P	Cpl.	Ranville, IIA-L-5
09/06/44	2378183	SPARKS J	Sigmn.	Ranville, IA-G-21
10/06/44	5778142	BOON F	Sigmn.	Hermanville, 1-E-20
13/06/44	4868422	COURTNEY S	Sigmn.	Ranville, IA-H-15
15/06/44	14333963	STAFFORD W A	Sigmn.	Ranville, IIA-F-12
16/06/44	6349668	JAMES J W C	Sigmn.	Ranville, IA-M-5
25/06/44	14506120	HILL D H	Dvr.	Ranville, IIA-B-2
06/07/44	5617160	SKIDMORE F	Sigmn.	La Delivrande, V-G-2
22/07/44	90173	SMALLMAN-TEW D.	Lt-Col.	Ranville, IA-B-6
23/07/44	14322744	THOMPSON K	Sigmn.	Ranville, IA-H-6
02/08/44	5121113	ALVARADO P M	Sigmn.	Ranville, IA-A-10
12/08/44	2377819	HEEKS B A	Sigmn.	Ranville, IIA-L-14
19/08/44	6923686	BOND F C	Sigmn.	Ranville, IIA-G-9
19/08/44	2374284	LEATHERBARROW R E	Dvr.	Ranville, IIA-M-14
07/10/44	5111378	PITT H W	Cpl.	Whistable, England, 3B-88
07/10/44	14203741	KNIGHT K J S	Sgt.	Middlesbrough, England, C-10453
01/11/44	2320894	GAMBLE D	Sgt.	St Nicholas at Wade, England, 360
01/11/44	3971876	GILRY A E S	L/Cpl.	

224th PARACHUTE FIELD AMBULANCE RAMC

Date	Number	Name	Rank	Location
06/06/44	97004379	HUTTON P	Pte.	Ranville, IA-F-13
06/06/44	97003462	LEACH J E	Pte.	Brucourt, 1
06/06/44	97004018	LEWIS J	Pte.	Brucourt, 2
06/06/44	97003318	SARGENT W P	Pte.	Ranville, IA-B-13
06/06/44	97003811	TINGLE L A	Pte.	M.I.A. Bayeux, P.18C.3
04/07/44	14552471	GARRAT C W	Pte.	Handsworth England, 10852
07/07/44	7379383	McLAUGHLIN W J	L/Cpl.	Ranville, IIIA-C-3
10/08/44	T 177854	AYERS M T	Dvr.	Ranville, VA-O-9
18/08/44	97005812	BASS A D	Sgt.	Ranville, IIA-K-14

225th PARACHUTE FIELD AMBULANCE RAMC

Date	Number	Name	Rank	Location
06/06/44	14292603	CLEMENTS J	Pte.	Ranville Church, 45
06/06/44	7266888	LEGGETT R	Pte.	Benouville, 18
07/06/44	14598987	LONGDON W R	Pte.	Ranville Church, 22
07/06/44	14557867	RIDOUT R S	Pte.	Ranville Church, 7
13/06/44	6026134	RUSSELL R F	L/Cpl.	Ranville Church, 36
13/06/44	T 777877	EMMETT R C	Dvr.	Ranville, IA-H-2
16/06/44	97001163	HARVEY T	Pte.	Ranville, IIA-F-7
07/08/44	7259757	CARTER H O	Sgt.	Ranville, IA-K-16
07/08/44	14245788	EARL G	Pte.	Ranville, IA-J-16

284th PARACHUTE FIELD AMBULANCE RAMC

Date	Number	Name	Rank	Location
25/08/44	7344644	FERRY O	Pte.	Ranville, VA-N-7

195th AIR LANDING AMBULANCE RAMC

Date	Number	Name	Rank	Location
06/06/44	7366078	HEARNE P	Pte.	Hermanville, 1-G-7
06/06/44	14260672	WORGAN L	Pte.	Ranville Church, 13

The night
of the paras

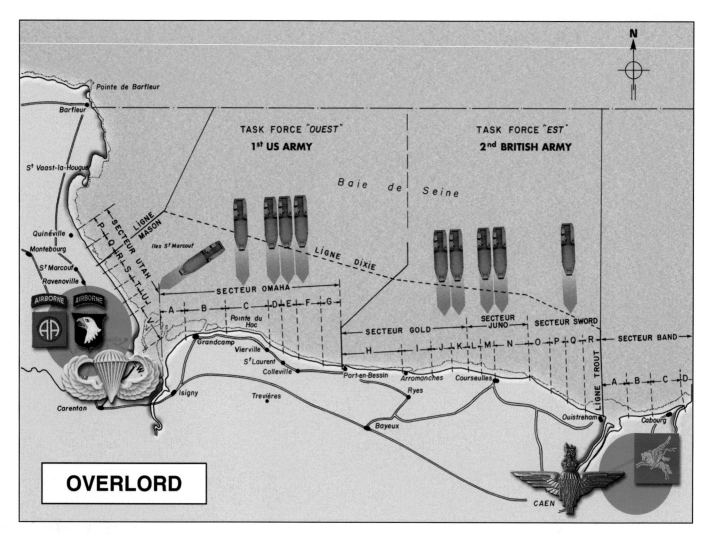

N

TASK FORCE "OUEST"
1st US ARMY

TASK FORCE "EST"
2nd BRITISH ARMY

Baie de Seine

OVERLORD

The airborne divisions covered the flanks of the landing beaches in Normandy. (Heimdal)

Overlord

The opening of the Second Front over the Normandy landing beaches was decided at the Trident conference held in Washington in May 1943. Normandy held sway in Allied thinking over the Pas-de-Calais as there were far fewer German troops stationed here, the low-lying beaches afforded easy access and the area was flanked by two useful ports, Cherbourg and Le Havre. It was initially decided to land between the Vire and Orne estuaries, but it soon became clear that this stretch of coast was far too restricted and the bridgehead would have to include the Cotentin peninsula ; at the same time far greater resources would have to be committed to the landing operation.

At the end of January 1944 General Eisenhower, the Supreme Allied Commander of Operation Overlord (SHAEF) was able to present the final plan and the men and material committed to it.

The First US Army, Lieutenant General Omar Bradley commanding, would land on the right, or western half of the bridgehead, and in the Cotentin (south of a line that leads to Saint-Martin-de-Varaville - Sainte-Mère Eglise), to a point west of Bayeux.

The Second British Army, Lieutenant General Miles C Demsey commanding, would land on the eastern, or left half of the bridgehead from Bayeux to a point north of Caen.

To cover and contain the landing beaches of Operation Overlord two solid flanking firewalls were assured by two US airborne divisions to the west, and one British airborne division to the east.

In the US VII Corps sector, this would consist of 82nd and 101st airborne divisions, whose mission was to establish a secure lodgement area inland and seize the main Carentan-Cherbourg highway by capturing the little village of Sainte-Mère Eglise, while at the same time securing the tracks leading away from Utah Beach where 4th Infantry Division would be landing. The two divisions would also need to control the road crossings over the flooded valley of the Merderet in order to extend the bridgehead in depth westward, across the neck of the Cotentin. Despite the initial confusion, this airborne operation was a complete success, as was the Utah Beach landing, where there were low casualties : the German coastal batteries found themselves completely cut off from the rear.

To the east, in the British sector, a single airborne division, 6th Airborne, was committed, using somewhat different methods and material. In the first place the division would not be committed in support of a seaborne landing, for example behind and between Sword beach and Caen, but would be deployed south-east of Sword, to form a bridgehead with its own battle lines, allowing the allied bridgehead to hinge upon its eastern 'shield'. But here too there would be bridges to be seized intact to allow the main body of seaborne infantry to link up, and others to be blown, to lock the enemy out and secure the front line. The sector would have to be held at all costs so that subsequent military operations, such as Goodwood in July, could be carried out. Before we examine the details of the plan, let us first turn to the means at the disposal of this division. First and foremost they were human : this was an élite division.

An élite division

1

In 1940, the British War Cabinet had been taken aback by the daring of the German paratroops in Norway, Holland (Rotterdam) and in Belgium (Eben Emael). Winston Churchill wrote to General Ismay of his War Cabinet on 22nd June : « *We ought to have a Corps of at least 5000 paratroops… »* At this time a paratroop training establishment, the Central Landing School, was taking shape at Ringway near Manchester, under the command of Major J.F.Rock, of the Royal Engineers. Airborne troops were placed under the orders of the RAF and the Army. From the outset this new type of warfare was modelled on German practice. It had as yet no history of its own :

1. This superb colour photograph taken in 1944 shows a paratrooper armed with a Sten sub-machine gun during exercises. His helmet is of the first type issued with a rubber strap and covered in camouflage netting. His shoulder patches show, from the top, the maroon cloth shoulder insignia of the airborne troops, his 'wings'or qualifying badge, and the divisional patch of the 6th airborne. (IWM)

2. The Pegasus, the insignia of 6th Airborne Division.

3. The horizontal « airborne » badge worn by an airborne division.

4. « Wings » worn by qualified paratroopers introduced on 28th December 1940 to indicate a certain number of jumps.

(Photos Heimdal)

1. This photo taken in he early part of the war shows British paras making adjustments to their equipment : both their parachutes and their jump smocks were based on German models. (DR)

2. During a training slight, these British paras are readying themselves to drop through the open hatch cut into the floor of a Whitley bomber. (IWM)

3. The jump was just as acrobatic out of an Albermale. (IWM)

4. Major General FAM Browning was the commander in chief of British airborne troops. (IWM)

equipment was untried, especially the jumping smocks, even the shape of the para's helmet was novel. Results from a mixture of individuality and experience soon made themselves apparent.

By early 1941 there were a sufficient number of paratroops trained to set up an airborne operation. The first took place on 11th February 1941 : 38 paras attacked the aqueduct at Tragino in Southern Italy. All were captured. The second operation was carried out on 27th February 1942 against a German radar station at Bruneval, north of Le Havre. Under the command of Major JC Frost, (whom we shall meet again at Arnhem in September 1944), the operation was a brilliant success.

In November 1941 Major General F.A.M.Browning was put in charge of all British airborne troops. The 1st Parachute Battalion, formerly the N° 11 Special Air Service Battalion, had been inflated by the arrival of new volunteers to form a 2nd and a 3rd battalion. In September 1941 the 1st Parachute Brigade was formed.

Major General Browning would breathe his own particular style into the British paras by introducing the red beret, leading to their nickname, the « Red Devils ». From the end of 1942 the paras would no longer jump from converted Whitley bombers but from modern Dakotas. General Browning's wife, the novelist Daphne du Maurier, chose the white winged horse, Pegasus, for its insignia.

Formed in September 1941 under the command of Richard N. Gale, promoted to the rank of Brigadier, **1st Parachute Brigade** was made up of 1st, 2nd, and 3rd Parachute Battalions. It underwent intensive training through the summer of 1942. Lieutenant

Colonel Flavell, who had commanded 2nd battalion, replaced Brigadier Gale when he was posted to the War Office. A number of officers would serve with distinction along the Orne in Normandy : Lieutenant Colonel S.J.L.Hill who took command of 1st Parachute Battalion in July 1942 ; his second-in-command Major Alastair Pearson. The second-in-command of 2nd Battalion was Major R.G.Pine-Coffin, who would take over from Lieutenant-Colonel Flavell in the autumn.

1st August 1942 would be a key date for the British paras since the War Office decided to merge all the parachute infantry units into a single Parachute Regiment, whose men would wear the cloth shoulder insignia bearing its name. Three further battalions, 4th, 5th and 6th, forming the new 2nd Parachute Brigade under the command of Brigadier E.E.Down were added to the original three of 1st Parachute Brigade. The 5th battalion were recruited from the Scots, 6th from the Welsh. It was part of British military tradition that these extra battalions should come to boost the ranks of the 'mother regiment' according to need. For the time being, the mission of this new brigade was to put in place an airborne division.

The landings into North Africa, « Operation Torch » was launched on 8th November 1942. Only 360 of the 3rd Battalion under Lieutenant Colonel R.J.Pine-Coffin could be parachuted over the Bône aerodrome. But the shortage of converted Whitley bombers – whereby the men had to drop through a hatch cut into the fuselage floor – had been replaced by the far more comfortable Dakotas. The rest of the brigade came ashore by boat into the port of Alger. The paras jumped again on 16th November near the Souk el Arba aerodrome. The brigade saw action and after being re-formed on 25th January 1943, was withdrawn from the front on 14th and 15th April. It became 1st Airborne Division and was dropped over Sicily in July 1943.

6th Airborne Division

But whereas the 1st Airborne paras were withdrawn from the field before being redeployed into Sicily, the British Airborne troops would receive considerable reinforcements. On 23rd April 1943 the War Office decided to form a new airborne division, 6th Airborne. From the 3rd May a skeleton HQ was formed, and Richard Gale, promoted to Major General from the 1st Parachute Brigade, took command the next

Major General Richard N Gale, after gaining experience commanding the 1st Parachute Brigade from September 1941, took command of 6th Airborne Division on 4th May 1943. At 48 he was one of the youngest British Generals. (IWM)

day. (1) His HQ was set up in Syrecot House in Fighel-dean, Wiltshire, and there he met his Chief of Staff, Lieutenant Colonel Shamus Hickie, his Quartermaster Officer Lieutenant Colonel John Fielding and his GSO1 Lieutenant Colonel Bobby Bray. This skeleton HQ became a hive of activity with the coming and going of secretaries, quartermasters, drivers etc. 3 weeks later, on 1st June, the HQ had 60% of its staff, and on 14th May Gale could issue his first Order of the Day.

(1) The most thorough book on the formation of the division is Go to it ! by Peter Harclerode, pub. Caxton Press.

Richard N Gale

Born in 1896, he was commissioned into the Worcestershire Regiment in 1915, transferred to the Machine Gun Corps on the Western Front In 1916, and there won the Military Cross. Between the wars he spent eighteen years on regimental duty, and by September 1939 he was a Major on the staff in the War Office in London. From December 1940 to July 1941 he commanded an infantry battalion and in September of 1941 took over command as a brigadier of the newly raised 1st Parachute Brigade. By 1943 he was a Major General and Director of Air at the War Office, and in April of that year he was ordered to raise and command the 6th Airborne Division, created on 3rd May.

Gale at once initiated a vigorous training programme to produce an élite division. 'Typically British', he was an officer with a forceful, robust personality, steeped in military history and a real professional. He would always be seen wearing his highly polished riding boots, and had a profound understanding of his men, who were trained as a close-knit family. At 48 he was one of the youngest British generals on D-Day. His honours included the Order of the Bath, Knight Commander of the British Empire (KBE), the Distinguished Service Order (DSO), and the Military Cross. He was a Commander of the United States Legion of Merit and of the French Legion of Honour and held the French Croix de Guerre with Palm.

He died in London on 29th July 1982.

Lieutenant Colonel Shamus Hickie. (IWM)

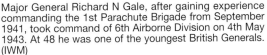

5

The division only consisted of one parachute brigade, **3rd Parachute Brigade**, commanded by Brigadier S.J.L.Hill D.S.O., M.C., recovering from wounds sustained in Africa. Brigadier Hill was a particularly outstanding officer, and at only 31, considered to be the ideal parachute commander.

This brigade was then made up of 7th Battalion, Somerset Light Infantry, 8th Battalion, Midland Counties, and 9th Battalion, the Home Counties.

It will be noted that while the paras came from the four corners of the country, each battalion was recruited regionally. They were below strength at this time, so reinforcements had to be sent to make up the ranks of 1st Parachute Brigade, following the losses suffered in the battles of Mateur and Sedjénane, in North Africa.

Apart from the skeleton headquarters and this parachute brigade, other units made up the division : 3rd Parachute Squadron the Royal Engineers, 224th Parachute Field Ambulance Royal Army Medical Corps, 2nd Battalion the Oxfordshire and Buckinghamshire Light Infantry, and 1st Battalion the Royal Ulster Rifles. The two latter battalions were light infantry who made up 1st Airlanding Brigade and were brought in seated in gliders.

At the end of May, Major General Sir Bernard Paget, Commander-in-Chief of Home Forces, was able to communicate some good news to Major General Gale. A battalion of Canadian paratroops had arrived on 28th July 1942, and by March 1943 was up to full strength. Under the command of Lieutenant Colonel G.F.P.Bradbrooke, it consisted of 31 officers and 548 non-commissioned officers and all ranks. They arrived at Bulford Camp and were integrated into the division in July. For the moment, their training fell into two parts or phases. In the first phase, the main effort was devoted to training specialists

and deputy commanders. Particular emphasis was laid on training marksmen : as the Canadians had remarked (2), in the initial assault supplies of ammunition would be low, so every shot counted and 'must find its target'. A Staff Sergeant turned up at Brisley to perfect their shooting skills, and they greatly improved : the ability of the men to fire accurately in Normandy saved many lives.

On **1st June** the Division was at last made up of 3 brigades. Apart from the initial 3rd Parachute Brigade, two infantry battalions which we mentioned made up **6th Airlanding Brigade**, while awaiting the third battalion. 5th Parachute Brigade arrived, under the command of Brigadier J.H.N.Poett.

It was only made up of 2 battalions, the 12th, recruited in Yorkshire, and the 13th, from Lancashire.

In August, **1st Canadian Parachute Battalion** rejoined the division, to be attributed to 3rd Parachute Brigade. Brigadier Hill had learnt back in May that this battalion would be integrated into his unit, and he was delighted ; he knew that these were the boldest and bravest of the élite of the Canadian army. On the other hand he would have to cede one of his battalions to 5th Brigade, which only had two. The choice would be a difficult one, and in the end 7th Battalion, the Somerset Light Infantry, the most senior of his units, rejoined 5th Brigade. The Canadian Battalion rejoined the 3rd Brigade on 11th August.

In **September,** 6th Airborne Division was at long last up to nearly full strength, and able to begin its training. On 22nd September the War Office ordered the topping up of the divisional units.

(2) H. St George Saunders, *the Red Beret*, Battery Press, 1985, p152

The airborne military chaplains, known as the parachute padres, on 1st May 1944. From left to right : the Reverend A. Buchanan, from Larne in Northern Ireland ; the Reverend E. Thimothy, from London, the Reverend Hales, from Netheravon (attached to Major General Gale's Headquarters) ; the Reverend J. Owen Jenkins, from Spittal in Pembrokeshire (chaplain to 12th Parachute Battalion). They wear their dog collars, and the uniform of the airborne, with its curved cloth shoulder patch ; below that the badge bearing the title Royal Army Chaplains, or RA. Ch.D. ; the insignia of the division ; and then the horizontal strip 'Airborne'. (IWM)

The Order of Battle

In 1943 a British infantry division consisted of 757 officers and 16,764 non-commissioned officers and other ranks. It would include two infantry brigades and a tank brigade. The organisation of an airborne division was somewhat different, with three brigades being made up of two paratroop brigades and an airlanding brigade, and was equipped with lighter arms, as we shall see.

6th Airborne Division was commanded by Major General Richard N. Gale from his Headquarters, helped by :

- *GSO 1 (Operations)* under Lieutenant Colonel Bobby Bray, transferred from the Duke of Wellington's Regiment to Chief Staff Officer at HQ.

- *GSO 1 (Air)*, under Lieutenant Colonel Bill Bradish of the Royal Irish Fusiliers. He directed all aspects of air training and the loading of aircraft.

- *GSO 2 (Operations)*, under Major David Baird of the Argyll and Sutherland Highlanders.

- *GSO 2 (Intelligence),* under Major Gerry Lacoste of the Royal Artillery, responsible for intelligence and the interrogation of prisoners of war. He was also a gifted artist and some of his pictures are on display in the Pegasus museum.

- Several *GSO 3*.

- The Assistant Adjutant and Quartermaster General, Lieutenant Colonel Shaemus Hickie of the King's Own Yorkshire Light Infantry (KOYLI), was responsible for divisional administration.

Other Headquarters staff made up the total, including General Gale's aide-de-camp, Captain Tom Haughton of the Royal Ulster Rifles ; also a Provost Company, 317th Field Security Section, and chaplains, with Lieutenant Colonel J.C.Hales.

6th Airborne Forward HQ in Normandy consisted altogether of 37 officers and 174 men, before the seaborne elements joined them between two and six days later.

A battalion of paratroops consisted of 550 men, recruited from all the territorial army units, keeping their regimental name as we have seen. A battalion had an HQ and a company command consisting of 3 paratroop companies, A, B, C, (5 officers and 120 men in each) with three sections of 36 men, again divided up into the basic fighting unit of a Sergeant, a Corporal and 8 men, which also made up a 'stick'. Transport aircraft normally carried 2 sticks each, together with their corresponding supplies.

3rd Parachute Brigade

Brigadier **James Hill** commanding, had served with the Royal Fusiliers before the war and with Lord Gort at his Headquarters during the Battle of France in 1940, when he had received the Military Cross. He had rejoined his airborne troops in 1941, before assuming second- in-command of the 1st Parachute Battalion, and then of the unit during the landings into North Africa.

In the fighting in this theatre of operations he was badly wounded, and was decorated with the DSO and the Legion of Honour. He then had three parachute battalions under his orders.

8th Parachute Battalion had been formed out of the Royal Warwickshire Regiment. Lieutenant-Colonel **Alastair Pearson,** a brilliant officer with a formidable reputation, commanded it. He had been an officer in the Territorial Army, in the Highland Light Infantry, had led 1st Parachute Battalion in North Africa, where he had been awarded 3 DSOs in succession – an amazing achievement – as well as the Military Cross. He was one of the few officers actually known by name to the Germans he was fighting.

Despite his frail health, he would remain as an officer in the reserve, finishing his career with the rank of Brigadier. On his death he would be the most decorated soldier in the British Army, C.B., D.S.O. four times over, O.B.E., M.C., T.D., C. St.J. In the 1970s he was the Lord Lieutenant of Dunbartonshire.

Lieutenant Colonel Terence Otway led 9th Parachute Battalion.

Each battalion was supported by a section equipped with 4 Vickers machine guns and another with 6 3-inch mortars.

9th Parachute Battalion was formed out of 10th Battalion of the Essex Regiment. Initially it was commanded by Lieutenant Colonel Martin Lindsay while still a Royal Scots Fusilier and one of the first men to undergo parachute training back in 1940. He had been replaced by Lieutenant Colonel **Terence Otway** of the Royal Ulster Rifles.

1st Canadian Parachute Battalion was then under the command of Lieutenant Colonel **George Bradbrooke.**

Opposite : 1st Canadian Parachute Battalion during a ceremony at Fort Benning in the USA in 1942. (Memorial Pegasus)

Above : Lieutenant Colonel George Bradbrooke led 1st Canadian Parachute Battalion. (IWM)

Below : The metal insignia worn on the beret by the men of 1st Canadian Parachute Battalion. (Photo Heimdal)

Below : Another picture of the royal inspection of 19th May 1944. We can see the men of 1st Canadian Parachute Battalion standing to attention for the King and Lieutenant General Browning. (IWM)

Above : A Sergeant's battledress of 1st Canadian Parachute Battalion. Note the special badges : the Canadian qualifying insignia sown above the left pocket, and the badge bearing the name and number of the unit. (Memorial Pegasus)

5th Parachute Brigade

Under the command of Brigadier Nigel Poett, he was the son of a Major General in the Indian Army, had been an officer in the Durham Light Infantry and would end his career as Commander-in-Chief Far East Land Forces.

7th Parachute Battalion was formed out of 10th Battalion the Somerset Light Infantry and led by Lieutenant Colonel Geoffrey Pine-Coffin, of the Devonshire Regiment. Here was another extremely courageous and outstanding officer, a landowner with an original turn of mind. On D-Day he bailed out wearing cowboy boots complete with spurs ! And his men were convinced Pine-Coffin had to be a code-name…

12th Parachute Battalion was formed out of 10th Battalion, the Green Howards – Yorkshiremen. It first was led by Lieutenant-Colonel Reggie Parker, also from the Green Howards, then from February 1944, by Lieutenant Colonel Johnny A.P. Johnson. The men in this battalion were allowed to wear a pale blue lanyard.

13th Parachute Battalion was formed out of 2nd/4th Battalion of the South Lancashire Regiment - Lancastrians - under the command of Lieutenant Colonel Peter Luard. Their motto « Win or die » was taken from the poem « They win or die who wear the rose of Lancashire » - and indeed the White Rose of Lancaster would be the battalion insignia.

Brigadier J.H.N.Poett led 5th Parachute Brigade. (Photo : General Sir Nigel Poett)

Below : Lieutenant Colonel Geoffrey Pine-Coffin led 7th Parachute Battalion. (IWM)

Lieutenant Colonel Peter J. Luard commanded 13th parachute Battalion. (Mémorial Pegasus)

1. Geoffrey Pine-Coffin's jacket, bearing the name, « Devon and Dorset » of his original regiment, but the rank of colonel to which he was later promoted. Note also the green and red stripe underneath it, the 1914-18 French Croix de Guerre. This recalled the action of the Devonshire Regiment at the Bois des Buttes, north of the River Aisne on 27th May 1918. Shortly before the outbreak of the Second World War, they were allowed to wear this stripe, as well as, for a short period, the lanyard of the Croix de Guerre that you also see here. (Mémorial Pegasus)

2. On the left sleeve beneath the stripe we can see the « Wings », the qualifying insignia of the paratrooper. (Mémorial Pegasus)

Lieutenant Colonel Michael Roberts. (IWM)

6th Airlanding Brigade

This brigade, under the command of the Honourable **Hugh Kindersley**, was brought in by gliders ; it had substantially more men as well as heavier equipment. It had its own HQ with its own command company, a reconnaissance section with 2 jeeps armed with twin Vickers machine guns, sapper-engineers equipped with a jeep with trailer, a company of engineers, a medical unit, and 3 battalions of infantry.

Two of the infantry battalions were regular army units which had existed before the war ; the other, the Devonshire regiment, was a more recent creation. It had been made up of the Devon coastal defence units, and was led by a Devonian, Lieutenant Colonel **Dick Stephens.**

2nd Battalion, the Oxfordshire and Buckinghamshire Light Infantry, the « 2nd Oxs and Bucks » for short, but commanded by Lieutenant Colonel **Michael Roberts.**

1st Battalion the Royal Ulster Rifles (R.U.R.) was led by Lieutenant-Colonel **Jack Carson.**

Each battalion consisted of about 750 men.

The insignia of the Devonshire Regiment worn by the men of 12th Battalion. (Photo Heimdal)

The cloth shoulder insignia of the Royal Ulster Rifles. (Mémorial Pegasus)

The cloth shoulder insignia and the beret badge of 2nd Oxs and Bucks. (Photo Heimdal)

Brigadier the Honourable Hugh Kindersley led 6th Airlanding Brigade. (IWM)

Captain R.E.H.Sheridan's Denison Smock, 1st Battalion the Royal Ulster Rifles. Notice the regimental Irish harp badge on his beret. (Mémorial Pegasus)

Reconnaissance

6th Airborne Armoured Reconnaissance Regiment, under the command of Lieutenant Colonel **Godfrey Stewart** of 13th/18th Royal Hussars, was made up of 3 squadrons of 29 officers and 267 men. It was drawn from various elements of 1st Armoured Division which, when it had set off for Sicily, had left its regimental reconnaissance regiment behind in England. It had a reduced number of effectives and relatively light equipment as it had to be brought in by glider.

It consisted of the Regimental Headquarters, equipped with 2 Tetrarchs – light tanks armed with a 3-inch (75mm) howitzer, a headquarters squadron with 2 jeeps equipped with Vickers machine guns for reconnaissance, and a jeep with trailer for the engineers.

The squadron of light tanks consisted of an HQ Troop of 4 Tetrarch light tanks, also equipped with 3-inch howitzer, while the 5 sections of sabre troops were each provided with 3 Tetrarch light tanks carrying 2-pounder guns.

This man from the Reconnaissance Regiment bears the name of his unit on his shoulder flash, and a yellow and green rectangle on his helmet.

During the Royal inspection of 19th May 1944 we can see an American-made 75mm M8 pack howitzer, of which 24 would be allocated to the Division within the 53rd Worcestershire Yeomanry Airlanding Light Regiment RA.

Major General Gale stands on the left of the Queen, Princess Elizabeth and King George VI, Colonel Reggie Parker, the Deputy Divisional Commander, Lieutenant Colonel Jack Norris, the Commander of Artillery, and Brigadier Kindersley, commander of th'e 6th Airlanding Brigade, stand to the right of her.

(IWM)

Above : A detail of Captain Thompson's beret, which he wore in 1944 commanding 210th Airlanding Light Battery R.A. This is the embroidered insignia of the Worcestershire Yeomanry. (Mémorial Pégasus)

Anti-tank artillery was available to each of the 2 brigades of paratroops : two batteries, **3rd Airlanding Anti-Tank Battery** led by Major Nick Cranmer, and **4th Airlanding Anti-Tank battery** under Major Peter Dixon. These two batteries had been constituted in July 1943, and each had its own headquarters and 4 'troops' of 4 six-pounders towed by jeeps or Bren Carriers, 16 in total.

By 1944 these batteries were re-equipped with 17-pounder guns, far more powerful, and able to take out Panzers. **6th Airlanding Anti-Tank Battery R.A.,** was equipped with 6-pounder anti-tank artillery for each reserve company for each of the 3 infantry battalions.

The division also had anti-aircraft guns : **2nd Airlanding Light Anti-Aircraft Battery R.A.** had been constituted in May 1943 and was placed under the command of Major W.A.H. Rowat. It consisted of 18 40mm Bofors guns and 48 20mm Hispano-Suiza (Oerlikon) guns.

The Engineers

All the Divisional Engineers were coordinated by the Commander Royal Engineers, Lieutenant Colonel Frank Lowman at HQ.

The Engineers provided 2 squadrons of paratroops to both paratroop brigades. **3rd Parachute Squadron R.E.,** under Major J.C.A. « Tim » Roseveare was attached to 3rd Parachute Brigade, and **591st Parachute Squadron R.E.,** under Major Andy Wood, to 5th Parachute Brigade. Each squadron brought together a command group and 3 'Troops' of 30 men each, each under a Captain and further broken down into platoons of 10 men.

249th Field Company R.E., under the command of Major Sandy Rutherford, was attached to 6th Airlanding brigade, and brought together a command group and 3 platoons, again each led by a Captain. This unit was very special : each platoon consisted of 3 platoons of 8 sappers, each platoon led by a Corporal. Each platoon was split into two, in order to duplicate the command structure ; one would be led by the Captain, the other by his second-in-command. One group would go in by glider, the other in an aircraft, and this was done in such a way that if one was lost, the other could continue to function at its objective.

Finally **286th Field Park Company R.E.,** under Major Jack Waters, was attached directly to the divisional HQ, and was responsible for supplying all the Engineer units.

On the 19th May 1944 an officer of 3rd Parachute Squadron R.E., explains to King George VI how a sapper's demolition charges work. Notice the trolley on the right, in front of Brigadier James Hill. (IWM)

Communications

6th Airborne Divisional Signals, under Lieutenant Colonel 'Pigmy' Smallman-Tew, were responsible for communications. This unit brought together a Headquarters Company and 3 Signals Companies. N° 1 Company was responsible for all radio and telephone links out of HQ to Army Corps and all units, and for links to aircraft. N° 2 Company provided signals platoons to each Brigade HQ, for the artillery regiment, the reconnaissance regiment and the engineers. Each platoon attached to the brigade HQ consisted of 2 officers and 73 non-commissioned officers and the rank and file – radio operators and telephonists. They had to ensure that radio and telephone links to the divisional HQ and to the different battalions were maintained. N° 3 Company handled radio traffic to the divisional base in England.

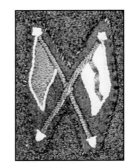

Cloth insignia for a signals instructor (until 1941 it consisted of a metal badge), worn on the left shoulder. (Mémorial Pegasus)

Above : Jacket and beret worn by William Stack, responsible for communications of the 9th Parachute Battalion. (Mémorial Pegasus)

Below : A Divisional communications motorcyclist in full gear. (Mémorial Pegasus)

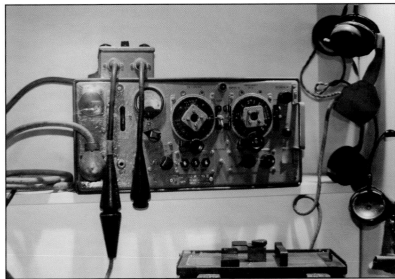

Radio Communications equipment. (Mémorial Pégasus)

Opposite : a small trolley, complete with special handles, used for unravelling telephone wire for divisional communications. (Mémorial Pégasus)

Above : On the 19th May 1944, King George VI and Queen Elizabeth inspected medical equipment of the 224th Parachute Field Ambulance, while General 'Boy' Browning peers into a satchel with his stick. (IWM)

Right : The Airborne division medical equipment. (RAMC). (Photo Heimdal)

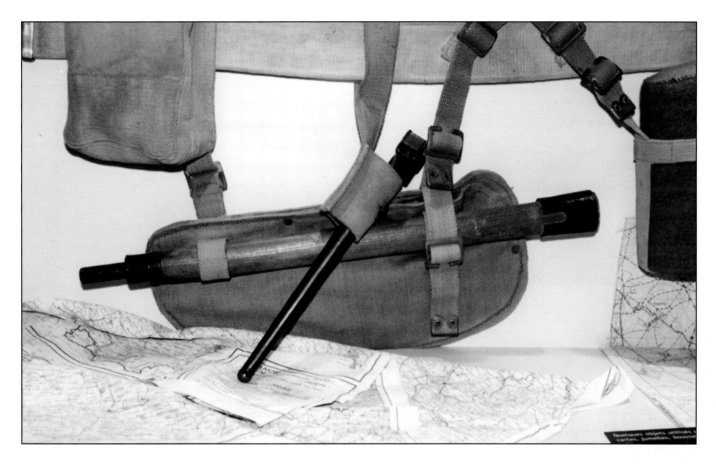

Medical Units

The entire Divisional medical corps, the Royal Army Medical Corps, or RAMC for short, was under the command of Colonel M. MacEwan. There were three 'Field Ambulances' : 224th Parachute Field Ambulance, attached to 3rd Parachute Brigade, was led by Lieutenant Colonel D.H.Thompson ; 225th Parachute Field Ambulance, attached to 5th Parachute Brigade, was led by Lieutenant Colonel Bruce Har-

vey ; and 195th Airlanding Field Ambulance RAMC, attached to 6th Airlanding Brigade, was led by Lieutenant-Colonel Bill Anderson. 224th and 225th had 9 RAMC officers and over 100 medics, the 195th rather more. In addition, each battalion in the division had a medical officer and medical section.

The division also had units affected to supply and services.

Detail of strapwork holding various tools and a bayonet. (Mémorial Pegasus)

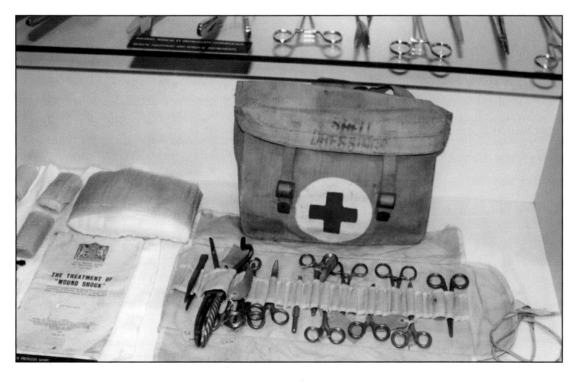

A military surgeon's pouch from 6th Airborne Division. (Mémorial Pegasus)

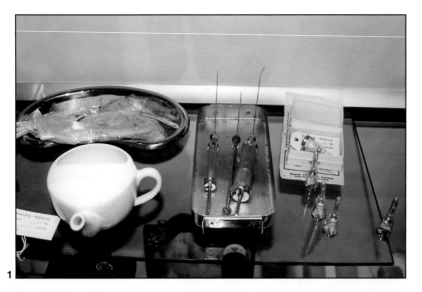

1. Morphine syringes.

2. Medical personnel of the division in England before D-Day.

3. Medical captain's jacket and trunk containing dressings and splints. (Mémorial Pegasus)

Transport, services

The **6th Airborne Division Ordnance Field Park,** the Royal Army Ordnance Corps (RAOC), consisted of about 80 men under Major W.L.Taylor. They were responsible for the equipment and had to be near the company workshops.

The Workshops

The Commander Royal Army Service Corps, Lieutenant Colonel J.L.Watson, was responsible for all the divisional services.

The workshop companies were brought together under the **6th Airborne Workshop REME,** led by Major E.B.Bonniwell. During an operation, the workshop would consist of an Advance Workshop Detachment parachuted into the field, the other would be brought in, along with their equipement, in 3 gliders. Each Horsa glider would carry 4 men, a Jeep, a light tank and other equipment.

The **Royal Army Service Corps (RASC),** for transportation and supply, were under Lieutenant-Colonel J. Lovegrove. They were made of several companies : 716th Light Composite Company, under Major A. Jones, brought together an echelon of com-

mand of which one was paratroop. It was equipped with jeeps, and had two trailers for carrying ammunition, supplies and other equipment. This company had to be in action alongside the first elements to arrive, in order to ensure resupply, and hence were parachuted in or brought in by glider. The other, more typical companies, were 398th Composite Company RASC, under Major M.E.Philipps, and 63rd Composite Company RASC, under Major A.C.Billetop.

The Army Air Corps elements

6th Airborne Division were brought into action in part by the **Army Air Corps,** which was attached to it. This was made up of the Glider Pilot regiment and the famous Pathfinders of 22nd Independent Parachute Company, integrated into the division.

The organisation of each airborne division, including the American airborne, included a unit of Pathfinders whose mission was to mark out the Drop Zones (DZs), or Landing Zones (LZs). The pathfinders would precede the main airborne assault to mark the DZs and LZs by day with smoke or with panels, and by night with radio beacons to guide in the aircraft.

22nd Independent Parachute Company, Major Francis Lennox Boyd of the Royal Scots Greys commanding, was attached to 6th Airborne Division.

There was a command section and three others, each with an officer and 33 junior ranks. Each stick was led by a Sergeant or Corporal, equipped with a Eureka ground-to-air radio homing beacon, which would send out a signal to be picked up by a Rebecca receiver installed in the transport plane. By day they were equipped with T-shaped panels to mark the zones, and by night they also had Holophane lamps powered by 6-volt batteries to mark out the Drop Zones. An orange-coloured lamp would be placed at the extremities of the 'T', and a green lamp at its foot.

60% of this 22nd Independent Parachute Company was, unusually, made up of German jews who had fled Nazi persecution, and once incorporated into the division, took on assumed names.

Right : Corporal « Jungle » Jones of 22nd Independent Parachute Company during the royal inspection of 19th May 1944. Before joining up Corporal Jones had been a PE instructor in the police. Notice the unusual placing of his 'wings', which a new regulation later had pushed up to the level of the shoulder. (IWM)

Below : This superb colour picture taken in the spring of 1944 shows a soldier of the 6th Airlanding Brigade, armed with a Lee Enfield rifle, in front of a Horsa glider. (IWM)

The German Forces

2

Generalleutenant Wilhelm Richter commanded 716th Infantry Division.

The insignia of 716th Infantry Division.

The main adversary awaiting 6th Airborne within their bridgehead would be elements of 716th Infantry Division which held the sector as far as the Dives to the east. The Seventh Army and 84th Corps (LXXXIV Armée-Korps) stopped here : beyond was the sector held by 711th Infantry Division answering to 81st Corps (LXXXI Armee-Korps) of 15th Army.

716th Infantry Division was activated in early May 1941 as an occupation division, made up of older soldiers recruited from the Wehrkreis VI, the military region of the Northern Rhineland. Stationed around Rouen in Normandy from July 1941, it was posted to Soissons and then Belgium, before returning to the Caen sector between the Vire and the Dives, with its HQ in Caen. In the western part of the sector it was, from February 1944, reinforced by 352nd Infantry Division. (1)

The division, commanded by Major General Wilhelm Richter, had two infantry regiments strung out along the coast, 726th to the west, and 736th to the east.

736th Grenadier Regiment, led by Oberst Ludwig Krug, straddled the Orne estuary, but principally stationed to the west of the river valley. This infantry regiment would have most of its battalions facing what would become Sword beach : 1/736 à Colleville, II/736 at Tailleville, and III/736 at Cresserons. The Regimental HQ was at Colleville in a position which the British termed 'Hillman', 2 H608-type shelters. These 3 battalions would find themselves confronting the British 3rd Infantry Division on D-Day.

But the regiment had a fourth battalion in position on the banks of the Orne, to the north of what would become the airborne bridgehead, Ost-Battalion 642 serving as IV/736.

Ost-Battalion 642 was made up of Russian volunteers ; its history goes back to 15th January 1943 when it was formed in the heart of the 4th Army in the Central Sector of the Eastern Front (Heeresgruppe Mitte). Its Headquarters was formed out of the company HQ (of the « Hopfgarten » battalion), and its men were drawn from 5 (Ost) Companie and Wach Battalion 582. Hundreds of thousands of Russian soldiers – deserters, prisoners of war or recruits, were conscripted into the German Army in the East, in units and small units made up into companies or battalions. This was the case of Ost-Battalion 642, largely made up of former Red Army soldiers, who joined 716th Division on 13th April 1944. It was 4th battalion of 736th GR and became IV (Ost) of 736th Gren.Rgt, its HQ at Amfréville. In May it was in the division's reserve. Consequently General Gale's principal adversary would be Russians formerly in the Red Army !

The fate of Ost-Battalion 642

This battalion fought 6th Airborne Division and took heavy casualties. In August it fell back to Alsace where it joined 19th Army. The unit was virtually annihilated, and in October survivors were transferred to Russisches Battalion 642. In November this battalion reached the Munsingen camp where it was absorbed into General Vlassov's « Russian Army of Liberation ».

This photo taken by the Canadians during the fighting in June 1944 shows Corporal W.S. Ducker treating a wounded soldier who was in fact a Russian in Ost-Battalion 642, as the cloth badge on his sleeve bears the letters ROA (« Russian Army of Liberation ») in the Russian colours. Corporal Ducker was killed on 16th June 1944. (Mémorial Pegasus)

716th Infantry Division also had an artillery regiment, **Artillerie-Regiment 1716,** under the command of Lieutenant-Colonel Helmut Knupe, based in Beuville, to the north of Caen, where 3rd Battery (3/AR 1716) was in position, in an apple orchard, ready for action. It was equipped with 100mm Czech-made guns (10cm leFH 14/19), which we will look at later. The three battalions of the group were equipped with this gun. The 2nd battery (2/AR 1716) was installed in Colleville, in the « Hillman » Fort, and its 4 100mm guns, originally set in open concrete turntables, were now under cover in concrete casemates. However these batteries only threatened Sword Beach. Only one other battery, 1/AR 1716, lay east of the Orne, and because, in contrast to the other two, it was set in a huge casemate which gave the impression of a much more powerful emplacement than it really was, the Allies decided it had to be put out of action : this was the gun battery at Merville which seemed also to threaten the entire Sword sector !

(1) See G. Bernage, Omaha Beach, Edition Heimdal 2001.

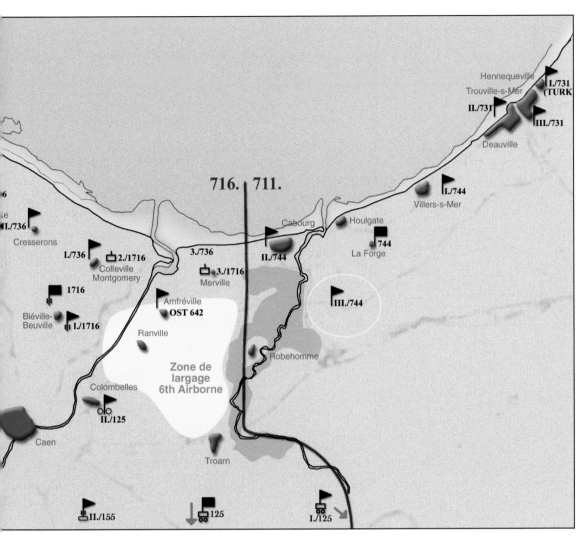

Left : On this map, we can see where the regimental and battalion headquarters were set up in the area to be attacked by 6th Airborne Division. Note the boundary line that separates 716th from 711st Infantry Divisions. Note also the presence of some units of 21st SS Panzer-Division to the south : the II/125, GR 125, II/155 and the 1/125. (Heimdal Map)

Below : One of the 100mm (10cm leFH 14/19 (t)) field Howitzers at Colleville (2/AR 1716), identical to the type at Merville. (IWM.)

The Merville Battery

This battery was equipped with light Czech-made 100mm Howitzers. The guns, the 10cm leichte Feldhaubitze 14/19 (t), or 10cm le FH 14/19 (t) for short, were manufactured at the Skoda factory in Pilsen, and had been widely used in the Czech army in 1938. Its Czech denomination was 10 cm houfnice vz. 14/19. The German Army used it in their own artillery units. Other guns of a similar type were picked up after the Polish campaign, and later in operation « Marita », between 1939 and 1941. It measured 2.4m long, the barrel itself 2.175 metres. It weighed 2855kg when combat ready. The shell weighed in at 16kg and it could fire 8 rounds a minute. Extreme range was 9800 metres, so it was not a powerful weapon. Its German equivalent, the 105mm light Howitzer (the 10.5cm le FH 18) could reach 12325 metres.

The battery was set up in the commune of Merville, between the centre of the village and the hamlet of Descanneville. The officers serving the battery, and its associated services, settled into the nearby château of Merville. Six horses were needed to move each 100mm gun into place. Until 1943 the 4 100mm Howitzers had no protection whatever, except the apple trees in the fields belonging to 3 local families, the Legrix, Duvals and Delfargueils.

The artillerymen spent their leisure time on the beach at Franceville, or in the nearby cafés, the Café Merville in the hamlet of Descanneville, or the Café Gondrée in Bénouville.

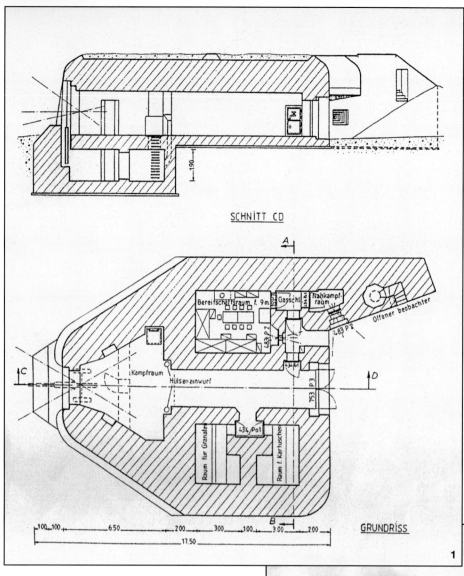

SCHNITT CD

GRUNDRISS

1

1. Plan and cross section of a type 611 casemate N°1. This huge construction even features a dormitory for the artillerymen. (Bereitschaftsraum). (Heimdal)

2. Plan and cross section of a type 669 casemate, which corresponds to the design of the 3 other casemates in the battery. These used far less concrete : 450m³ as against 1330 m³ for type 611.

3. The embrasure of the type 669 casemate. (E.G. Heimdal)

4. The rear of the casemate was quite straightforward, a double swing door sufficiently wide to allow the 100mm gun to be moved in and out as required. (E.G. Heimdal)

3

4

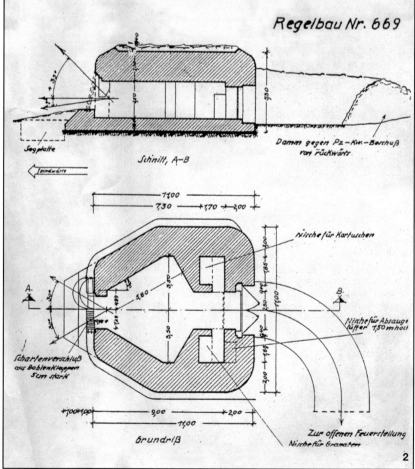

Regelbau Nr. 669

Schnitt, A-B

Grundriß

2

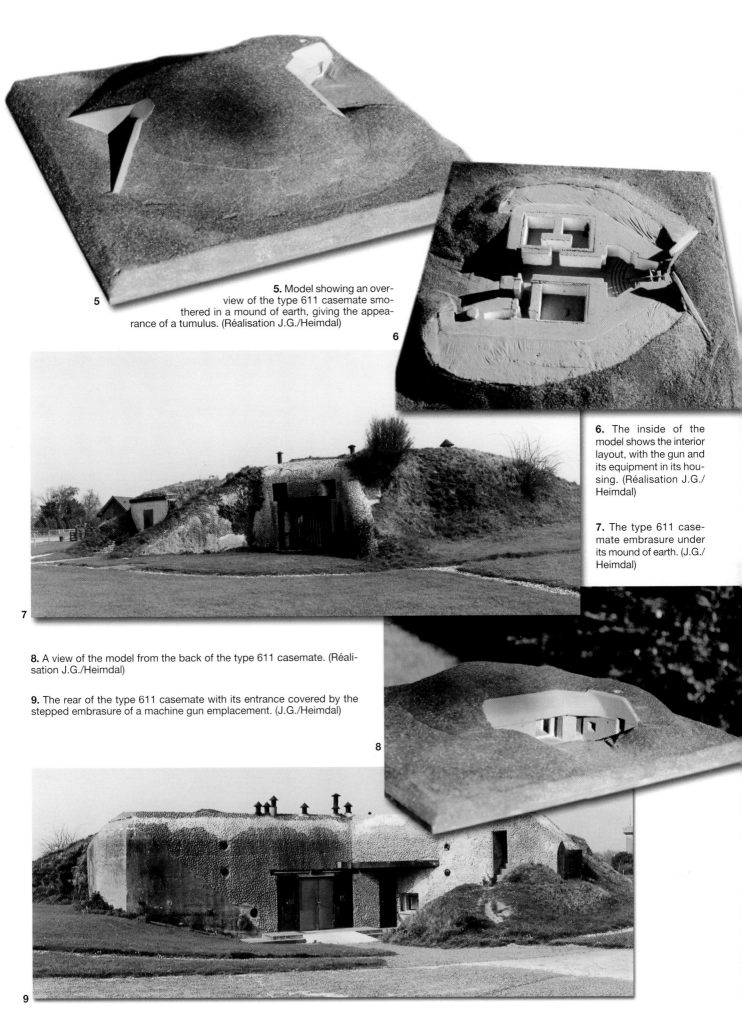

5. Model showing an overview of the type 611 casemate smothered in a mound of earth, giving the appearance of a tumulus. (Réalisation J.G./Heimdal)

6. The inside of the model shows the interior layout, with the gun and its equipment in its housing. (Réalisation J.G./Heimdal)

7. The type 611 casemate embrasure under its mound of earth. (J.G./Heimdal)

8. A view of the model from the back of the type 611 casemate. (Réalisation J.G./Heimdal)

9. The rear of the type 611 casemate with its entrance covered by the stepped embrasure of a machine gun emplacement. (J.G./Heimdal)

The type 611 casemate

In the spring of 1943 work on the first casemate began. The task was entrusted to the Rittmann Company in Paris, supervised locally from Houlgate through a regional directorate in Rouen. There was still time and the means to build a relatively 'com-fortable' type 611 casemate (Regelbau 611). Apart from the gun housing itself, the access corridor and the two ammunition stores (one for shells, the *Raum für Granaten,* and one for cartridges, the *Raum für Kartuschen*), the casemate also had a shelter for 9 artillerymen *(Bereitschaftsraum für 9 Mann),* a gas extraction chamber *(Gasschleuse)* and a flanking machine gun embrasure covering the rear entrance *(Nahkampfraum).* At 17,50m long, it was huge, recalling the two type 650 casemates at Azeville in the Cotentin : this type of casemate required over 1330m³ of concrete, 700m³ of soil to be excavated, and 65 tons of steel reinforcing rods ; the three other casemates at Merville, built later, were three times less massive, requiring 450m³ of concrete, 120m³ of soil to be removed, and only 20 tons of steel !

This enormous casemate was covered in an earthen mound akin to a megalithic tumulus in appearance. Apart from the open embrasure at the front for the gun itself, its rear was protected by a stepped embrasure to house a machine gun, and atop the abutment, a tobruk hole *(Ringstand)* for another machine gunner. The unique size and scale of this casemate would eventually attract the attention of Allied air reconnaissance. The housing could potentially conceal a 150mm gun, an altogether different beast compared to the feeble 100mm. American air reconnaissance reported in November 1943 that the Merville Battery had to be equipped with « *a 155mm howitzer and other guns* ». This misapprehension in the intelligence assessment remained in place right up to D-Day. Another, British report dated 28/4/1944, confirmed : « *Intelligence Information up to April 28 1944 : 4 ? 150mm (5.9 in) Howitzers. Range 14,600 yds. Rate of fire about 5 rpm. 96-Ib shell. Centre line NE Arc of fire 130°. At present mounted in open circular emplacements, diam. 36 ft, probably with concrete beds ; wheels of gun-carriage shackled to pivots of mounting. In front of each existing emplacement a concrete casemate is being constructed. Work started in June 1943. N° 1 Casemate complete ; n° 2 nearly complete ; n° 3 & 4 - work proceeding slowly. No I earthed over, earth banked up to cover roof. Gap left in near for entrance, and one in front for gun port. These casemates contain gun compartments with embrasure in front, room for detachment on duty and one or two magazines. Thickness of concrete probably 6ft 6in. Open emplacements and casemates arranged in an arc facing ORNE estuary. The Battery in casemates will have an arc of fire of 90°-130° but guns in open emplacements have all-round traverse. Slight camouflage, of roads and services. Accomodation at gun positions, men and stores in concrete casemates and a few older concrete shelters underground. Off-duty personnel billeted*

1

3

2

4

5

in Merville-Franceville village. Battery OP almost certainly within Infantry Strongpoint on R bank of ORNE 138789. Communications : buried cable and probably also wireless. Armament 3 x ?20mm AA guns possibly not all present. Identity : ? Army Static Coastal Troops. (Text in Assault on the guns of Merville, Alan Jefferson, p. 198-199.)

So the Germans had put in place a weak gun battery, able to fire at a range of under 10km only, while the Allies had estimated its range to be over 13km : the difference was enough to make it a priority target. American intelligence believed the battery not to be directed by the Army *(Heer)*, but by the Navy, a coastal battery using naval guns such as at Longues. The source of this error can be found in the huge type 611 casemate. If the Germans had simply left their guns under the apple trees as before, the Allies would not have taken much notice. With hindsight we can see that on D-Day the gun batteries protected in concrete, having first been the target of a number of bombing raids, were quickly silenced by naval bombardment or overwhelmed ; that the splay of the embrasure limited their effectiveness, even if, as was sometimes the case, it was possible to pull them out of their protective housings to swing them round a full 360°. Only the batteries at Azeville and Crisbecq really did the job they were designed to do. At Longues for example, one of the positions was quickly put out of action and the others, limited in their objectives, were taken from the rear on D-Day +1. However the field guns dissimulated among the apple trees, hard to spot and easy to move, would be far more effective, as was particularly the case on Omaha Beach. Whatever the efforts to camouflage the guns in concrete by painting them as houses, stretching netting over them, cladding them in stone or mounds of earth, it was all so much romantic nonsense and bore no relation at all to efficient defence procedures. Allied aerial observation spotted and tracked every phase of the highly visible works by the Organisation Todt. Very often the Resistance were able to provide additional information, as was indeed the case at Merville. The Allies knew the exact thickness of the casemate : 2 metres.

Two sisters, Denise and Jacqueline « Bernard » (see Alan Jefferson p80ff) were the mistresses of two regimental officers, - Denise of Captain Wolter, the battery commander, - for the express purpose of obtaining information for London.

At 1.30 am on 19th May 1944, while Denise and Captain Woleter lay in each other's arms in the château, 15 Lancasters and 51 Halifax heavy bombers of the Royal Canadian Air Force dropped in. The battery was wrecked and they were both killed : their bodies were pulled from the rubble next day. Denise had provided London with information only to be killed by Allied bombs.

The two sisters were not the only civilians to provide information. The network Zéro-France had been set up in July 1940 in Belgium before spreading into northern France and along the Channel coast. Its mission was to glean intelligence about the fortifications of the Atlantic Wall. Locally the network was based in Dives-sur-Mer. Among its members, René Denis, postmaster-general at Merville-Franceville, was probably the source of transmissions of information coming in from other members of the Zéro-France network, from men such as M.Delanoë in Cabourg, Paul Marion in Hôme, and Joseph Danlos in Merville itself. Unfortunately the network would be penetrated and dismantled by the Gestapo, with the help of local auxiliaries working for the German police. Joseph Danlos would die in the camp of Neuengamme on 8th January 1945. Louis Bourdet was a valuable member of the network. He was an electri-

cian who had to read the meter in the bunkers ! A cheerful cove, there was nothing he liked more than a good laugh with the Germans – while slipping his hand as opportunity arose into the gun to measure its calibre. And what happened to that priceless information that could have brought the calibre estimates down from 150mm to 100mm ? Such disdain on the part of the Allies would lead to many deaths.

By the time the type 611 casemate was finished, works had been in progress for two years. The command bunker, the bunkers to shelter the reserve and the ammunition, then the kitchen facilities followed. The three other howitzers stood in the open air for 7 months.

On the west bank of the Orne, the 3rd battery (3/AR 1716), commanded by Lieutenant Karl Heyde (who would later become the deputy commander of the regiment) found himself in a much more exposed position, his guns stuck out in the field among the cows. During an inspection tour, the Kommandeur of the regiment expressed his surprise at the state of affairs, given the increase in RAF activity. Heyde replied : « I cannot agree Colonel, cows are the best camouflage possible » He was quite right : 3/1716 would never be spotted by air observation and would remain untouched, fully justifying his remark : all too often that mass of concrete would prove a complete waste of time and effort.

The fate awaiting the battery

In early 1944 the battery was commanded by Captain Karl-Heinrich Wolter, with his second-in-command, Lieutenant Rudi Schaaf, esconced in their command bunker. They had an officer and two non-commissioned officers to help them carry out two important tasks.

Johannes Buskotte, from Osnabrück, was the Chief Sergeant Major who knew all there was to know about the battery. Peter Timp was an observation officer billeted in Descanneville with a platoon of infantrymen of the 3/GR 736th, his battle station being set up in the forward rangefinder emplacement built on the fringes of the Sallennelles Bay. His observation post was linked to the battery by deeply buried telephone cables. Sergeant Fritz Waldmann, 37, a mathematician by training, was responsible for adjusting the guns' range-finding settings.

The GFM Erwin Rommel had been appointed head of the Heeresgruppe B towards the end of 1943. For six months N°1 casemate had been completed while the other three howitzers stood in the open vulnerable to air attack. Rommel's inspection would change all that. On 6th March, while heading for Caen, he stopped off at Merville. His big black Horch drew up at the gate and he leapt out to be greeted by Captain Wolter. The GFM was with his second-in-command, with General Meise, the general in charge of Heeresgruppe B engineers, General Dr Hans Speidel, his Chief of Staff ; and Vice-Admiral Friedrich Ruge.

He found the OT works dragging on, and gave orders for the pace of work to be stepped up. His visit lasted twenty minutes.

On 20th March, before the first air raid over the battery, allied air reconnaissance took its last pictures of the site as yet undamaged. About 30 men had been recruited locally, and others had been conscripted into labour service out of Caen, from where two German lorries brought them each morning to work on the battery, all under the supervision of the Rittmann construction company.

Leutnant Steiner.

1. Field Marshal Rommel's inspection of Merville on 6th May 1944, just a month before the airborne operation ! He is being welcomed by Captain Karl-Heintz Wolter who would be killed in the raid of 20th May. (Mémorial Pégasus)

2 and 3. From left to right : Hans Buskotte, Major Karl Werner Hof, and Captain Schimpf, on 25th May 1944. In the background you can see a house and the same spot as it appears today in the picture to the left. (Mémorial Pegasus and photo Heimdal)

4. and 5. General Dollmann, Head of the Seventh Army, inspecting the site on 25th May 1944, five days after a catastrophic air raid. Leutnant Steiner, wearing the helmet, walks on the left. The house you see in the background and in the picture to the right, was a reference point in reports coming from the Resistance. (Mémorial Pegasus and photo Heimdal)

During the raid of 20th April over the Descanneville crossroads, the labourers were digging an anti-tank ditch to the west of the battery : 7 civilians were killed.

The first raid over the gun battery came as a profound shock to the German troops after so many months of peace and quiet.

It was so terribly frustrating to have to 'take the punishment' with nothing more than an 'Erika' 20mm Flak to fire back with. In the night of 9th –10th May, a raid by 56 Lancaster bombers, dropped their loads to the south of the Battery. This mis-aiming helped to boost the morale of the garrison a little, and the following report was drawn up :

« Of over 1000 bombs dropped, only 50 landed anywhere near the battery, and of those, only 2 actually struck a casemate. However an outbuilding at the local farm at La Mavais was flattened, the big farm of La Buisson took a massive bomb in the vegetable patch, and at Descanneville nearby, all the windows in the village were shattered. Casualties include 27 cows ; 40 missing, fled from the scene. The rabbit hutches have suffered severe damage. »

On the 15th May the Kommandeur of the Artillerie-Regiment 1716, Colonel Andersen, was taken ill and had to be sent back to Germany. He was replaced by Major Helmuth Knupe, promoted to the grade of lieutenant-colonel. He transferred Lieutenant Schimpf to Merville (to get him away from the HQ at Colleville). In the night of 19th –20th May the 20th air raid struck the battery, killing, as we have seen, Captain Wolter and his mistress. Schimpf crumpled before these responsibilities and got leave to return to Germany : it seemed he wasn't the man for the job. So Lieutenant Colonel Knupe gave Raimund Steiner, 24, command of the battery, a simple sub-lieutenant and former Alpine chasseur (Gebirgsjäger) from an old bourgeois family in Innsbruck, Austria. Knupe trusted him, but Steiner's family was anti-nazi, and had suffered persecution : his father had died while being deported.

He left Colleville for Merville on 20th May. Three days later the head of the LXXXIV.AK, General der Artillerie Erich Marcks, turned up unexpectedly at the battery and struggled up onto the top of the casemate to get a view of the site. He had lost a leg in Russia : Steiner offered to help but he would have none of it. Steiner asked when the « temporary » Howitzers would be replaced, but Marcks declared it was a strategic decision and he would be informed in due course. On 25th May, at 2pm, General Friedrich Dollmann, head of the 7th Army, turned up, and seemed most especially interested in the effect of the bombing. And just after he left, there would be another massive raid, the heavy bombs stretching the nerves to the limit. An unexploded bomb, rammed into the earth at an angle of 50° (delivered therefore by a figh-

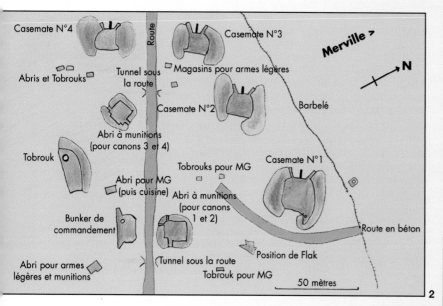

1. Aerial photograph taken by allied observation shortly before D-Day. You can see the anti-tank ditch quite clearly. On 29th April 1944 local labourers were working on the site when the bombers struck. The battery would take many raids, churning up the ground around the site, and levelling most of the outlying buildings. The raid of 20th May was devastating. (Photo RAF)

2. Ground plan of the battery today. (Heimdal)

Books concerning Merville's Battery

- Alan Jefferson, *Assault on the Guns of Merville*, John Murray, London, 1987.

- Sylvie Hée and Annie Fettu, *Merville Franceville plage*, Editions Cahiers du Temps, Cabourg, 1998.

- Alain Chazette, *Le Mur de l'Atlantique en Normandie*, Heimdal, Bayeux, 2000.

- Terry Gander and Peter Chamberlain, *Small Arms, artillery and special weapons of the Third Reich - An Encyclopedic survey*, Macdonald and Jane's Publishers Ltd, London, 1978.

ter-bomber), lay buried just outside the entrance to casemate N°3. This bomb was extremely dangerous : the General in charge of engineers came to see for himself what it consisted of. But the 2-metre thick walls had stood firm.

There would be a succession of further bombing raids.On the night of 26/27th May, the rain had churned the ground into slippery mud : at midday, on the 27th Rommel was present when a shout alerted the assembled officers to two low-flying Spitfires. As the aircraft opened fire everyone threw themselves into the mud, wrecking their smart uniforms… except Rommel, who impassively remarked : « *Come the invasion, it will soon be over.! »* Everyone expected the Allies to be thrown back into the sea, except Steiner, who, as an anti-nazi, thought their defences would be quickly overwhelmed. On the following night 55 Lancasters attacked, the Allies attracted like a magnet to the battery. Once again everything was thrown into disorder, 3 of the 4 MG proximity machine guns were destroyed, reducing the defences once more. Yet another raid took place in the evening of the 2nd June. On Sunday 4th June a platoon of engineers, the 'death commandos » consisting of deserters, Russian prisoners of war, Poles, Yugoslavs, came to dig out the unexploded bombs while Lieutenant Steiner reorganised his defences. D-Day was only two days away !

711th Infantry Division
The Dives Marshes

6th Airborne Drop Zone was bound by the course of the River Orne to the west and the Dives to the east. The Dives valley had been flooded by the Germans to create an area that could only be crossed with great difficulty. The valley had indeed originally been a deep estuary at a time, two thousand years ago, when the sea came to the level of the present N13. The estuary had gradually filled in and, in the tenth century, after the Vikings had settled in the area, been used for salt pans.

Nowadays it is a low, flat plain just a few metres above sea level and dotted with a few hummocks of higher ground, bearing Scandinavian names like Robehomme (holm = a Norse word meaning « island »). This plain has become a vast and well-drained meadow criss-crossed by many irrigation canals which in winter is always flooded owing to the high level of rainfall. A system of sluice-gates allows the water levels of the drainage canals to be regulated, and it was this which the Germans exploited in order to flood the area permanently, thereby creating a formidable east-west barrier and isolating the coast.

To the east of this great water-table began the sector of a new army, the 15th, a new Army Corps, the 81st, and a new infantry division, the 711th. This division had been constituted on 1st May 1941 in the Wehrkreis XI (the military region of Hanover). It was the product of a 15th wave of recruitment. In August 1941 it was sent to the North-East of France ; in December it was stationed near Rouen, under the command of Generalleutnant Friedrich Wilhelm Deutsch from July 1942 to March 1943, and then under Generalleutnant Josef Reichert to the end of the war. In the spring of 1944 it shifted further west, into the coastal area extending from the Seine estuary in the east to the Dives to the west. Its HQ was moved to Pont-l'Evêque. This division was therefore stationed in the Pays d'Auge and would be on the western flank of the future allied landing.

Generalleutnant Josef Reichert was helped by his first staff officer and operations officer Colonel Dr Polenski. The Division only had 14000 men, with two infantry regiments, 731st Grenadier Regiment and 744th Grenadier Regiment. The former was stationed on the coast, under the command of Oberst Enno Erich von Limburg, who had his HQ in at Trouville. This regiment was quite unusual in its racial composition, since 1st battalion, 1/Gren.Rgt of 731st was also made up of men recruited out of the Eastern Front (Ost batallion), Turkeman volunteers, « Mongols » (as the locals called them), belonging originally to 781st Turkestanisches Bataillon, and before that to the Red Army. They were under the command of Hauptmann Klaus and based in Hennequeville. 2nd

1

2

Generalleutnant Josef Reichert led the 711th ID.

The insignia of 711 Infanterie-Division, stationed in Normandy in June 1944.

Cloth insignia worn by volunteers from Turkestan, sewn into the right sleeve of their uniforms. (Photo Heimdal)

1. Deauville. Men of II/731st are walking though the concrete sea wall towards the beach. Notice the roof of the famous Normandy Hotel in the background. (BA/293/1485/27)

2. Some Turkeman volunteers drawn up as a guard of honour in front of the church of Saint Arnoult, near Hennequeville. (BA)

The clay 'Vaches Noires' cliffs, near Auberville and Villers-sur-Mer crumble chaotically into the sea. A landing here was so unlikely that it was only very lightly defended. We can see a machine gun emplacement with a primitive wooden parapet. One of the soldiers is waving at his comrade as he walks by, back from leave. These men belonged to 4th company of 744th Grenadier Regiment…

(BA/295/1568/23)

and 3rd battalions were based in Deauville-château and Touques respectively.

2nd infantry regiment, 744th Grenadier-Regiment, under the command of Colonel German Maier, was deployed further west, opposite the future airborne bridgehead. Its HQ was a type H608 concrete bunker in the village of La Forge, to the south-east of Houlgate. 1st battalion HQ was set up in Favrol, a village to the south of the seaside town of Villers-sur Mer. 2nd battalion (II/744) was stationed behind Cabourg and 3rd (III/744) had its HQ in the château of Dramard, near Gonneville-sur Mer. This regiment was equipped with 12 Schmeissers, 7 machine guns, 56 mortars (all types), 30 searchlights, 60cm and 90cm Flak searchlights, 37 5cm Pak anti-tank guns in fixed emplacements, three 7.5cm and six 4.7cm Paks. The first two battalions spread their

companies and heavy material along the coast, so were not available as a counter-attack force. 3rd battalion (III/744) was held in reserve. And as the flooded area represented an obstacle to the Germans as well, reinforcements could only be deployed in counter-attack against the airborne bridgehead to the north, between Cabourg and Merville.

This division had **1711th Artillery Regiment** attached to it. A few army gun batteries made up the coastal defence, such as 3/KHAA 1255 at Houlgate-Tournebride. Four horse-drawn gun batteries could be used to bolster the beach defences or, if necessary, used in the land battle, since they could be moved about. 3rd/AR 1711, equipped with four 7.62cm FK39 guns, was stationed at Saint-Vaasten-Auge, near the village of Grands Jardin. 4th AR/1711 was based in Gonneville-sur-Mer near Fortes Terres. 6th AR/1711 was based behind the Château at Dramard, known as Bruyère Mannet. Here the allies would have found what they so much feared at Merville : four powerful French-made 155mm Howitzers ! (15,5cm SFH 414 [f]) 7th AR/1711, equipped with similar such guns, was based in Mont de Grangues.

711th Division had other units at its disposal, but measured at company strength only, not battalion strength : an engineers company, Pionier-Kompanie 711, a company of anti-tank fighters (Panzerjäger-Kompanie 711) equipped with a dozen obsolete French R-35 tanks stationed at Bonneville-sur-Touques, to the south of Deauville, and a signals company, Nachrichten-Kompanie 711.

According to Allied intelligence this division was pretty weak, running at 40% strength in its static defence rôle and a mere 15% of its counter-attack capabilities : it had only one battalion in reserve behind what would be the airborne bridgehead. On the other hand there were quite a few dangerous gun batteries lurking in the background.

The Turkestan Legion

In May 1942 the Germans created the Turkestan Legion, presided over by Kajum Khan and his National Committee of Turkestan. In the event of a victory over the Soviet Union the Germans promised to help the Turkemans set up a state of their own, bringing together the republics of Kazakstan, Turkmenistan and Ouzbekistan, and the tribes that lived in them : the Turkemans, Karapalkes, Kazaks, Kirguizs, Tadjiks and Ouzbeks. From the end of 1943 16 battalions of these 'Turkemans', some 16000 men, had been constituted, most of them racially 'Mongol' in appearance and turkish language, and Muslim in religious practice. When the German army collapsed, their dream of independence was put on ice until the Gorbachev era, who would give the green light to the creation of Central Asian republics to the north of Afghanistan.

Right : ... but only a few hundred metres away lay the underground complex at Auberville. Here we can see one of the two entrances to it, bearing the notice « Hermann's Hole (Höhle) », and some of the men of a platoon of 4th company of the GR744 for whom it was designed as a dormitory (2 rooms) and munitions store (4 rooms).
(BA/295/1568/9)

Below : one of the corridors of the underground Auberville complex.
(BA/295/1568/6)

21st Panzer Division

A third division was drawn up alongside the others where the 6th Airborne would be engaged in battle, and this time it was an armoured division.

After its destruction in North Africa, it had been reconstituted in France out of Schelle Brigade West, created on 22nd March 1943. On 17th June it became Schnelle Division West, and then 21 Panzer-Division (neu) on 6th July : « neu », or new, to distinguish it from the former division destroyed in North Africa. It was set up outside Rennes on 15th July 1943, and began to be moved north towards Caen between the 26th and 30th April 1944. The two grenadier regiments were deployed either side of the Orne : 192nd Panzergrenadier-regiment's HQ was at Thury-Harcourt, its 1st battalion at Verson, its 2nd near Cambes-en-Plaine, to the west and north of Caen. However 125th Panzergrenadier-regiment was based to the east of Caen and the Orne, in the school at Vimont, 13km away.

125th Panzergrenadier-Regiment was led by Major Hans von Luck. This Prussian officer of the old school, 33 years old, of a family whose military history went back to the days of Frederick the Great. He had been taught by Erwin Rommel in the Reichswehr, and it was under his orders that he had got his baptism of fire when attacking Poland on 1st September 1939. He had led a reconnaissance platoon in 7th Panzer Division in 1940 in France, still with Rommel. Von Luck fully understood the offensive principles of his master, who in turn well appreciated the offensive qualities of his officer. Von Luck fought in Russia and, again under Rommel, in the Afrika Korps. It was inevitable he form part of the reconstituted division, and was given command of 125th Panzergrenadier Regiment, carrying the rank of Major (to be further promoted to Lieutenant Colonel in July). Hans von Luck had little sympathy for his National-Socialist masters, but he fought for his country with determination.

His 1st battalion (1/125), equipped with half-tracks, was led by Hauptmann Schenk zu Schweinsburg, and was based at Fierville-la-Campagne, 18 km to the south-east of Caen. It brought together 3 combat battalions, the 3rd under Leutnant Gerhard Bandomir. The « heavy » company was led by Oberleutnant Wendorff : his 2nd battalion (II/125), under the command of Hauptmann Kuron, had its HQ at Colombelles, 5km north-east of Caen, 5th company (Oberleutnant Brandenburg) was stationed in Troarn, 6th « heavies » (Hauptmann Ackermann) in Banneville, 8th, and 10th (schwere Werfer, heavy rocket launchers) in Colombelles. It is not known where the 7th and 9th were situated.

The division also had a regiment of tanks, Panzer-Regiment 100, whose HQ was at Aubigny, 3km north of Falaise. 155th Panzer-Artillerie-Regiment positioned its guns to the north and south of Caen, for 1st and 2nd troops respectively. However 4 batteries of III/155 were in position to the south-east of Caen at Saint Aignan de Cramesnil and Bourgébus, quite close to Major von Luck's regimental sector. The reconnaissance battalion (Panzer-Aufklärungs-Abteilung 21) under Major Waldow was stationed to the south-east of Condé-sur-Noireau, but its highly mobile material was able to rejoin Major von Luck in double-quick time come D-Day.

1. Major Hans von Luck commanded 125th Panzer-Grenadier-Regiment of 21st Panzer Division. His unit, based in the south of the zone affected to 6th Airborne Division, represented the greatest single threat to the British paras. Here Major von Luck is perusing a map and listening to Leutnant Gerhard Bandomir's report (left), commander of 3rd company. (BA)

2. and 3. Hans von Luck (2, right) and Gerhard Bandomir (3, left) returning to the battlefield in 1989. Both are now dead. (Photos Heimdal)

Above : A Panzer IV (Panzer-Regiment 100) in position south of Ranville. (BA)

Opposite page : An assault gun of Sturmgeschütz-Abteilung 200 group under Major Becker equiped with a 7,5 cm Pak 40 : given the power of its material, this group represented a formidable threat. A fearsome 105mm howitzer was also mounted on a French Hotchkiss tank chassis (10,5cm Feldhaubitze 18/40). It had a 12 km range and could fire at a rate of 6 to 8 rounds a minute : it was particularly effective when used in artillery support against tanks. (BA)

Left : A map dated 28th April summing up the Allied intelligence assessment of the disposition of the German forces between the Seine and the Orne, where 6th Airborne would be landing. The allies put German strength at 13000 men in 711 Infanterie-Division, armed with 20 anti-tank weapons, 60 medium artillery pieces, and 35 tanks, and well placed to counter-attack. It also enjoyed the support of the coastal guns at Le Havre, while 3 armoured divisions were, to a greater or lesser degree, within useful distance : 21st SS Panzer Division (very near), 12th SS Panzer Division (fairly near) and the Panzer Lehr Division. 116th Panzer division stationed outside Rouen can also be noted.

Specialised Airborne Equipment

1. The British Para's equipment : his red beret with the winged parachute badge, alongside a couple of grenades lying on a Denison Smock. (Photo Heimdal)

2. The parachutist ready to jump, his uniform and equipment protected by a parachute smock, kitted out in his parachute webbing and here wearing an inflatable life-belt. The helmet is covered by camouflage netting. (Mémorial Pégasus)

The airborne division was trained to use specialised equipment adapted to a swiftly deployed force, starting with the paratroop units equipped for the purpose.

The men of the Parachute Regiment

On the 9th July 1940 the first soldiers of the British Army to follow paratroop training were the B and C Troops of N°2 Commando. Everything at first had to be improvised, modelling their equipment on the German example. Their instructors, naturally enough, were RAF : RAF pilots and crews already received instruction in bailing out at Henlow. After training inside two converted hangars at Ringway, the first jumps took place out of a Whitley bomber – through a hole cut in the floor of the fuselage. From the beginning, the organisation of a 'stick' of ten men was equivalent to the smallest combat infantry unit.

The **parachute** itself was based on the damaged parachute and steel helmet of a Fallschirmjäger brought to the training school at Ringway. Two British firms, which before the war had been in competition one with the other, set about combining their efforts to manufacture thousands of examples of the new parachute and harness for use by the airborne troops. The 'statichute', whereby the parachute opened automatically was well-known, widely used, and improved upon over time. Usually the canopy was made out of nylon, or sometimes cotton, and had a diameter of 28 feet or just over 9 metres. The parachute was folded up inside its envelope : a process which took a specialist 25 minutes to carry out, including all checks after use. It was not permitted to leave it folded for more than two months, or to use it for more than 25 jumps. WAFs, the Women's Auxiliary Force were normally used for this vital task as they were judged particularly skilful at it.

The 1942 model of the **parachute smock** was copied from the German type : it hugged the body, came down to the thighs and could be done up with a zip and 3 snap buttons. It could be adjusted by a belt and harness straps which could however snag during the jump. It had to be worn as a matter of security. Usually the paratroops divested himself of it on landing.

The **Denison Smock,** introduced in 1941 and named after its inventor, Major Denison, was peculiar to the

1

2

British paratroops; it was a roomy cotton outfit made out of heavy-duty windproof material, with large pockets and worn between the battledress and the parachute smock. After tearing off the parachute smock, this immensely practical garment was worn into battle.

There was also the Airborne Forces sleeveless over-smock, officially termed the Jacket, Parachutists, 1942 Pattern, a version of the parachute smock with 4 pockets in the front used, among other things, for grenades. Despite its designation as the « 1942

model », it was in fact only introduced shortly before D-Day.

The battledress was the classic British soldier's uniform : khaki jacket and trousers, but with a slightly different cut and a large pocket for maps on the right thigh.

The paratroops were all volunteers recruited out of regiments whose uniforms they would have been wearing when they arrived at their new unit. From that moment on they would above all be distinguished by their maroon red beret which had been introduced on 29th July 1942, according to Regulation

1. Paratroops embarking on a Dakota. (IWM)

2. It took about 25 minutes to check and fold a parachute, a vital task, as the notice hanging above the WAFs declares : *Life depends on every parachute you pack.* Women were usually given this job as they were deemed to be the more skilful at it. (IWM)

3

3. Two men from a Parachute Battalion of the 6th Airborne Division picking up their parachute at the military stores. (IWM)

1. A combat-ready para : once on the ground he has divested himself of the Parachute smock, revealing the Denison combat smock beneath. He is armed with a MK5 Sten gun machine-pistol with wooden stock and grips. (Mémorial Pegasus)

2. The 6th Airborne sleeveless parachute smock, issued shortly before D-Day. (Mémorial Pegasus)

Various insignia worn by British paratroops. **1** and **2**, cloth shoulder insignia of the Parachute Regiment. **3.** The new Parachute Regiment beret badge introduced in May 1943. **4.** The cloth qualifying badge introduced on 17th June 1942, worn by anyone not a member of a paratroop unit. **5.** The 'wings' or cloth qualifying badge introduced on 28th December 1940. A refusal to jump could lead to its being withdrawn. (Photo Heimdal)

1

2

ACI 1596. Major General Frederick « Boy » Browning, commanding airborne forces from November 1941, had noticed during a military parade at the Wellington Barracks, that the Guards wore different coloured berets unique to these troops. It struck him how a coloured beret could indicate membership of an élite : hesitating between blue and maroon, it is said that his wife, the novelist Daphne du Maurier, opted for the latter. Certainly the colour would seem to evoke the blood of sacrifice. Since, the red paratroop beret has been an unqualified success as a symbol of the most trustworthy, élite troops in places well beyond British shores.

Wearing the red beret is only permitted after having performed a number of qualifying jumps and obtained their wings. The Parachute regiment's original metal qualifying badge, introduced on 1st August 1942 showed an eagle topped by a crown landing on the letter AAC, « Army Airborne Corps ». In May 1943, nine months later, a new insignia was introduced. Reflecting the parachutists' qualification, it represented a deployed parachute flanked by wings and topped by the Crown and Anglo-Norman 'leopard' or lion. The badge took its firm place in tradition, symbolising British airborne operations from May 1943 onwards.

On the shoulder a cloth badge was sewn for all airborne divisions, the Pegasus horse, again an idea of Daphne du Maurier.

On 28 December 1940, Order N°1589 instructed the creation of a cloth qualifying badge for the parachutist.

It featured pale blue wings, a white parachute on a khaki background (1) and was sewn onto the right

6

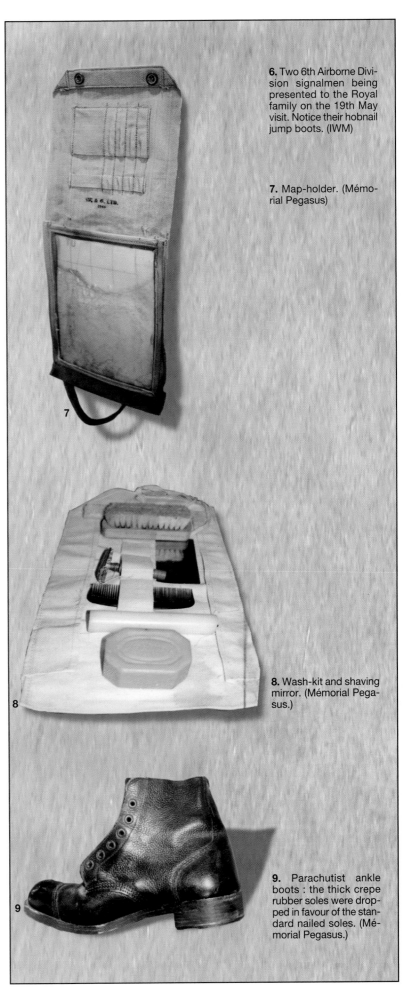

6. Two 6th Airborne Division signalmen being presented to the Royal family on the 19th May visit. Notice their hobnail jump boots. (IWM)

7. Map-holder. (Mémorial Pegasus)

8. Wash-kit and shaving mirror. (Mémorial Pegasus.)

9. Parachutist ankle boots : the thick crepe rubber soles were dropped in favour of the standard nailed soles. (Mémorial Pegasus.)

sleeve, between the shoulder and the elbow ; it had to be worn at all times, even when not serving in a parachute regiment. A regulation of 12th February 1941 specified its withdrawal on a refusal to jump, and a further regulation of 17th June 1942 (ACI1274) specified that the badge was to be worn 2 inches (5 cm) below the line of the shoulder.

Another cloth badge was introduced by this same regulation : a straightforward white parachute on a background of the drab khaki colour of the uniform. This was the qualification badge for 'non- regular parachute trained personnel,' in other words, men who did not form part of a paratroop unit.

On the shoulder each member of the airborne division wore a curved cloth insignia bearing the name of his regiment or specific unit. Paratroops bore the words : 'Parachute Regiment.'

The parachutist had a specially designed camouflage-netted round helmet with a chin strap that framed the ears. The ankle boots originally had thick crepe rubber soles, but as this proved unnecessary, the shoes were issued with standard nailed soles.

(1) *Cloth worked with pale blue wings and a white parachute on a background of drab material.*

The Bren Gun mounted on its tripod. (Mémorial Pegasus.)

Weapons

A paratrooper had to bear light arms : the Colt 38, the Webley 38 MkII revolver, the 9mm Browning automatic or the Mk2 Sten gun carried in the webbing of his parachute, the 1928 Thompson A1 machine-gun, the Bren machine-gun, or the standard Lee Enfield 4 Mark 1 rifle. Then there was always the silent weapon of war : the Sykes-Fairburn dagger.

The PIAT gun was not much use against tanks. Additional weight to their attack could be brought to bear by a number of weapons : the Gammon grenade with its hessian bag packed with plastic explosives, 2 types of mortar, light, easily portable mortars, and the 3-inch (75mm) mortar that could be carried on the back of two men in two parts, or in a jeep. The US M8 **75mm pack howitzer** was a light, compact, American-made field piece designed to be towed by a jeep. Other artillery pieces were the classic 6-pounder anti-tank gun and the 17-pounder anti-aircraft gun.

All the artillery pieces and vehicles had to be brought in by glider, and the weight distribution within the aircraft had to be precisely calculated to maintain equilibrium in flight. The lighter vehicles, like the **jeeps,** often fitted with Vickers machine-guns, were brought in by Horsa gliders with their trailers, which were immensely practical for carrying war material, ammunition or explosives. Heavier vehicles had to loaded into Hamilcars, capable of carrying small lorries, Bren

The Sten Gun Mk 5 machine-pistol with its wooden stock, was well adapted to the needs of the paratroops.

The light PIAT bazooka was widely used but not very efficient : here you can see it displayed for royal inspection on 19th May 1944. Some of these men are snipers wearing their cloth camouflage ribbons. (IWM)

A US M8 Pack Howitzer is being made ready for action here by artillerymen of the (53rd Worcestershire Yeomanry) Airlanding Light Regiment RA during an exercise. This very compact field piece had been specially designed for airborne operations. (IWM.)

Carriers, or even light Tetrarch tanks. This tank was also part of the specialised armoury of the airborne troops. In 1937 Vickers had worked on a new tank project to replace the light MkVI tank. This would be the MkVII, proposed and realised by the War office in 1938. This little tank, also known as the A17 Light Cruiser linked speed with plate armour. An initial order of some 120 was made but, with the outbreak of war and the Blitz difficulties began to arise and only 177 were run off the assembly lines. The experience of tank battles in 1940 put the whole concept of the light tank into question ; reconnaissance scout cars were preferred, fitted with machine guns.

The army cast about in vain for some use to which they could put the Tetrarch MkVII light tank until the development of airborne divisions provided the ideal solution. Weighing in at only 7.5 to 8 tons when combat ready, its compactness, speed (40mph on the road, 25mph off road) made it the perfect machine – just when it was scheduled for the scrap-heap ! They were issued to the 6th Airborne Reconnaissance Regiment.

Specialised military material

The airborne troops would enjoy a number of peculiar methods of locomotion ; such as the folding bicycle, which allowed them to get about the country quickly. It was the second of the two models developed that would be used in Normandy. A pack could be strapped into the frame.

Then there were two specialised motorbikes with the Welbike .... Collapsible Motorcycle, nicknamed the Corgi, designed specifically for the airborne troops in 1942 and parachuted in in its own container. It could be assembled quickly and operational in minutes.

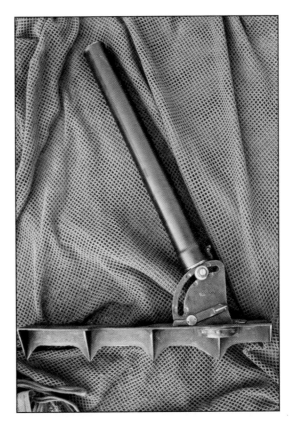

Above : Light, easily portable mortar. (Photo Heimdal)

Below : The 3 -inch (75mm) mortar, a powerful weapon which could be carried on the backs of two men, in two parts. The jeeps were brought in by gliders. (Mémorial Pegasus)

The Tetrach Mk VII

Technical Specification :

- Crew : 2 men, tank leader and driver

- Engine : Meadow, 12 cylinders, 175cv

- Length : 4.05m

- Width : 2.20m

- Height : 2.10m

- Weight combat ready : 7.5 – 8 tonnes

- Speed : 40mph on road
  25mph off road

- Range : 120km/ 70 miles

- Ditch straddle : 1.5m

- Armour : 4mm – 14mm

- Guns : 1 2lb (40mm) gun, 50 rounds ; l 7.52 Besa machine gun, 2025 rounds ; or 3 » (75mm) mortar. (Tetrarch ICS type)

A Tetrarch light tank being unloaded from a Hamilcar glider by men of 6th Airborne Reconnaissance Regiment during exercises at the RAF airbase at Tarrant Rushton. (IWM)

A Tetrarch tank being secured inside a Hamilcar glider by two men of 6th Airborne Reconnaissance Regiment. (IWM)

A Tetrarch tank is firmly secured by steel straps. Notice the different markings : the divison insignia, the number 85 in white on a red background, and on the right a wooden ladder to gain access to the cockpit. (IWM)

Another, larger, but very light motorbike with a two-stroke engine was designed for and used by men in reconnaissance and liaison missions.

A light, highly practical, collapsible two-wheel trolley helped to shift material about easily, and small featherweight trailers could be shunted about by a strong pair of arms. Various packs and bags secured by webbing straps allowed for the easy transport of material, for example the 3-inch mortar could be strapped to the back of two men in two pieces.

1. An exercice in London using the second model of the folding bicycle : note the transport pack strapped onto the frame. (IWM)

2. The bicycle could be quite easily folded in two. (IWM)

3. The second model of the folding bicycle allowed the rider to get about quickly. This one was used on D-Day around Ranville. (Photo Heimdal)

Long cylindrical containers that split open along their length, and sturdy rectangular wickerwork baskets were used to drop this equipment safely.

6th airborne division signals units used light radio sets which could be strapped to the chest, and even had the use of carrier pigeons parachuted in drum-like boxes !

The most impressive of all their specialised equipment were the gliders which we will examine, along with training and operational preparations, in the following chapter.

Below : A mini motorbike nicknamed the 'Corgi '. (Photo Heimdal)

Above : One open and one closed container used to parachute in all kinds of supplies. (Mémorial Pegasus)

Below : A light motorbike fitted with a two-stroke engine designed for used by airborne troops. (IWM)

A container is being emptied of its collapsible motorbikes, straightway assembled on the spot by the paras. (IWM)

Lieutenant Colonel Shamus Hickie, King George VI and Princess Elizabeth inspecting a cane basket used to deliver supplies. (IWM)

Webbing straps secure the wickerwork basket and its parachute. (Mémorial Pegasus)

Carrier pigeon and its parachute used specifically by communication units. (MP). (Mémorial Pegasus)

Towards D-Day

At 11am on 17th February 1944, Lieutenant General F. 'Boy' Browning came to Major General Gale's HQ with the splendid news that they had been looking forward to hearing : that General Eisenhower's final plans for Operation Overlord, the amphibious assault into Normandy, would involve the 6th Airborne Division. After all their efforts, all the long years and months of hard training, now at last it would all bear fruit.

However when they began to look at the plan in more detail, it was disappointing to see that inadequate air transport and only a single parachute brigade, with one anti-tank battery in support, were to be committed. The brigade would be under the command of the 3rd Infantry Division in a seaborne landing on Sword Beach, and its only objective would be the seizure of the two bridges over the Orne and the canal, the bridges of Ranville and Bénouville ! The plan lacked the ambition in keeping with the deployment of an élite division. Major-General Gale decided that the 3rd Parachute Brigade under Brigadier James Hill, should be chosen for the task. Hill, an outstanding leader of men, felt that the coup de main operation would be far better carried out by light infantry in gliders than by paratroops. Major General Gale made his feelings known that a single brigade was simply not enough, and on **23rd February** it was decided to attribute RAF Groups 38 and 46 to the operation, thereby allowing the whole division to be committed, and under the direct orders of the 1st British Corps !

Thus the airborne division would be entrusted with securing the whole left flank of the 1st Corps of the British 2nd Army. The staff officers of the 6th Airborne Division set up their command structure at 1st Corps HQ at Ashley Gardens, London, to begin the more detailed planning process for the airborne assault. Then, to put the finishing touches to the airborne operation the Planning Group moved into 'The Old Farm' of Brigmerston House near Milston, a village between Netheravon and Bulford in Wiltshire. There, every element within the division was represented, including the staff liaison officers of the 1st Special Service Brigade, and the N°38 and 46 RAF Groups. In the final phase, the headquarters moved to Scotland to liaise with the 3rd Infantry Division.

Lieutenant General F.A.M. Browning.

Major General R.N. Gale.

The Objectives

First the division had to seize intact the two bridges over the Orne river and Canal, at Ranville and Bénouville, a key mission already part of the initial plan. The bridgehead had to be held at all costs. Then the next objective would be to take out the Merville gun battry before seaborne troops came ashore at Sword beach : allied intelligence had overestimated its capacity to inflict casualties on the troops disembarking

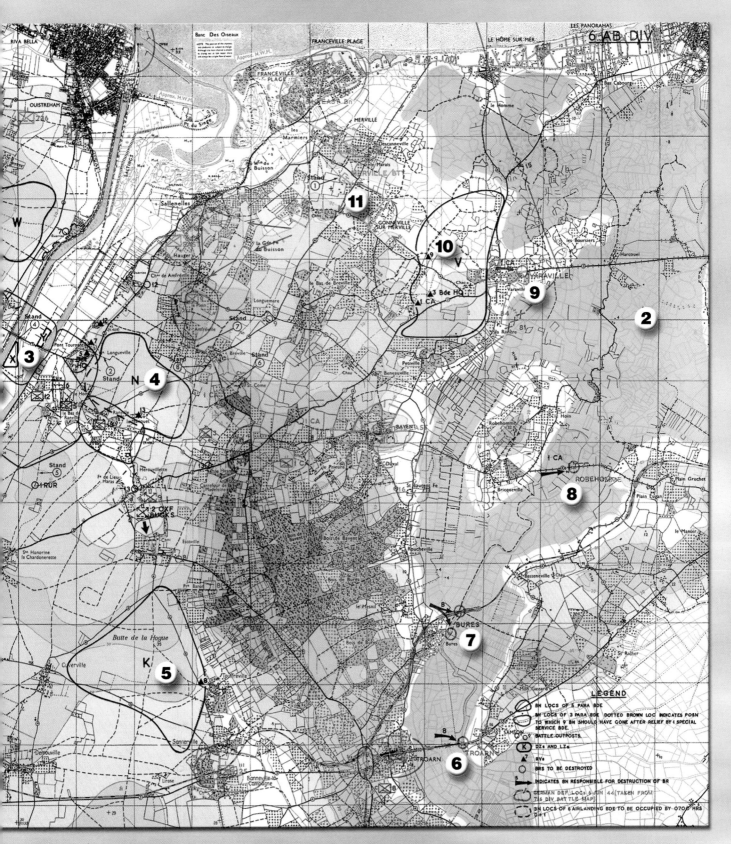

there at that range (see chapter 2). Thirdly, five fixed bridges had to be blown over the river Dives at Varaville, Robehomme, Bures and Troarn, to stop any German counter-attack across the flooded valley in its tracks.

There would be two other secondary missions : to clear the entire lodgement area between the Orne and the Dives of the enemy, and hold it. They were also to take the villages of Sallenelles and Franceville to the north, and the whole coastal area between

This map clearly show the 6th Airborne Division objectives. **1.** The Orne, with the canal to the west of it. **2.** The flooded marshland valley of the Dives. **3.** The sector for Major Howard's 'coup de main party', seizing the Orne river bridge at Ranville (LZ 'X') and canal bridge at Bénouville (LZ 'Y'). **4.** Ranville and LZ 'N', the landing zone for the 5th Brigade. **5.** DZ 'K', to the south, for gliders of the 8th Battalion. **6.** The bridge at Troarn, to be blown. **7.** The bridge at Bures, to be blown. **8.** The bridge at Robehomme, to be blown. **9.** The bridge at Varaville, to be blown. **10.** Drop Zone 'V'. **11.** The Merville Gun Battery. **12.** Landing Zone 'W', for the 6th Airlanding Brigade.

them as far as Cabourg on the Dives estuary in order to protect from coastal batteries the incoming seaborne troops landing east of the Orne. Once secure in this bridgehead, the division must repel German counter-attacks which could be expected from the east and south-east, effectively creating a shield behind which the seaborne troops at Sword Beach would be able to advance south and capture Caen.

However, despite the commitment of 2 RAF groups, there would be insufficient aircraft to bring in the whole division in one lift. Two parachute brigades would have to be dropped the night of the 5th- 6th June, Operation Tonga, and an airborne brigade, along with heavy equipment and the rest of HQ would be brought in by glider at the end of the afternoon of D-Day, Operation Mallard.

The Plan

Operation Tonga

The pathfinders and the coup de main over the bridges.

At **0h20**, 60 Pathfinders of the 22nd Parachute Independent Company would be dopped out of 6 Albermarle bombers onto 3 Drop and Landing Zones N, V and K, to guide in the others. At the same instant, the 'coup de main party' would seize the bridges at Bénouville and Ranville. Six Halifax bombers towing 6 gliders would bring in Major John Howard and Company D of the 2nd Oxs and Bucks : 3 gliders would land at Landing Zone X, near the cantilever bridge at Bénouville, and the other 3 at Landing Zone Y, the old swing bridge at Ranville. The mission of Major Howard and his men was to capture and hold these two bridges. Meanwhile 21 Albemarle would be dropping the first echelon of 200 paratroops of the 3rd and 5th Brigades.

The Parachute Brigades and the HQ

At **0050hrs** 108 C47 Dakotas, and 17 gliders would bring in 2500 paratroops of the 3rd Parachute Brigade under Brigadier James Hill onto Drop Zone K, east of Caen between Cuverville and Sannerville, and on Drop Zone V, to the west of Varaville, where the company HQ would be set up. These two Drop Zones would constitute the south-east and north-east corners of the bridgehead, out of which the raiding parties to blow the Dives bridges would be launched.

At the same time, 91 Stirling bombers would bring in 2600 paratroops of the 5th Parachute Brigade under Brigadier Nigel Poett onto Drop Zone N, near Ranville and to the east of the Orne bridges. 21 C47 Dakotas and 19 Albermarles would bring in the divisional headquarters.

The missions of the 5th Parachute Brigade

Major General Gale gave out precise instructions to each of his units regarding their missions in France. The **5th Parachute Brigade** was to take and hold the Bénouville and Ranville bridges intact, for which vital task Company D of the 2nd Oxs and Bucks was attached to the brigade. Pine-Coffin's 7th Parachute Battalion was to support the company and stand firm against all German counter-attacks, including armoured attacks, towards the Bénouville/Ranville/Bas de Ranville sector. These bridges had to be in Allied hands by 0020hrs when the Pathfinders would start jumping to guide in the aircraft bearing gliderborne troops and the divisional headquarters.

At **0320hrs,** in Landing Zone N, again outside Ranville, 68 Horsa gliders would land bearing 1200 men, HQ troops (artillerymen, engineers, medical support), 4 huge Hamilcar gliders bringing in the 4th antitank battery, attached to the 5th Brigade.

The missions of the 3rd Parachute Brigade

A detachment of the 22nd Independent Parachute Company, a platoon of the 4th Airlanding anti-tank battery ; the 3rd Parachute Squadron Royal Engineers, and the 224th Parachute Field Ambulance were all in support of the 3rd brigade.

At **0020hrs,** the reconnaissance company of the 9th Parachute Battalion would be dropped by 4 Albermarles to set up the 'coup de main party' against the Merville Battery. 2 Albermarles would drop pathfinders to mark out DZ V, near Varaville, for Otway's 9th Parachute Battalion and the 1st Canadian Battalion. The pathfinders for the 8th Parachute Battalion would mark out DZ K for Pearson's 8th Battalion north-east of Troarn.

At **0050hrs** 71 C47 Dakotas would drop the 9th Parachute Battalion, the 1st Canadian Parachute Battalion, and bring in 11 Horsas onto LZ V. Pearson's 8th Parachute Battalion would be dropped to the south, onto Drop Zone K with 6 Horsas in support on Landing Zone K.

At **0430hrs** 3 Horsa gliders would bring in a detachment of the 9th Parachute Battalion, which would land on the Merville Battery.

Meanwhile the 3rd Parachute Brigade had to carry out an important mission : the blowing of five bridges over the Dives. At 0050hrs Major Roseveare's 3rd Parachute Squadron Royal Engineers, with the 8th Parachute Battalion, would jump over DZ K. The first section – engineers – would blow the bridge at Troarn with demolition charges.

The second platoon would blow two bridges at Bures. These two platoons would be protected by paratroops of the 8th battalion. Both platoons would be equipped with jeeps and trailers.

The third section of this specialised squadron would jump – each man bearing 5kg of TNT - further north, onto Drop Zone V. With the 1st Canadian Parachute Battalion, their mission was to blow the bridges at Varaville and at Robehomme, east of a slight isolated rise out of the marshes. They too would be equipped with jeeps and trailers to help carry their explosive charges.

At 0500hrs, with the bridges blown, the 3rd Parachute Squadron RE would mine the roads around Brigadier Hill's 3rd Brigade sector to create an interdiction area between Varaville and Plein.

Towards midday the airborne bridgehead would be supported by the 1st Special Service Brigade under Lord Lovat, which would have landed on the beaches with the 3rd Infantry Division. This commando brigade would link up with the 6th Airborne Division, cross the Bénouville and Ranville bridges, and reinforce the airborne bridgehead to the east.

Operation Mallard

Towards the end of the evening of D-Day, around 9pm, Operation Mallard would bring in further reinforcements of the 6th Airlanding Brigade, brought in by 220 Horsas towed behind Stirling and Halifax bombers of the RAF 38 and 46 groups. They would land in Landing Zone W, to the west of the canal, and on Landing Zone N at Ranville. This airlift would also bring in elements of the 6th Airborne Reconnaissance Regiment RAC with their famous Tetrarch tanks in 30 Hamilcar gliders towed by Stirlings.

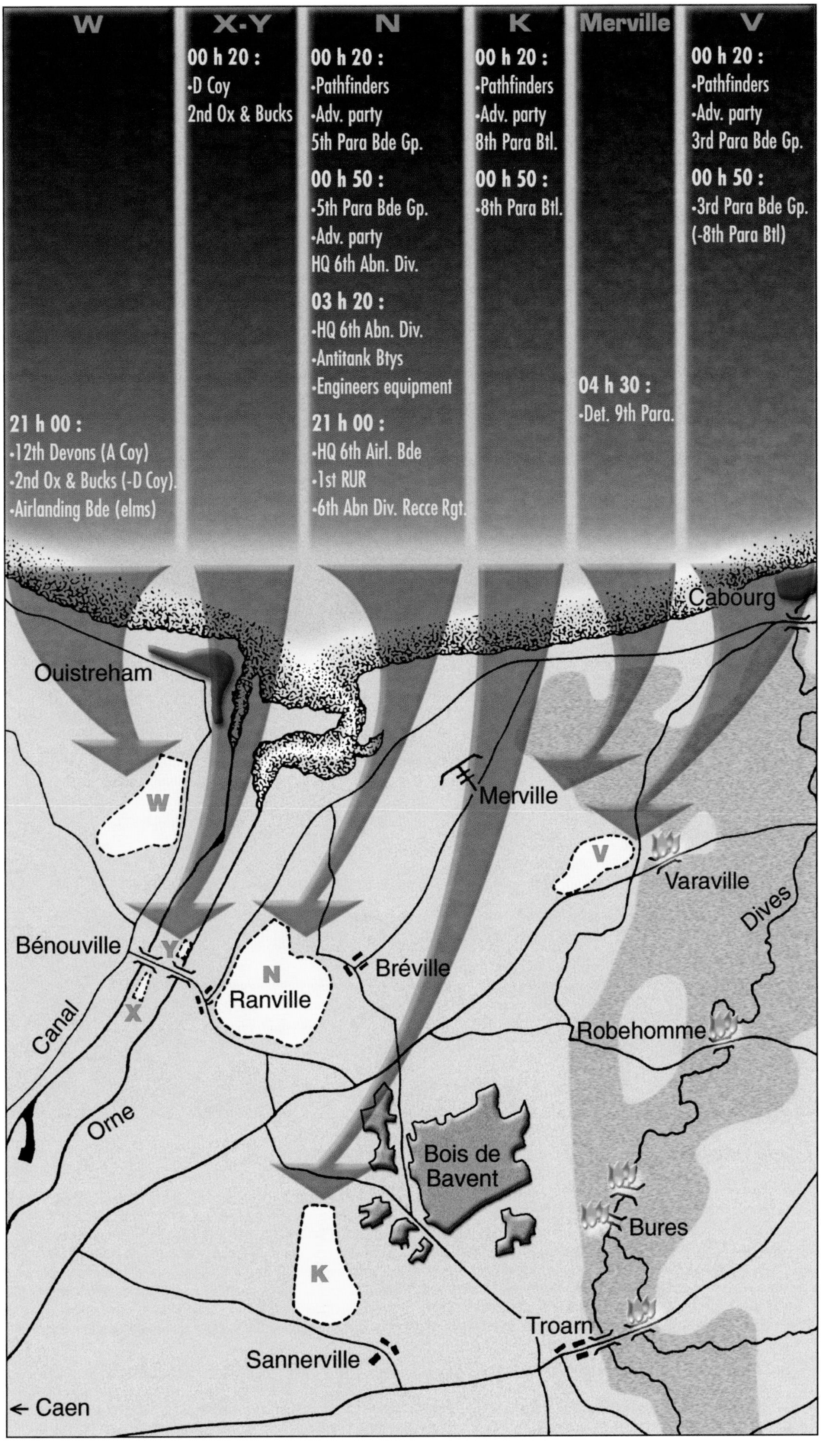

W	X-Y	N	K	Merville	V
	00 h 20 : •D Coy 2nd Ox & Bucks	**00 h 20 :** •Pathfinders •Adv. party 5th Para Bde Gp.	**00 h 20 :** •Pathfinders •Adv. party 8th Para Btl.		**00 h 20 :** •Pathfinders •Adv. party 3rd Para Bde Gp.
		00 h 50 : •5th Para Bde Gp. •Adv. party HQ 6th Abn. Div.	**00 h 50 :** •8th Para Btl.		**00 h 50 :** •3rd Para Bde Gp. (-8th Para Btl)
		03 h 20 : •HQ 6th Abn. Div. •Antitank Btys •Engineers equipment		**04 h 30 :** •Det. 9th Para.	
21 h 00 : •12th Devons (A Coy) •2nd Ox & Bucks (-D Coy). •Airlanding Bde (elms)		**21 h 00 :** •HQ 6th Airl. Bde •1st RUR •6th Abn Div. Recce Rgt.			

Map showing D-Day landings by parachute and gliders of the 6th Airborne Division east of the Orne.

Cabourg

Ouistreham

Merville

W

V

Varaville

Dives

Bénouville

Y

N

Bréville

X

Ranville

Robehomme

Canal

Orne

Bois de
Bavent

Bures

K

Troarn

Sannerville

← Caen

Training

Now that the detailed plan was in place there remained the months of training up to D-Day itself. This time would be used to concentrate the men on preparing for their specific and concrete objectives, the 'coup de main' by glider to seize the bridges intact, the neutralisation of guns, the blowing of bridges by demolition etc

All this preparation required meticulous planning and organisation, and all the while maintaining the strictest secrecy. The skeleton HQ under Major General Gale was set up in a modest villa, « pleasantly hidden among the trees near the river Avon. » (1) These elaborate precautions were effective but somewhat exaggerated at times. For example only one officer would be responsible for the one key that gave access to the one door where the planning staff would meet, and one day, when he was delayed, he found a throng of eager planning officers – most of them of field rank, in a state of high indignation, for the door « was fast locked and entry by any other means was impossible, since all the windows were barred. They had to pass the time in the church cemetery in silence, or talking about trivial matters unable to discuss what was most uppermost in their minds » (p.155, Red Beret).

the sheep from the goats : the men were subject to close observation to see who were fit enough to serve in a paratroop unit, and if you did not make the grade, you would be sent back from whence you came labelled 'RTU' : Returned to Unit.

Those who passed muster at this first selection procedure went off to the famous N°1 Parachute Training School at Ringway, near Manchester. In the first of two weeks training the emphasis was on the practical : how to jump correctly out of an aircraft, how to control his parachute so as to arrive safely on the ground. A life-size wooden model of the trap door in the Whitley bomber was set up. The 'trapeze' allowed the men to learn how to hang from the rigging of their parachute. Nothing was simpler to learn to control the fall : a toboggan whose ramp came to about 2 metres above the earthen ground allowed the future paratroop to 'fall and roll'. A 20' platform (6.7m) with a system of compressed air ejected at the moment of impact simulated the effect of landing on the ground. The men were suspended from a 100' (33m) metal tower under their parachute canopy from a metallic arm and there had to learn the proper reflexes when in this position. Once he was 'comfortable', he would be released and would drop to the ground under his parachute. This contraption

Frank Gleeson of 12th Battalion.

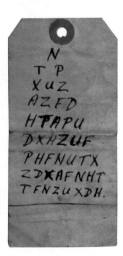

Frank Gleeson's luggage label on which he had prepared for an eye test, having poor eyesight. (Photo Heimdal)

The Paratroops

When the division had been formed, only four of six battalions, the 7th, 8th, 9th and the 1st Canadian Battalion, had been constituted. The 12th and 13th Battalions were formed out of infantry units merged into the airborne division. Only half of the original effectives had volunteered in the division, ready for parachute training ; their ranks were topped up by other volunteers to serve as paratroops. Their training as paratroops began in the airborne forces depot at Harwick Hall. This initial training was to sort out

(1) See The Red Beret, the Battery Press, 1985 p155 by Hilary St-George Saunders.

was invented by the men of the 1st Polish Parachute Brigade.

After this first week of exercises, the trainee would then pass to an exercise which was rather disagreeable to most of the initiates. They had to go up to 700' in an anchored balloon and suffering perhaps from vertigo and air sickness, the trainee would await his instructions to jump. He would be with three other trainee paratroops in a 'stick', sat around a hole in the ballon basket, looking down into the sickening void.

When the order from the instructor came – « GO ! » each had to throw himself through the round hole and rip open his parachute 120' (40m) below the balloon. On the ground an instructor would be bello-

1

Among the young volunteers for the 12th Battalion (Yorkshire) the Parachute Regiment was the 19 year-old Frank Gleeson. A sports fanatic, he was bored in his artillery unit and volunteered for the airborne. On the day of his medical he learnt that anyone wearing glasses was failed – and he needed them. So he thought up a ruse to get round the problem. He learnt by heart the lower lines of letters usually required to be read off during the eyecheck, and on the strength of his unusual height, excellent physical condition, and « good eyesight », his candidature was accepted. He would have the privilege of throwing himself through the hatch of a Stirling at 0107hrs precisely on D-Day ! Until his recent decease, he had always worn glasses.

1. Training in hangars out of a model of the fuselage, from which hung the trainee parachutists. (IWM)

2. Jumping from a toboggan and rolling on the ground was part of the necessary initial training for the parachutist. (IWM)

3. A trainee preparing to jump from a 100' tower. (IWM)

Below : Some training jumps. (Mémorial Pegasus)

2

wing instructions through a loud-hailer when adjustments were necessary. Despite these grim acrobatics, there were relatively few accidents.

After two such jumps, five jumps out of an aircraft would follow. Initially this would be in sticks of 5 men, and then in the regulation stick of twenty. Jumping out of a hole in the floor of a converted Stirling or Albemarle always risked twisting the parachute : it was so much easier out of the side door of a Dakota !

After completing 11 jumps at Ringway, the trainee parachutists were at last awarded their qualifying badges : their 'wings' stitched onto the right shoulder of their uniforms.

3

The gliders

With the parachute troops, the spearhead of the airborne attack would be men and material brought in by glider units. The British used two types of gliders, the Horsa and the giant Hamilcar. They would be piloted by men of the Glider Pilot Regiment, whose creation went back to the early days of the development of British airborne forces.

The Glider Pilot regiment

In 1940 the United Kingdom was both in its darkest and most glorious year, having suffered heavy defeats on the continent, leaving behind most of its military equipment on the beaches at Dunkirk. But the summer of 1940 had also brought a miracle : the saving of the daylight skies over Britain by the pilots of the RAF, thereby denying a German invasion threat. The air arm, which had been neglected between the wars, acquired enormous prestige. An airborne army began

me *Wings*. The Glider Pilot Regiment, still attached to the Army would be under the command of the now-promoted Brigadier George Chatterton with two 'wings', each consisting originally of six squadrons, each squadron made up of four flights. N°1 Wing was under the command of Lieutenant Colonel Iain Murray : his C Squadron would be equipped with Hamilcars. N°2 Wings was under the command of Lieutenant Colonel John Place. An Independent Squadron would be committed to battle separately, fighting in North Africa, and the landings into Provence, France.

The Hamilcar

This giant glider was perhaps the most unusual piece of equipment used by the airborne troops. The Germans had thought up the idea of a monstrous glider called the Me321 Gigant which was very difficult to fly. The British were far more successful with the same concept. They called their glider the Hamilcar, in honour of the Carthaginian General who took Hannibal's elephants over the Alps into Italy.

At the start of the war all the British had was a light glider, the Hotspur, but the idea of a much heavier glider quickly took shape in the hands of General Aircraft and construction started in 1941 in the Birmingham railway carriage works. This glider was referred to as a « whale with wings » - a wing span of 110 feet (37m), a height of 25 feet (8.30m) and a total length of 67 feet 6 inches (over 23m).

The prototype was half 'life-size', but time was pressing so it was given a wooden air frame. In March 1942 the first full size Hamilcar took to the air and incredibly, this great leviathan of an aircraft flew like a dream. Its designers had brought to bear a remarkable concentration of talent. Brigadier Chatterton decided to carry out a test flight from Netheravon to

1 and 2. Cloth shoulder insignia of glider pilots.

3. The Army Flying Badge was adopted following decision N°768 of 11th August 1942, to be worn above the left pocket of all Air Observation Post Pilots and glider pilots.

4. Glider co-pilot badge, adopted by regulation ACI1128n on the 19th August 1942*.

5. Badge for glider trained infantry, an unofficial badge authorised by the airborne HQ for those who had participated in landing operations.

6. Glider Pilot insignia to be worn on the beret, bearing the letter AAC (Army Air Corps).

(Photo Heimdal/Memorial Museum of Bayeux)

Right : Glider pilot's flying helmet. (Mémorial Pégasus)

to take shape under General 'Boy' Browning at this time.

Major George Chatterton, an RAF pilot back in 1930, was bored to the back teeth with manning a coastal defence unit in the south of England. Then an advertisement for glider pilots brought him one snowy and freezing day in the second winter of the war to Salisbury station where a jeep was waiting to take him across the bleak, chalky Wiltshire downs to Netheravon airfield. He was received by General Browning, at 46, a lean athletic figure with a pencil moustache and a beautifully cut, belted uniform. The General was a man of real presence and charm ; Major Chatterton came under his spell and found himself two weeks later selected as second-in-command to Lieutenant Colonel Rock, commander of the 1st Battalion, the Glider Pilot Regiment : Chatterton's experience as an officer in both the air and army had served him well. There was only one battalion in this unusual regiment, formed out of army pilots, as the insignia of their beret indicated : AAC or Army Air Corps. A second battalion was created and Major Chatterton put in command. However during a nighttime training exercise Lieutenant Colonel John Frank Rock, the pioneer of airborne troops, crashed his glider and died later in a military hospital. So Chatterton was given the 1st Battalion, and command of the 2nd passed to Lieutenant Colonel Iain Murray.

In the end, in 1943 the two battalions were redesignated according to tradition in the air arm and beca-

Tarrant Rushton. When he came up to the beast he was amazed at its sheer size. The only hope of getting it towed was by calling upon the services of a four-engined heavy bomber such as the Handley Page Halifax, and even this looked puny alongside the giant glider. The cockpit stood 8 metres from the ground and could only be reached by a wooden ladder ! The two pilots sat in tandem one behind the other in relative security since there was bullet-proof glass to the sides and front and a sheet of armour plating below them. The whole air frame was in wood and metal, weighing in at seven tons or 18000 pounds ; it could bear its own weight, making the total loaded weight 14 tons, and was capable of carrying a Bren Carrier, a light Tetrarch tank, a small Morris truck or a 17-pounder anti-tank gun.

Brigadier Chatterton could hear the pilot of his Halifax tow through the headphones : the rope became taught, the great glider slid along the grass, and on the second gentle bounce, became airborne : it would be his first test flight, and to his great surprise the glider seemed incredibly light. After a smooth run to the south coast, the tug was released, and he could begin to feel how wonderfully sensitive the craft was to the controls. « It was amazing to think that this great wooden monster had been contructed entirely on the basis of guesswork, a really fine piece of work by General Aircraft. » (2) He turned the aircraft to return to base, and when he came in to land, the glider seemed to gently float to a stop !

Brigadier George Chatterton handed the command of his great gliders to Major Dickie Dale : the Hamilcar Squadron would be C Squadron of N°1 Wing. Training began in November 1943, but come January 1944 there still remained a lot to be done. But thanks to the skills of Group Captain Tom Cooper and his flight commanders, such as Squadron Leader « Buster » Briggs, the training programme was able to increase in intensity. 1200 drops were achieved in February and March, as against only 311 up to that time. Landing speeds were reduced from 105 mph to 75mph. Over 400 drops were carried out at night, and with the spring, training became more intense than ever.

In April Brigadier Chatterton watched as, for the first time, a Tetrarch tank was stowed in the fuselage. No-one had tried to place such a load into the aircraft before : a light tank with all its crew inside it for added safety. All went well, but the last Hamilcar came in too quickly, at 110 mph. It bounced, bounced again, slithered across the airfield and crashed into a group of Nissan huts. The two pilots could look down from their perch at all the destruction, but the

A giant Hamilcar landing. (Mémorial Pegasus)

tank, which had been projected into the building at 80 mph, catapulted out of the glider and came to a halt 50 yards (45m) further on, smothered in the wrecked wood and metal fragments of the huts. Chatterton ran towards the Tetrarch and saw the driver emerge out of his hatch, his face covered in dust. « Are you alright ? », a worried Chatterton asked. The driver replied : « Yeh, but I'm covered in muck ! » (3) It would be the fastest tank in history.

This demonstration flight showed at any rate that it was possible to transport a light tank by air. The tank crews however had also received a special training, for as the glider came into land, the pilot was in contact with the tank crew through his telephone, and would give the signal for the driver to start up the engine before landing in order to warm it up. The exhaust was connected by a pipe to a little trapdoor in the plywood fuselage. Once on the ground, a landing trip was automatically released, the nose of the glider sprang open and the tank could drive straight out and into battle, all within 15 seconds of landing.

By the time the training programme was over, 2800 tows had been effected, or nearly 50 tows per glider

(2) See *The Wings of Pegasus, Battery Press,* 1982, p. 124-5.
(3) *Op. Cit.,* p. 125-6.

Model of a Giant Hamilcar. The wings bear the 'invasion stripes' into Normandy. This giant glider could carry a payload of 7 tons. (Mémorial Pegasus)

crew, which was a truly remarkable achievement. Above all great credit should be given to the RAF Halifax pilots who had quite a performance struggling to tow the giant Hamilcar in a steady line. 7 glider pilots were killed during these exercises.

The Horsa

The Horsa Mark II had a wing-span of 88 feet (29m), was 68 feet long (22m) and when empty, weighed 3.5 tons. It could carry 4.3 tons maximum. It had a removable undercarriage which became detached while landing on uneven ground. When under tow, it flew at 165mph. Once released it flew at 100mph, and could reach over 200mph in a gliding dive. It carried 28 fully armed troops, plus pilot and copilot, or two jeeps, or either a jeep with a 6-pounder anti-tank gun plus ammunition and crew, or a jeep and a 75mm howitzer plus ammunition and crew. Loading was carried out through a side door on the left-hand side of the fuselage.

Final training

By February 1944, when Major-General Gale received his divisional orders of engagement for the Normandy campaign, the state of readiness of the Glider Pilot Regiment left a lot to be desired. A worried Brigadier Chatterton said as much, pointing out that the last major exercise had been back in September 43. N°1 Wing, operating with the RAF's 38 Group, had only received the basic RAF training ; N°2 Wing was in an even more parlous state : a third of the unit was in Sicily and yet had not flown for months. A few pilots had managed to acquire some valuable experience in North Africa but most men hadn't even seen an airfield for at least 6 to 9 months ! The pilots had about 150 flying hours, but most of them were accumulated at flying school : indeed many instructors leading the training programme had barely more flying hours that the men they led.

A lot of problems remained unresolved. The biggest of them was how to bring the largest number of gliders in a single space of time and onto the same

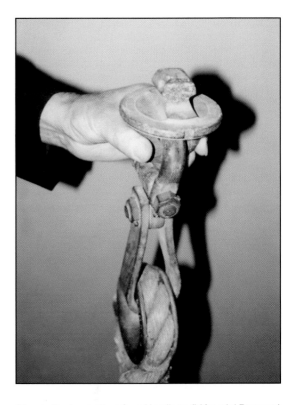

Above : towing system for a Hamilcar. (Mémorial Pegasus)

Below : A trapdoor in the Hamilcar to allow tanks to start up their engines before landing. (Mémorial Pegasus.)

Below : To reach the highest levels of skill, from February 1944 onwards glider pilot training increased in intensity. Here we can see preparations for a training flight : pilots are studying maps under the watchful eye of their instruction officer who often had barely more flying hours that their trainees. Notice also their flying helmets and the GPR insignia on their berets. (Museum of Army Flying)

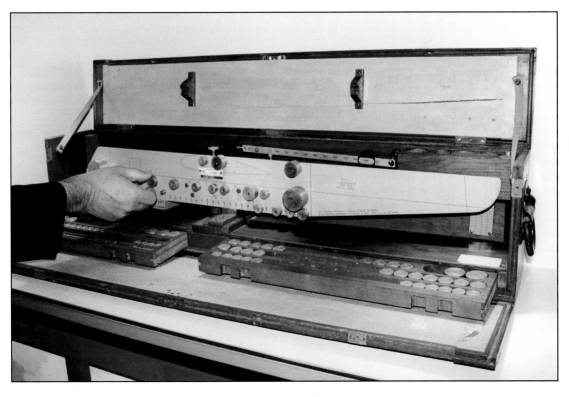

This instrument was designed to plan the weight distribution inside the glider. Armed with the weight statistics of each item of equipement to be loaded, their eventual position had to be carefully calculated in order to maintain the equilibrium of the aircraft. This model fuselage was used by the pilot to be balanced out by a system of small weights which represented the elements to be placed inside the glider. (Mémorial Pegasus.)

objective. To avoid collision and risk on landing, a 'funnel system' was perfected whereby during landing procedures each glider followed the glider in front as if it were passing through a funnel, so that each would land at regular intervals and come to rest one behind the other. The system proved its worth as dozens of gliders had to land at 30-second intervals. To refine their procedures still further pilots used tracing paper to copy the aerial reconnaissance photographs of their landing zones, and mark in where each glider would end up. All this organisation worked remarkably well, and the old rivalries that had dogged relations between the RAF and the Glider Pilot Regiment were a thing of the past, as they got on with the job in a spirit of total cooperation.

Another procedure which was perfected to allow an even greater degree of precision in finding their objectives was the use of 'target gliders'. These bore special markings and would land first on the target objective, followed by the others, in keeping with the 'funnel system'.

A serious difficulty had to be over come in the meantime : loading the material onto the glider. On a Horsa glider this took place through a side door. Experience of operations in the Mediterranean had demonstrated that although the gliders landed onto their objectives, it was all too often impossible to unload anything since the doors were either twisted or jammed on impact ! Some pilots resorted to using a belt of explosives to blow off the tail of the glider, but this all too often resulted in wrecking the equipment they had striven to bring : one can imagine how disappointed the hapless pilots would have felt in such circumstances ! Faced with this problem, Brigadier Chatterton found himself mulling over the problem with the engineer officer of 38 Group when the solution came to him in a flash : noticing the ring of bolts bracketing the circumference of the fuselage he declared, « My God, do you think we could just unbolt the thing ? ? » (4) The whole rear of the glider could then simply fall away. The finishing touches to such a system was developed so that the war material could be tipped out of the snapped-open fuselage.

A Horsa coming in to land : note the great surface area of the flaps. (Mémorial Pegasus.)

By D-Day the whole nose on some Horsa gliders could even be lifted up.

It took time to get to the point where large-scale military exercises could be mounted. The first took place on **2nd March 1944** out of Welford aerodrome. 97 bombers towing gliders (some of which were American) took to the air, and only 3 gliders missed their targets !

The greatest concentration of aircraft to that date took place on 23rd April when 38 and 46 Groups brought 185 gliders to their objectives at Southrop, Brize Norton and Harwell. 38 Group brought N°1 Wing, and, for the first time, 46 Group brought in N°2 Wing, henceforth its responsibility.

There were also large-scale night-time exercises, in which 90 to 100 gliders would land in a single ope-

(4) In the Wings of Pegasus, p. 122.

port training when they were in the 1st Airlanding Brigade. The 12th Battalion the Devonshire Regiment had still to get used to this means of transport.

In the Horsa glider, up to 30 men were securely strapped in with lap belts and sat on wooden benches facing each other along the length of the aircraft. The flight was really rather unpleasant. First, as the tug gathered speed and took off, the tow rope would snap taut, the plane jerk forward and the men would be thrown against each other. As the glider pitched and rolled, the men would start heaving and throwing up, and no remedy known to man could put a stop to it ; worse, the buffeting backdraught from the engines of a vast formation of heavy bombers would cause the tow ropes of the gliders in the rear to worryingly tighten and slacken over the turbulence, causing the glider to jerk and jolt. Even then, the worst was yet to come : the landing. In the final approach, the pilot would put his head through the door to the cockpit and bellow at his miserable passengers : « BRACE ! BRACE ! » They would then put their arms round each other's shoulders, and lift their feet up off the floor in anticipation of the landing.

As soon as the glider slithered or rolled to a halt, they would exit the aircraft through the side doors, or unload any equipment in the glider.

On the 1st June, the Brigade's training was over. Lieutenant Charles Sneezum commanded 9th Platoon of the A Company of the 12th Battalion, the Devonshire Regiment.

Back in 1939 Jeff Sneezum was so bored in the bank that he volunteered to join the army at the declaration of war only to find himself ...back at a desk job. So he volunteered to join the commandos and took part in the raids on Bayonne and Boulogne, carried out by N°1 Commando. He then trained as an officer and was promoted to lieutenant in November 1943. He was transferred to 12th Battalion of 6th Airborne Division.

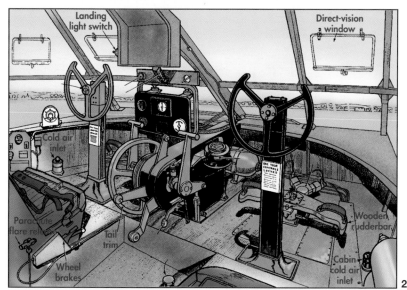

1. A Horsa pilot at the controls of his aircraft. (IWM)

2. The Horsa cockpit, showing the controls. This picture was printed in the Aeroplane magazine on 26th May 1944, just a few days before D-Day. (Coll. Memorial Museum, Bayeux)

3. The wheel of a Horsa glider, an emergency axe, and a glider pilot's insignia. (Photo Heimdal)

ration. This huge nocturnal armada was Brigadier Chatterton's 'grand vision', requiring a very high level of training made possible by the degree of cooperation between the RAF and the Glider Pilot Regiment, under the direction of Air Vice Marshal Hollinghurst. The gliders were guided in to land near Netheravon by parachutists who set up in advance 'T'-shaped signs hung with small lamps.

Airborne Infantry

The gliders would not only be bringing in war material, but also the men of the 6th Airlanding Brigade. 2 battalions of this brigade, the 1st Battalion the Royal Ulster Rifles (the RUR), and the 2nd Battalion the Oxfordshire and Buckinghamshire Light Infantry (Oxs and Bucks) had already received their glider trans-

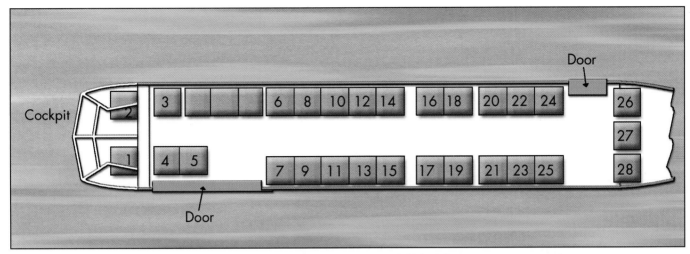

Cockpit

Door

Door

The layout of a Horsa fuselage showing the seat plan for the men to be disembarked. (Heimdal)

Henceforth Lieutenant Sneezum and his men would be training on the bleak chalky downs north of Stonehenge on the Salisbury Plain. The announcement of the campaign to come was greeted with joy : Sneezum was a volunteer, but this will to « go to it » was for the men, conscripts for most part with wives and children, a matter of getting the job over with in order to get back to a normal life at home as soon as possible – and more altruistically, to free their mates in German prisoner of war camps. Many of their buddies or neighbours had been captured at Dunkirk and were 'behind the wire'.

The Germans had to be defeated, and quickly, to bring home their own as soon as possible. More ideological motives, such as freeing the French, were not uppermost in their minds. Fear of death doesn't seem to have figured in their preoccupations, as they had immense confidence in what they were doing. Lieutenant Sneezum recalls : « *Every evening we saw fleets of heavy bombers heading off to Germany and with such an impressive display of airpower we felt we were certain to win. What we didn't know at the time was that a certain number of aircraft would not be making the return trip.* »

A Halifax bomber towing a Horsa glider off the runway. (IWM)

Above : Lieutenant Geoffrey Sneezum commanded 9th Platoon of A Company of the 12th Battalion, the Devonshire Regiment of 6th Airlanding Brigade. (Heimdal)

Left : This photograph shows how the tail of the Horsa glider was removed on D-Day to exit material. (IWM)

JUNE	1	ALBEMARLE	1616	SELF	4 CREW	AIR·TEST & FORMATION FLYING
JUNE	4	ALBEMARLE	1616	SELF	F/O CROKER . F/S HANSEN.	'OPERATION TONGA 9. PARATROOPS
					F/S LAWSON. SGT STUART.	3 CONTAINERS DROPPED NORTH OF
						CAEN NR RIVER ORNE . NORMANDY

Above : Flight log book for the paratroops' 4th June drop.

Jim Wallwork's glider pilot qualifying badge. (Mémorial Pegassus.)

Left and right : Staff-Sergeant Jim Wallwork piloted glider N°1, bringing in Major Howard and his men right up to the bridge. (Mémorial Pegasus.)

Staff-Sergeant Stanley Pearson flew Glider N°5.

Staff-Sergeant Roy Howard flew Glider N°6. On the left we see his own photograph, and on the right a lifelike waxwork in his battledress. (Mémorial Pegasus)

In the evening of 4th June Lieutenant Sneezum and his men had watched as the paras left the aerodrome, and now, several hours later, they were coming back, their faces blackened, declaring 'It's tomorrow !' The whole operation had been put back a day. The wait was extremely frustrating – but the Devonshires would not be sharing the inconvenience since they were due to be sent into Normandy some twenty hours after the first drops, once the initial landings had secured the bridgehead. Lieutenant Sneezum suggested his men get a good night's sleep before the big day. They spent the night under canvas in sleeping bags laid over mattresses. Lieutenant Sneezum's platoon was proud to be part of the only company in the 12th Devons which would land on D-Day in Normandy. Company A would be integrated into the 600-man Parker Force (so called after its commander), made up of Company A itself, an infantry company equipped with four jeeps, a company of engineers, an artillery battery and a reconnaissance company. Once landed this tactical group's mission was to cut the Mézidon-Cagny railway line, and the national highway Caen- Paris RN13, and locate 21st Panzer. Lieutenant Sneezum and his men were provided with just 3 days of food rations, after which time it was supposed they could be shipped back to England, mission accomplished.

Final Preparations

Special Operations

Thousands of turboprop engines throbbed through the night of the 4th June to drop their loads onto German positions, but among them a single Albermarle set off on a little-known operation, Operation Tonga. The crew was made up of 4 men, Flight-Officer Crocker, Flight-Sergeants Hansen and Lawson, and Sergeant Stuart. Their flight logbook recorded « Operation Tonga : 9 paratroops, 3 containers dropped north of Caen, near River Orne, Normandy ».(MP)

So 24 hours before D-Day, nine paratroops were to be the first Brits to land in Normandy, preparing the ground for a particularly important operation, the 'coup de main' party. So where did these paras bunker down while they awaited the critical hour ? To the northwest of Bénouville Bridge, opposite the Café Gondrée, stood another café. Its proprietor, M. Louis Picot, had links with the resistance, and would be killed in the first hours of D-Day. Later his daughter would say that she had been forbidden from going down into the cellar in the days preceding 6th June – so were the paras hidden there after their mission had been carried out ?

Chargement des planeurs

How to load equipment into the gliders had been an important feature of their training. During the flight the equilibrium of the glider had to be strictly maintained by working out the precise centre of gravity. There were a number of anchor points through which steel cables were threaded to hold the material securely in place. These cables had to be sufficiently strong to withstand the shock of a rough landing : if the cables snapped free and a jeep or a 6-pounder gun came adrift inside the fuselage, both pilots could be killed, as indeed sometimes occurred during operations. Similar precision had to be given to the planning of landing on specific targets, such as the coup de main party over the bridges, or onto the Merville Batteries.

Preparation of the « coup de main party » over the bridges.

The outcome of the whole invasion hinged on the ability of 6 gliderpilots to land spot on to their targets. 3 gliders were to land at Landing Zone X, (Euston I) next to the Bénouville cantilever bridge, and 3 at Landing Zone Y, (Euston II) by the Ranville swing bridge. For greater security 8 gliders of C squadron had carried out realistic night-time exercises onto sites that closely resembled their real objectives, for example the 'twin' in England of the rectagular field next to Ranville. Flight Lieutenant Tommy Grant, who directed the training, had announced to his 16 pilots on their last training flight that the the next time would be 'the real thing'. The 6 gliders to be deployed for the coup de main party were as follows :

For the Bénouville bridge at LZ X :

N° 1 glider and platoon, flown by Staff Sergeant Jim Wallwork, 24, and S/Sgt John Ainsworth carrying Major John Howard and Lieutenant Brotheridge.

N°2 glider and platoon, flown by S/Sgt Oliver Boland and S/Sgt Hobbs carrying Lieutenant David Wood ;

N°3 glider and platoon, flown by S/Sgts Barkway and Bogle carrying Lieutenant 'Sandy' Smith, 22, and Doctor Vaughan.

For Ranville bridge at LZ Y :

N°4 glider and platoon flown by S/Sgts Lawrence and Shorter carrying Captain Brian Priday (second-in-command of Major Howard's Company D, the Oxs and Bucks) and Lieutenant Tony Hooper.

N°5 glider and platoon, flown by S/Sgts Stan Pearson, 21, and S/Sgt Guthrie, carrying Lieutenant Sweeney.

N°6 glider and platoon, flown by S/Sgt Roy Howard, 21, and S/Sgt Baacke, carrying Lieutenant Fox.

It was now time for the plan to be unveiled to the Glider Pilots (GPs), now billeted in tents alongside Tarrant Rushton aerodrome. The attack would take place at night, the 6 gliders would be released at 6000 feet (2000m) over the Normandy coast at Cabourg. Each glider would transport 28 men and one or two officers, 23 infantry riflemen of the Oxs and Bucks, and 5 sappers.

Staff Sergeant **Stanley Pearson,** 21, piloting glider N°5 to land at LZ Y near Ranville bridge, had volunteered in 1939 to join the East Riding Yeomanry territorials, at the tender age of 16, by lying about his age. He was found out and sent to a battalion of 'young'uns' and from there joined the RAF and finally the Glider Pilot Regiment. His first flight piloting a glider was on 31st January 1942, and on 1st July he took eight men on board : a year later he was engaged in the Sicily campaign. Taken prisoner by the Italians, he was quickly freed by the allies. His training intensified and a few weeks before D-Day he rejoined C Squadron at Tarrant Rushton to meet the tug pilots. The GPs slept on base in Nissan huts ; then the training for the mission itself began. A V-shaped field borded by trees at a place called Homes Camp was picked out as best resembling the area to the south-east of Benouville bridge. A nearby rectangular field with trees along one side was marked

with flags on the other three to suggest the « coup de main » operational site at Ranville. In this way meticulous preparations had been laid down for the future mission.

Staff Sergeant **Roy Howard** – not to be confused with the Major of the same name – would fly glider N°6. At the age of 21, after 18 months training, he had passed his pilot's licence test with 'flying colours'. His high marks « well above the average » had certainly influenced his superiors in choosing him for a mission of such importance. Operational training had begun 6 weeks before D-Day. Quite apart from the need to spring a surprise on the enemy, they had to land as close as possible to the bridges. Each night the gliders, loaded with steel weights to simulate the 28 fully-equipped men spread along the fuselage, glided unaided for over ten minutes before coming down to land on the two tiny plots of land set up to look like their objectives.

Then the men they were due to transport were presented to the glider pilots, the engineers, and Company D under the command of Major John Howard.

John Howard was born on 8th December 1912, the eldest son East End working-class family of 9 children. To get away from the street life of that part of London, and out of his love for sport and the open air, John joined the scouts. He was an outstanding pupil, especially at maths, but because of his family's straitened circumstances, he had to leave school at the age of 14 and take up office work. He started taking evening classes to better his position, but the brokers he worked for themselves went broke and he found himself out of work. So he took up the King's Shilling in the form of the King's Shropshire Light Infantry. Those early days were hard ; he found his barrack-mates « vulgar and violent ». However this extraordinary peace time army offered a lot of sport and John Howard became a PT instructor and was promoted to Corporal. In June 1938 his army contract expired, so he joined the Oxfordshire Constabulary. He rejoined his old regiment, the KSLI, on 2nd December 1939, by which time he was married (to Joy Browley, on 28th October 1939). In just a few weeks, this 'old soldier' had been promoted to Sergeant, Sergeant-Major in early 1940, then Chief Warrant Officer with higher officer rank in prospect. The new British wartime army lacked officer material and John Howard stood out. He went to the Officer Training School in June 1940, and emerged to join the Oxfordshire and Buckinghamshire Light Infantry (the Oxs and Bucks). As a former Oxfordshire police officer, he was attracted to this regiment linked to the old university town, but he encountered a problem : most of the officers were of a different social class altogether, and the working class, ex-policeman oik in their midst was an embarrassment. Lieutenant Howard was hurt by this treatment, but once again his personal qualities won through. Appreciating his skills in platoon manoeuvres, his Colonel had him promoted to the rank of Captain, in command of a company.

In early 1942, 2nd Battalion, the Oxs and Bucks, was attached to the airborne. For the time being however, regulations only allowed volunteers to join : 60% accepted, 10% were rejected on medical grounds, and John Howard found himself briefly in charge of a platoon, with the rank of Lieutenant. Soon however he was in command of a company once again and promoted to Major in May 1942, commanding Company D of 2nd Oxs and Bucks. Their traditional regimental badge, proudly worn on the red beret, was a hunting horn. Men from all over Great Britain strengthened the battalion, not a few being Cockneys like Howard, and some, the street urchins of his youth. They were all volunteers, in peak physical

Major Howard's helmet, with the Regimental colours of D Company, the Oxs and Bucks stenciled on it. (Mémorial Pegasus)

Major John Howard commanded the coup de main party over the bridges. (Airborne Forces Museum)

The hunting horn, the insignia of the Oxs and Bucks.

condition and 'rarin' to have a crack at the enemy. High Command had decided to form an élite unit : on 2nd May 1944 Major Howard was summoned by Brigadier Nigel Poett of 5th Parachute Brigade to be told that Company D was being detached from the brigade to carry out a special mission of capital importance to the Allied landings : the seizure of the cantilever bridge at Bénouville and the old swing bridge at Ranville. According to British intelligence these bridges were garrisoned by 50 Germans armed with 6 heavy machine guns and 2 light antitank guns. A concrete shelter was being constructed and demolition charges had been placed under the bridges. It was essential these bridges be taken intact as they were the only means whereby the seaborne troops brought across Sword beach could link up with the airborne bridgehead. The bridges had to overwhelmed in a lightning assault, before the Germans realised what was happening and blow them. Success depended utterly on the coup de main party : they would have to arrive at night, when the Germans would be off their guard, and with the discretion and precision that only a gliderborne assault could supply.

This operation would prove difficult, but not impossible. But once taken, they would have to face up to the German counter-attacks. The coup de main party would take place around midnight. Paratroopers of the 5th Brigade would drop east of the Orne at 0050hrs and link up at Ranville bridge. The Benouville bridge was thought to be the more threatened of the two by German counter attacks estimated to have started by 0100hrs. Major Howard would later be informed that the 7th Battalion would be coming in at 0230hrs to reinforce the position. Once the bridges were in British hands, Major Howard would be required to deploy two-thirds of his men in a defensive position either side of the bridges and commit the other third to offensive patrols holding off and seeking out the likely German counter-attacks. For the coup de main he would have 6 gliders to bring in Company D and a platoon of 30 sappers reinforced by paratroops. 3rd Infantry Division would begin landing at 0725 on Sword Beach, to the west of Ouistreham. Commandos of N°1 Special Service Brigade under Lord Lovat were to land at 0820 hrs and then thrust forward to join up at the bridge around midday * (H- Hour +4hrs), so Major Howard and his men would be expected to hang on through 11 hours of German attacks ! So it was this selfsame 2nd May 1944, in the Planning HQ set up in an old country house at Broadmore, with its low beams and rickety staircases, that Major Howard read his mission detail for the first time. He looked up at Brigadier Poett across the table : never in his whole life had he felt such intense emotion, as it dawned on him that it would be he and his men chosen to be the first to touch French soil on D-Day ! (5)

(5) For more details see Stephen E. Ambrose, *Pegasus Bridge*, Allen & Unwin, 1984.

1. The Ranville swing bridge over the Orne ; a pre-war photograph. (Archives du Calvados.)

2. Aerial photo of Bénouville bridge, seen from the north-west. (R.A.F.)

3. The cantilever bridge at Bénouville, seen from the west bank, in a pre-war photograph. (Archives du Calvados.)

Major Howard was given a free hand to train his men as he thought fit, and Brigadier Poett undertook to provide all the help possible. Thanks to the endeavours of the resistance on the spot, passed on to British intelligence, Howard would soon know everything about his objectives, how the Germans passed their time, every change in their routine would be noted and London informed within one or two days ! Madame Vion, the director of the maternity hospital set up in the superb eighteenth century château of Bénouville just to the south of the bridge and overlooking it. In the report dated 17th May there was so much detail that an extremely accurate 4-metre long model could be made. When the Germans demolished 2 small buildings, the model buildings were straightway removed as well. 2 bridges very similar to those to be seized were located near Exeter, and Howard and his men spent six days simulating attacks on them. Everything was checked down to the smallest detail : yet on each occasion Howard always found something which hadn't thought of previously and which needed improvement. Soon all was ready. His main worry was how to take out a small bunker which covered the bridge to the northeast, and which was where the demolition charges were stored.

After the last practice flight on 30th May, Flight Lieutenant Tommy Grant told his men that the next would be for the invasion proper. The glider pilots and Major Howard and his men were grouped together at Tarrant Rushton, summoned to a Nissen hut where the model was kept and thus began the first of a series of briefings over the next few days. In the morning Major Howard explained everything about the site He knew the site in all its detail, the height of the hedges (10 to 15 feet), the width of the river and the canal, the flow of the current...Each day after lunch they had instruction on the airborne operation. They were shown aerial photographs of the bridges and the surrounding area, and even a film reproducing their flight over the Normandy countryside once they would have crossed the coast. In this way they soaked up every aspect of the battle to come. The men also had to have their seats allocated in the gliders, their names chalked onto the back of the seats. Four of the men (two to a door) had the job of tearing open the doors at the critical moment.

Finally the GPs came to the HQ on Salisbury Plain and were shown a model of the whole invasion area. They then returned to Tarrant Rushton. In the evening of 5th June 1944, the weather began to improve for their take off at 2245hrs !

Preparation of the Coup de Main party

A second group of gliders would have an even more delicate mission to perform : three gliders would land right among the Merville guns, a hugely risky undertaking which could only involve volunteers. Brigadier Chatterton drove to the airbase at Brize Norton to seek his volunteers – and every pilot stepped forward and asked their commander Ian Toler to choose their crew.

To guide the three gliders to the Merville battery, unusually, a Rebecca receiver would be carried on board, while a paratrooper, equipped with an Eureka radio beacon would be dropped near the barbed-wire perimeter. To reach a perfect pitch of combat readiness, a life-size copy of the Merville Battery was even constructed. The gliders would have to land in and among the guns in the dead of night, a drop which involved enormous risk.

English Map - Bénouville, Ranville, Ecarde Quarry, Le Mariquet, Amfréville, Bréville, Hérouvillette... and the bridges.

Major Howard's compass. (Mémorial Pegasus.)

This map shows the aerodromes and air corridors that extend over the airborne bridgehead. The estimated position of the allied fleet at H-Hour – 5 is indicated **(1)**, as is the area under flak out of Le Havre **(2)**. The first air corridor would be used at H-5 **(3)**, the others at H-2 **(4)**. Operation Mallard, on D-Day afternoon **(5)** and the return flight paths **(6)** are also shown.

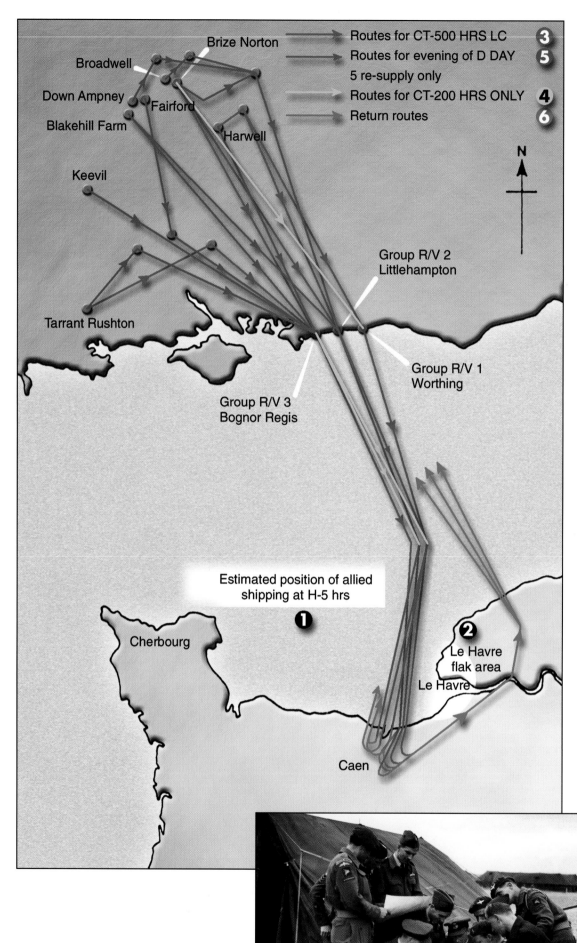

Routes for CT-500 HRS LC **3**

Routes for evening of D DAY **5**

5 re-supply only

Routes for CT-200 HRS ONLY **4**

Return routes **6**

N

Brize Norton

Broadwell

Down Ampney

Fairford

Blakehill Farm

Harwell

Keevil

Group R/V 2
Littlehampton

Tarrant Rushton

Group R/V 1
Worthing

Group R/V 3
Bognor Regis

Estimated position of allied
shipping at H-5 hrs

1

Cherbourg

2

Le Havre
flak area

Le Havre

Caen

Right : A Pilots and paras briefing before the 'big day'. (IWM)

1. Glider pilots receiving flight instructions to Normandy. The flight paths can be seen on the huge map fixed to the wall (see opposite), indicating the different aerodromes from which they would be taking off. Their route would take them over Bognor Regis, Little-hampton and Worthing. One can also see the ground plan of an aerodrome : take-off pro-cedures would be most precise. (IWM)

2. Glider Pilots listen attentively to last-minu-te advice. (IWM)

3. and **4.** Lieutenant Bob Midwood of 22nd Independent Parachute Company, giving instructions to his stick of path-finders on the requirements of their mission. They would set up radar homing beacons in advance of the main assault, thereby being the first to jump into Normandy on D-Day (IWM)

Equipment being loaded onto gliders

1. The 6th Airlanding brigade are making their final preparations for Normandy. The Horsa glider was designed to take both equipment and parachute-borne elements during the night. Here we can see men heaving a jeep in through a side door.

2. Here, thanks to a wooden access ramp, a 6-pounder anti-tank gun is loaded : it had to be tipped up in order to get it inside. (Photos IWM)

3. A fully loaded, covered trailer is being pushed into the Horsa.

4. The huge Hamilcar glider has a well-secured Morris truck fitted into the nose. The royal inspection of 19th May 1944 is attended by the King and General Gale

(Photos IWM)

1

2

1. Wooden boxes are being prepared, to be placed into the wickerwork baskets alongside. (IWM)

2. This interesting photograph shows the men being issued with their 'invasion currency' by military bursars. A Lieutenant of the Parachute Regiment is handing out the bank notes under the intrigued gaze of an RASC (Royal Army Sevice Corps) Corporal. Their cloth shoulder insignia can be clearly seen. A Sergeant of the Royal Corps of Signals on the left pores over a list, as does a Corporal at the other end of the table. (IWM)

6

3

4

3. This picture was taken at the same time from the other end of the table, with the same Parachute Regiment Lieutenant, and a Captain. A Royal Signal Corps soldier (see his insignia) is leaning over the table and counting out his money. The words 'invasion currency' are clearly visible on the box full of banknotes. General de Gaulle would have nothing to do with this currency, and shortly after the landings had the national currency restored. (IWM)

4. In this close-up we can see a hundred-franc note. (IWM)

6

5. Taken at RAF Fairford on Saturday 3rd June, Signalman John Easby (left) is showing his banknotes to signalman Douglas Davis see also page 97. (IWM)

6. An English-French-German phrase book used by the troops. (Mémorial Pegasus)

Below : the Horsa glider which brought in Major General R.N.Gale to Normandy left from Harwell aerodrome with the number 70 chalked on its side door. This 22-metre long glider had two side doors, one for the exiting of passengers, and the other, wider door for material. The 'invasion stripes' were painted on to avoid 'friendly' anti-aircraft fire shooting down allied aircraft. (DCA) Often this was crudely slapped on with a broom. (Painting by Vincent Dhorne/Heimdal)

Background photograph : long lines of Hamilcar gliders are drawn up on the runway. 355 gliders would take part in the invasion (Operations Tonga and Mallard), and only 10 would be lost. Notice also the Stirling bombers that would tow them to Normandy. (IWM)

3

4

5th June 1944, a few hours before take-off.

1. Major General Gale addresses a group of paratroops who give him their undivided attention.

2. Trucks bring men and equipment up to the Harwell aerodrome. The Pathfinders are about to clamber on board the Albermarles parked along the runway.

3. General Gale goes over some last points with some men whose faces are now blackened for the imminent operation.

4. Parachutes are piling up at the foot of an Albermarle, waiting for their owners.

(IWM)

The paras getting ready for the big jump.

Preparations were every bit as meticulous for the paratroops. The 'redoubtable' Lieutenant Colonel Pearson knew that his men would be engaged in fighting in the Bois de Bavent, so they had to learn the techniques of combat in woodland. Training on Salisbury plain therefore posed a problem ! He would eventually locate a wood suited to perfecting their training.

1. The paras inspect the new sleeveless jump suits they have just received. (see p32).

2. and **3.** These paratroops are blackening their faces to better camouflage themselves for the imminent jump. They are also wearing a specially designed life-belt.

4. The beret badge shows these men to be in Signals. They would jump with the paras and are putting a homing pigeon into the special box (see p39) in which it would be parachuted out of the aircraft with the men.

(Photos IWM)

5. Ted Lough, Deputy Assistant Quartermaster General (DAQMG) of 5th Parachute Brigade with other members of the brigade HQ at Fairford airfield. Each is straining to touch their lucky mascot. Captain Radmore, the brigade signals commander stands partly hidden on the extreme right. (Photo IWM)

The photos poo 72 were taken by Captain Malandinc on the RAF base at Harwell from which General Gale left for France, in the last hours of June 5th 1944.

1. All is ready, the men are waiting at the edge of the runway. Major-General Gale's glider, chalked with the number 70, looms ghostlike in the background. Its pilot with his toughened leather flying helmet is standing in the middle of the photo.

2. Surrounded by RAF personnel, the paras play at cards to while away the time prior to departure. They will be among the first to jump into Normandy : in the background is the outline of an Albermarle.

3. Next to it, pathfinders of 22nd Independent Parachute Company set their watches. From left to right : Lieutenants De La Tour, Wells, Vischer and Midwoop. ? De La Tour would be killed in Normandy.

(Photos IWM)

Everything was now ready for the big jump. 423 aircraft in 15 squadrons of 38 and 46 Group were made available by the RAF. In the night of 5th June Air Chief Marshal Sir Trafford Leigh-Mallory, the Overlord Air Commander, called in on each of the aerodromes from which British and American paratroops would be setting forth.

All the men were highly trained for this moment, but many had never been engaged in combat operations before. On a clear, moonlit night,

50 minutes before midnight, Squadron Leader Merrick took off from Harwell to lead the first of six Albermarles taking the paras of 22nd Independent Parachute Company. With him was Air Vice-Marshal Hollinghurst.

Paratroops prepare to climb aboard a converted Albemarle bomber, capable of carrying 10 men in a stick. These men would form part of the first wave, dropped at 0020 into Normandy. The aircraft, crudely painted with 'invasion stripes', also carried the men of 22nd Parachute Independent Company and the advance parties ahead of the two parachute brigades. (IWM)

The Harwell air base.

Above : Major General Gale is getting ready to climb aboard his glider which has 70 crudely scrawled in chalk on it. The aerodrome commander is proferring a pot of jam ; by 0100hrs Gale would be over Ranville bridge.

Right : The paras on board a Dakota heading for Normandy. As Major General Gale would often say : « *Go to it !* »

(Photos IWM)

72

That Monday 5th June was characterised by feverish activity for the men of the 6th Airborne division as they made their final preparations for their flight to Normandy. They had been consigned to transit camps since 22nd May, and at last the time had come to go. But from the German perspective, these days were the usual routine.

Night watch for Major von Luck

For Major Hans von Luck Normandy was showing its nastier side that blustery 5th June ; it had rained all day long and the violent gusts of wind were getting him down. Come the evening, the worst of it at last began to lift. He was billetted in a house on the edge of Bellengreville, to the west of Vimont. Spread out in front of him were his regimental training maps. His second-in-command, Lieutenant Helmut Liebeskind was in the regimental HQ in the middle of the village ; both men were waiting for the report following a night-time exercise in the Troarn-Escoville sector, near the coast, by 2nd battalion (II/125). 1st Battalion, equipped with armoured half-tracks, was meanwhile stationed in the rear, awaiting orders. Hans von Luck, formed by Rommel's offensive spirit, had made it clear to his battalions and companies that in the event of a landing they were individually and immediately to throw themselves into a counter-attack, and to take no notice of orders from High Command telling them to await their instructions. Nor was Hans von Luck at all happy about the conditions for his motorised and mechanised unit, trained for offensive action yet contrained to wait for weeks for something to happen.

A little further north lay the village, or rather villages, of Ranville, since it was a community not clustered round the church but spread out in a scatter of hamlets, some at a considerable distance from each other, like Longueville and Longueval, with others, like Le Mariquet and le Bas de Ranville, flanking the village of Ranville itself closer together. Although the church tower had been restored in the 19th century, tradition had always had it that the remains of an English soldier of the Hundred Years War had been placed under the cap stone. A D-Day shell would soon shatter that particular legend...

The old swing bridge at Ranville to the west of the commune had long since become a fixed bridge with the construction of the canal parallel to it ; the opening of the cantilever bridge at Bénouville took place in 1935.

At the western end of Ranville bridge was a German guardpost, rather like that of a prisoner-of-war camp, and 24 hours a day 2 sentries paced up and down the 'Eiffel bridge'. The 'Horsa bridge memorial' marks the spot. On the opposite, eastern end of the bridge stood 2 stone houses, the northernmost of the two being a café, the other the old keeper's lodge, used in the days of a functioning swing bridge.

The café had been requisitioned for use by the two guards, and on this critical shift of 5th-6th June, from 8pm to the following morning at 6am, it was one Adolf

1. Ranville bridge at the turn of the last century, looking east with the café on the left.

2. The same spot today, with the bridge rebuilt, but the former café is still visible. (EG/Heimdal.)

3. On the night of 5th June 1944 the German troops were undertaking military exercises which used dummy ammuntion you see here. (Photo Heimdal.)

Houlbey, 59, and Pierre Avice 67. These civilian conscripts had set up a sentry box next to the café to protect them from the weather when on duty. Between shifts they could pop into the keeper's lodge opposite to eat or sleep. To furnish it, 4 white wooden bunks with 'used' mattresses, a white wooden table and two benches had been obtained from the German guard post at Bénouville. Their creature comforts also included a cast-iron saucepan. In the garden below street level, a shelter had been constructed under the road. Apart from the bridge guards, who doubled as technicians to keep an eye on the bridge lifting gear at Bénouville, there were other categories of guard : road sentries and guards on the telephone cables ; all were locals conscripted by the German authorities, who hoped to limit acts of sabotage by designating hostages on the strength of good behaviour.

The two French conscripts were going to be rubbing shoulders with the German guards whose average age was in the forties. Pierre Avice left his house in the Bas de Ranville and set out along the Chemin du Hom towards the Orne river bridge.

At Bénouville the cantilever bridge was particularly well-defended on its eastern bank, covering the lifting mechanism. On the south of the road, a 50mm gun in its own concrete housing, shelters and trenches formed a complex on the bridge approaches. On the north side of the road was the keeper's lodge, a concrete shelter, a machine-gun emplacement, more trenches, and barbed wire fencing. The German garrison was made up of about 50 men armed with six 50mm MGs, an anti-aircraft gun and a machine gun. All the surrounding land was flooded, reedy marshland, crossed by the road bet-

ween the two bridges. There were two other machine guns on either side of the road covering the approach to the bridge on the Bénouville side of the canal

Here, on the right-hand side of the road was the Picot café, where the proprietor, M. Louis Picot, 40, seems to have been hiding a group of paras since the 4th June. (see p52) To the north-west the massive square bell-tower of the local church dominated the near horizon. On the south side of the road, opposite the Picot café, and hard by the bridge, was the Café Gondrée, owned by Mr and Mrs Gondrée. A number of German soldiers would come for a drink there, and Madame Gondrée, would came from Alsace, would listen to their conversations. Two conscript guards, Auguste Delaunay, 67, a retired customs officer from Ranville, and Alexandre Sohier, 74 from Bénouville, would both be among the first civilian victims.

Tension was mounting that evening. Félix Picot, 28, a peasant farmer, and Paulette Fabre, 18, a seamstress, were neighbours and engaged to be married. They were back from Argences in their horse and cart, having been held up by a road block at Hérouvillette, around 9.30pm, and another near Château Bruder around 10pm (the German HQ at Eranville, now 6, Rue du Général de Gaulle). Just what was going on. It was 11pm when they finally got back to le Bas de Ranville. Was it more manoeuvres ? Were the patrols out looking for a downed pilot ?

Then there was the strange noise of massed aircraft in the sky, the country was suddenly lit up, the Germans were everywhere. All the locals knew was that the Germans billetted on them were out on night exercises.

The Bénouville cantilever bridge, the objective of Major Howard and his men. Today it has been replaced by a modern replica that tries to imitate the original, this having been moved to a site in the grounds of the Mémorial Pégasus Museum. (Photo Heimdal.)

Objective : the Bridges

Major Howard and his men were now climbing on board their gliders. Their objectives were code-named Euston I and Euston II.

Euston I, or Landing Zone X consisted of :

N°1 glider and platoon flown by Jim Wallwork ; he carried Major Howard, and Lieutenant Brotheridge who had to run across the bridge to the opposite bank. Corporal Wally Parr had chalked the name of his wife, Lady Irene, on the aircraft.

N°2 glider and platoon carried Lieutenant Wood, whose mission was to wipe out the defenses on the east bank of the canal.

N°3 glider and platoon Lieutenant Smith had to reinforce N°1 Platoon on the west bank.

Euston II, Landing Zone Y at the Ranville Bridge consisted of :

N°4 glider and platoon, transporting Captain Priday, the second-in-command ; N°5 glider and platoon with Lieutenant Fox ; and glider and platoon N°6 with Lieutenant Sweeney. At 2256hrs Wallwork gave the signal to the pilot of his Halifax that he was ready for take-off, and the five other gliders followed him at one-minute intervals. They would be over their objectives roughly an hour later, twenty minutes before the pathfinders.

S/Sgt Stan Pearson, piloting glider N°5 heard the crackling voice of the Halifax Wireless Officer Peter Bain ask him « Everything all right back there ? » Shortly after midnight, British Double Summer Time - it was 1am in France - Peter asked : « Can you see the Orne estuary ? » When Pearson said yes, he cast off the cable as they crossed the coast directly over Cabourg. Now in free flight, Pearson took control of the glider and banked towards course bearing 187. Both Stan and Len realised that they were overloaded and plunging too fast. A barrage of flaming orange Flak shot past the aircraft as it dropped to 4000 feet. Clearly they were going to miss the bridge, so they changed course and at 3000 feet (about 1000metres) they were able to make out lights springing up around the canal bridge sector (Euston I). They remarked to Lieutenant Sweeney that battle seemed to be under way near the Bénouville brid-

ge : the engagement for the men in gliders 1, 2 and 3 had begun 5 minutes earlier.

In N°6 glider S/Sgt Roy Howard, his tug's navigator informed him that he was ready to cast off the tow now they were in their correct position between Cabourg and Ranville, at a height of 6000 feet. Again the speed was excessive, so he decided to move the two men seated closest to him to the rear of the glider in the event of a crash. All the gliders were in fact overloaded. The glider passed through a number of clouds and some Flak until, at 1200 feet (400m), the river and bridge suddenly hove into view. How small the field he had to land in then seemed ! And the battle was already raging down there on the ground, in LZ X.

Euston I

Jim Wallwork's N°1 glider was also badly overloaded. On his final approach at a gut-wrenching speed the bridge loomed before him. The ground rushed up, trees threatened to his left and right, the fields were flooded and marshy. The barbed wire, which Wallwork had been asked to break through with the nose of the Horsa, was straight ahead. If he hit an antiglider pole the wings of the aircraft could be torn off, which might slow the aircraft... or kill them. He was going to have to use his drag chute, an untried and dangerous procedure and a prospect he dreaded. He was going too fast yet could not stop too abruptly either, in case N°2 glider slammed into the back of him. Wallwork yelled at his co-pilot Ainsworth to deploy the parachute : it billowed out, the nose wheel buckled, the whole glider then bounced back up into the air, all three wheels now torn off ! The second order was to jettison the parachute, and the glider crashed onto its skids, sending out a shower of friction sparks until it buried its nose in the barbed wire, which crumpled under the impact. The crash sent the pilot and co-pilot, still strapped to their seats flying forward through the cockpit glass and onto the ground. Inside the glider everyone, including Major Howard, was thrown from their seats and knocked unconscious. On the bridge, the German sentry, Helmut Roemer (of 3/716) had heard the uproar from the crash of splintering wood but had put it down to another chunk of bomber wing falling out of the sky. His failure to sound the alarm saved the glidermen from being wiped out.

1. N°1 glider, piloted by S/Sgt Wallwork, crash landing by the bridge as depicted by Malcolm Winter. This was a difficult landing ; the plane lost its wheels after the drag chute was deployed, before coming to a standstill in the barbed wire. The accuracy of the landing was an incredible achievement. Picture in Mémorial Pegasus.

2. A wooden Horsa skid. That of N°1 glider sent showers of sparks in the final moments of landing. (Mémorial Pegasus)

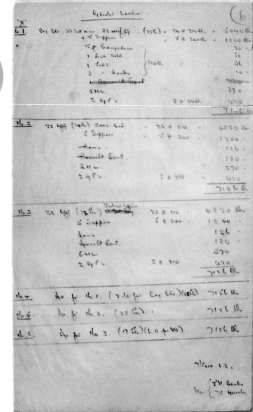

1. Major Howard's notes for loading the glider. All the gliders were badly overloaded, and came down too quickly onto their objectives. (Mémorial Pegasus)

2. Shortly after the crash-landing, Lieutenant Brotheridge led his men up to the road entrance to the bridge. (Model Mémorial Pegasus)

3. N°3 glider came down with a roaring crash. It was 0018hrs (detail of painting in Mémorial Pegasus)

Despite the violence of the landing, it was a masterpiece of accurate flying. The men regained consciousness within eight to ten seconds, cut their way out of the aircraft, incredulous before total silence that greeted them. Lieutenant Brotheridge sent 3 men off to destroy the concrete bunker housing the machine-gun to the north-east of the bridge. At this point N°2 glider came down, just a minute after the first ! It too had to use its drag chute to avoid colliding with N°1 glider, but S/Sgt Boland had to swerve to avoid it, and in doing so broke the back off his own glider. He came to a stop right on the edge of a pond : the only casualty of the landings would be a man from this glider drowned in the pond here. David Wood and his men set off at full tilt from the broken glider to join Major Howard.

With enemy fire coming at them Howard sent Wood to clear out the trench from whence the firing came, on the other side of the road. Glider N°3, its drag chute deployed came skidding in with a resounding crash. Lieutenant Sandy Smith was thrown out of the glider, and stunned. It was 0018hrs.

Meanwhile on the bridge, the German sentry, seeing Lieutenant Brotheridge and about 20 men rushing at him, ran back towards the western end of the bridge to raise the alarm. Another soldier drew his pistol, but Brotheridge gave him a full clip from his Sten and cut him down, the first German to die. A huge explosion came out of the concrete shelter attacked with grenades, and with their mission accomplished, the 3 men took up position near the Café Gondrée while the sappers cut the wires under the bridge that could be used for demolition charges.

The first shots had alerted the Germans. As Brotheridge reached the other end of the bridge, he took a bullet in the neck just as he lobbed a grenade into a gun pit. Corporal Billy Gray knocked out the other. Sergeant Hickmann sprayed the bridge with two clips from his MP40 machine pistol, but the four inexperienced young soldiers with him, softened by the cushy life in Normandy, were petrified and not up to it ; he decided to pull them all off.

4. A small bunker containing a machine gun to the north of the bridge road would be blown by 3 men. (Model, Mémorial Pegasus)

5. Lieutenant Brotheridge led his men across the bridge. (Model, Mémorial Pegasus)

6. Corporal Greenhalgh was drowned in the pond by his glider N°2, from which he was thrown on landing. (EG/Heimdal)

7. Corporal Greenhalgh's machine gun, discovered during a Staff College Battlefield Tour in 1967. Greenhalgh is buried in Douvres-la-Délivrande military cemetery. (Mémorial Pegasus)

8. In the detail from this painting, we can see glider N°1 at rest right by the bridge. The café Gondrée can be seen across the canal. (Mémorial Pegasus)

1. Lieutenant Brotheridge was fatally wounded in the neck as he reached the far end of the bridge, and died shortly afterwards. (A model of the bridge in June 1944, to compare with p74, Mémorial Pegasus)

2. Hip flask belonging to Lieutenant Brotheridge, conserved in the Mémorial Pegasus.

3. N°1 glider came to a stop in the barbed wire, here visible in a photograph taken a few days after the operaiton. The square control tower of the bridge can be seen in the background. (IWM)

However there were other German soldiers and the exchanges of gunfire continued. The bridge sentries, Auguste Delaunay and Alexandre Sohier were two silhouettes in the night shot dead in the first minutes of the assault. Louis Picot thoughtlessly – and spontaneously – greeted the arrival of the Brits on the west bank of the canal with a shout of « Vive les Anglais! ». Waving his arms about in full view of the soldiers on his own front porch, this enthusiastic greeting however attracted the wrong kind of attention since a German soldier posted on M. Picot's own terrace gunned him down for his pains. All three Frenchmen have 'Morts pour la France' written on their death certificates.

Lieutenant 'Sandy' Smith reached the western end of the bridge. In an exchange of fire he killed one German with a round from his Sten, thereby just avoiding a grenade from being lobbed at him. George Gondrée chose this moment to emerge from the cellar where he and his family had been hiding since the first sound of gunfire. Lieutenant Smith spotted his silhouette behind the café window and sprayed it with a clip from his Sten, fortunately missing M. Gondrée, who beat a hasty retreat.

0021hrs. Howard's three platoons had wiped out all German resistance. The bridge garrison were either killed, or had fled, and the survivors bunkered down in their dug-outs had no chance since there would be no prisoners. High-explosive and phosphorus grenades cleared out the remaining positions. Then the men started looking for 'Danny' : Lieutenant Den Brotheridge who lay slumped in the middle of the road opposite the café, choking on his own blood ; he would die shortly afterwards. On the other end of the bridge

Lieutenant David Wood was wounded in the leg from an isolated burst of MG40 machine-gun fire. But from this point on Major Howard was in command of the Bénouville position, and at 0022hrs he set up his HQ in a slit trench to the north-west of the bridge.

Euston II

Meanwhile S/Sgt Pearson was at the controls of glider N°5 and as yet there was no German reaction. As they approached Ranville Bridge four men in the rear threw open the side doors, but they were going too fast, and at 200 feet the pilots decided to bring

4. Major Howard's beret bearing a hunting horn badge, the insignia of the Oxs and Bucks, and his cloth shoulder badge which reads 'Fifty-Second', recalling that the Oxs and Bucks was also the 52nd Light Infantry. (Mémorial Pegasus)

5. John Howard by Bénouville bridge in 1990. (Photo Heimdal)

6. Gliders 1,2 and 3 can be clearly made out in this aerial photo as well as the German slit trenches leading up to the bridge. (R.A.F.)

7. This map shows the 2 bridges where the gliders ended up. N°6 glider landed quite close to Ranville Bridge, N°5 much further north. (Carte Heimdal.)

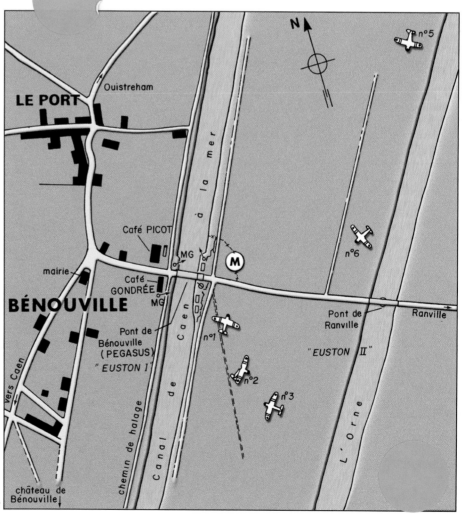

her down. Len Guthrie hit his flaps hard, forcing the glider down onto the ground. Lieutenant Sweeney was flung against the cockpit as the pilots read off their exact position. « Get out of the glider you lot and follow us to the bridge », Sweeney ordered. However they wouldn't be the first, since S/Sgt Roy Howard had performed a textbook landing in glider N°6, carrying Lieutenant Dennis Fox. He jumped out of the plywood fuselage to tell Fox that they were in the right place and all they had to do now was take the bridge. He then took off his pilot's kit and became an ordinary soldier, his mission to help those he had brought safely in and onto their objective. He began to realise that his was the only glider that had ended up where it was supposed to be, since, as we have seen, glider N°5, having been held up by procedural requirements of the final run-in had hit an air pocket and slumped onto the ground 700 metres north of the bridge. As for glider N°4, transporting Captain Brian Priday and his men, the tug pilot had mistaken the two bridges at Périers-en-Auge for their target, so the gliders had landed over 7 miles away to the east ! This navigational error would lead to the wiping out of a resistance network a few weeks later.

Lieutenant Dennis Fox's platoon was therefore the first to reach the bridge, joined shortly by Lieutenant 'Tod' Sweeney's platoon. There was no opposition – the sentries had run off when the first mortar had been fired outside the glider. Lieutenant Sweeney sent Stan Pearson and Len Guthrie off to tell Major Howard the news that Ranville bridge was taken.

Major Howard, who had set up his N°3 platoon (Smith) to the west of the bridge, and his N°2 platoon (Wood) to the east, was, despite the flush of victory, deeply saddened by the news of Brotherid-ge's death, and concerned that all three platoon commanders were out of action.

Lieutenant Smith had been wounded in the wrist on reaching the other end of the bridge, and Lieutenant Wood had taken three bullets from a Schmeisser MP40 in his left leg. But the news from Ranville was marvellous, and he was now able to send back the coded message that the two undamaged bridges were in British hands : « Ham and Jam ». « Ham » was the code name of the Bénouville bridge, and « Jam » the code name of the Ranville bridge. « Jack » would have been the message signifying the destruction of the canal bridge, but Howard had just learnt from sapper Jack Neilsen that no explosive charges had been fitted to the wires made ready for them under the bridge deck ! These charges would be found next day in a nearby hut. So altogether the 'coup de main' party had been an outstanding success, and Major Howard could instruct Corporal Tappenden to send out repeatedly into the night the magic radio message : Ham and Jam - Ham and Jam.

The pathfinders arrive

At 0020hrs 6 Albermarles were to drop 60 Pathfinders of 22nd Independent Parachute Company on Zones N, V and K in order to guide in the following formations of aircraft. The aircraft of 38 Group consisted of the 6 Halifax tugs towing Howard's 6 gliders, 6 Albermarles to drop the pathfinders, and 15 other aircraft bringing in parachute-borne units and heavy equipment in support. But the Pathfinders of 22nd Independent Parachute Company would not have the luck enjoyed by Major Howard and his men. Only the men dropped at 0020hrs out of 2 Albermarles onto Zone N (Ranville) were able to fulfil their missions as planned. 'Eureka' radio transmitters would produce a radar homing beacon to be picked up by 'Rebecca' receivers carried on board aircraft in the 2nd wave. A large number of Aldis lamps were also dropped to be ready to provide a visual signal.

One of the two Albermarles bearing the Pathfinders destined for Zone K, near Touffréville, to the south, were dropped short onto Zone N, which led to 13 sticks of paras of the 3rd Parachute Brigade being dropped there in error during the 2nd wave. All went well however for the other Albermarle, and this second group of Pathfinders was able to fulfil their mission for the 3rd Brigade in Zone K.

As for Zone V, between Varaville and Merville, the drop was satisfactory for the men, but most of the containers ended up lost in the marshes, an error which risked seriously compromising the mission of Lieutenant Colonel Otway's 9th Battalion.

Now the time had come when the men on the ground, Major Howard's 140 soldiers, the 60 Pathfinders and the 200 men who had landed ahead of the principal body of paras, were waiting for the 5000 paratroops who had taken off from England in 110 Stirling and Albermarle bombers of 38 Group. 6 of the Albermarles were towing Horsa gliders, and 13 of 146 C47 Dakota aircraft of 46 group were towing Horsas, 6 of the gliders laden with jeeps, demolition groups and other heavy material. (2 would land correctly, 3 would land in error in DZ N, and one would be lost, owing to the disorientation of the Pathfinders) It was 0045hrs. 5 minutes later, there was a renewed throbbing in the skies over Normandy : the largest airborne convoy of all was rumbling out of the night : the paras were coming !

Above : Staff Sergeant Roy Howard carried out a textbook landing of his N°6 glider : an extraordinary achievement. We see him here in his combat gear. (Mémorial Pegasus)

Right : This commemorative stone marks the spot to the north–west of Ranville Bridge where the German guard room used to stand. (Photo EG/Heimdal.)

6ᵗʰ Airborne
on D-Day

A troop of artillerymen of 3rd Airlanding Tank Battalion, RA, with their two tug pilots and those of the glider attending their last briefing in the evening of June 5th. Their 17-pounder is housed inside the Hamilcar behind them, itself covered in chalked graffiti. (IWM)

Artillerymen of 4th Airlanding battery RA are enjoying a last mug of tea before setting off in the night of June 5th-6th. (IWM)

Above : Medical personnel of the Parachute Field Ambulance are sharing a last cigarette with the RAF crew. (IWM)

Below : The paras are emplaning, to jump at 0050hrs, 6th June. (IWM)

Operation Tonga

With the Orne and canal bridges in British hands, the Eureka I and Eureka II operation had been an outstanding success. But the partial failure of the Pathfinders of 22nd Independent Parachute Company was going to have a knock-on effect on the incoming paras. As we have seen, 2 Albermarles managed to fulfil their mission objectives by dropping their men over DZ N. The Pathfinders' task consisted of setting up Eureka radio homing beacons to be picked up by Rebecca receivers on board a number of aircraft in the second wave, and also in laying out a large number of Aldis lamps on the ground to give out a visual signal. However one of the two sticks destined for DZ K was dropped short, onto DZ N, leading to 13 sticks of men being dropped here in error.

5th Brigade

The clear signals given out by the DZ N Pathfinders would lead to an accurate drop by Brigadier Nigel Poett's 5th Brigade paratroops.

Over a period of 23 minutes, 123 aircraft dropped 2026 men and 702 containers onto the right spot. Poett was the first of the 5th Brigade to drop. He had decided he would be in a better position to reach a decision in the event of a failure in the coup de main party bridge mission if he accompanied the Pathfinders. He took with him a skeleton tactical HQ. However, despite their earlier training, Poett had never before actually been on ops with the paras, nor had he ever jumped out of an Albermarle : neither had his HQ staff. Wearing cumbersome lifebelts around the waist they were not unlike Michelin Men, having to squeeze themselves through the circular hatch in the floor of the fuselage. Poett was the first to have to jump, and when he came to try and raise the hatch cover, he realised that there wasn't the room to do it with all his men stacked up standing behind him. Briefly he had the horrible thought that he might have to return to the UK without having been able to jump, while his own men were fighting it out on the ground ! However they at last managed to heave it open and the green light lit up a moment later. He slammed into the ground – but was safe and sound in Normandy, with absolutely no idea where he might be. It was so dark he couldn't even make out the church tower of Ranville. The exhausts of the departing aircraft heading for Ranville came him some idea, so he set off in that general direction. All was silent, there was no sound of gunfire, and on the way he picked up a private, a member of his stick. Then suddenly there was a great fracas of machine gun fire and explosions, and the sight of flares, announcing Major Howard's assault on the bridges : the perfect signpost as to where he should be headed ! Other gunshots could be now heard towards Ranville. Poett, without yet knowing it, had just lost the officer he had planned on meeting there, his radio operator, Lieutenant Gordon Royle.

Brigadier Poett arrived at the Orne bridge some 30 minutes after his landing. Lieutenant Tod Sweeney briefed him in detail : all the objectives of the coup de main party had been realised.

Brigadier Nigel Poett.

Lieutenant Sweeney.

Heavily laden, rather strained looking paratroops are ready to jump, their leg bags at their feet. (IWM)

Then at 0050hrs the rumble of dozens of approaching aircraft filled the sky as 5th Brigade paratroops were dropped onto DZ N. By now however the German garrison in Ranville was on full alert and was starting to lob mortars and machine-gun the DZ.

7th Battalion

7th Battalion, Light Infantry was commanded by Lieutenant Colonel R.G.Pine-Coffin, a veteran of the North African campaign. He and his men were woken from a last nap taken after their final preparations, a last

check was carried out through their pockets to ensure, as was the practice for all battalions, that there was nothing which might identify the unit. The battalion almoner, the Reverend G. Parry, a highly popular priest with all the men in the unit, gave a short communion service before the men set off in 33 trucks to 33 Stirlings awaiting on the tarmac. Before climbing on board they had a mug of tea and blackened their faces with a special camouflage cream or, since when it dried it was liable to flake, with soot collected from the bottom of the men's tea kettles. Some of the officer's and men of Major Nigel Neale's

Lieutenant Colonel Pine-Coffin.

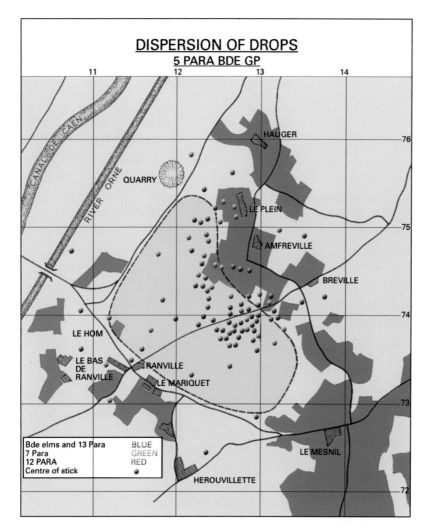

DISPERSION OF DROPS
5 PARA BDE GP

Bde elms and 13 Para	BLUE	
7 Para	GREEN	
12 PARA	RED	
Centre of stick	●	

Map showing the dispersion of drops of 5th Brigade : in blue Brigade elements and 13th Battalion ; in green, 7th Battalion ; in red 12th Battalion. The circle represents the centre of the sticks. The quarry was the rv for 12th Battalion. (Parachute Assault Normandy)

B Company had been lumbered with rubber dinghies packed into kitbags. These were in case Major Howard's coup de main operation failed and they would have to cross the canal and/or river. Major R Bartlett's C Company was only carrying light equipment in order to reinforce Howard's position as quickly as possible.

The Normandy coast came into view. The men were in high spirits, confident in the outcome of their mission, even joking. Their training had been intense and they were now ready. They couldn't know that all was not well with the men of the Advance Party battalion who had been parachuted in with the pathfinders to mark out DZ N : they were still floundering about vainly trying to rally at the rendezvous at Le Hom near the Orne river bridge.

On the dot of **0050hrs** 31 Stirlings were right over their objective : two were shot down by flak, taking all their men with them. The paras found themselves overburdened with all their equipment, and this held up the drop, scattering them over longer stretches of country than planned. 7th battalion with its rubber dinghies was particularly spreaed out. Leader of A Company, Major **Nigel Taylor** met up with Brigadier Nigel Poett, shouted « *Double, Nigel, double !* » and they both ran over the bridges to turn left into the village of Bénouville and try and find out some news about the German positions from the local populace. He got into a small cottage, and in his own words :

You know what it is if you ask the way in the country, you always manage to get the village idiot. I didn't get the village idiot, but I did get the oldest inhabitant. They were naturally very frightened and took a

lot of convincing that we were not Germans on an exercise. But they eventually realised who we were and then the trouble was gettigng out, they were so pleased to see us. They knew nothing. We pressed on, moving with sections staggered each side of the road. It was dead quiet by now. Suddenly a German motorbike appeared and came towards us. Every man in my leading platoon took a shot at him, and hit him. He swerved across the road and crashed, the engine still roaring, the bike on top of him. He was dead, but underneath him was my platoon commander, and he died about twenty minutes later. This was not good ! » Ready for anything p155. In fact Lieutenant Bowyer, who commanded the platoon, was mortally wounded by his own batman who accidentally let off some ordnance.

Captain Webber, the second-in-command of A Company would be the second officer to make it to the RV. Following his CO's orders he had kept on his jump smock where normally he would have discarded it to avoid being aimed at : a large green triangle was painted on the back, and officers and sergeants had a circle above that ! From his position he could hear the noise of battle which turned out to be the ammunition exploding inside the German half-track in front of Bénouville bridge. At this point he found himself the most senior officer present, but he wasn't sure if he should help out at the bridge or stay where he was : then he was relieved to see Major Taylor who took charge of the situation and the rest is known.

Lieutenant Rogers, one of the advance party, was equipped with a green Aldis lamp which was intended to signal the location of the battalion RV. As the main drop came in he started to flash it from where he was at that time, still some distance from the RV location. A number of men saw the lamp and moved towards it, amongst them the Commanding Officer Lieutenant Colonel Geoffrey Pine-Coffin (1), who had jumped wearing cowboy boots and spurs ! Bursts of tracer bullets were winging their way around the paras by the Germans who had been roused by the pathfinder drop. As Lieutenant Colonel Pine-Coffin recalled : It was a most desperate feeling to know that one was so close to the dropping zone but not to know in which direction it lay... it was impossible to pick up a landmark until a chance flare dropped by one of the aircraft illuminated the church at Ranville.

The church was easy to recognise because its square stone tower, built in the Hundred Years War against the English marauders, is separated by several yards from the nave. Geoffrey Pine-Coffin rejoined his RV where he found Lieutenant Rogers and his Aldis lamp, and Private Chambers who sounded the regimental call continuously on his bugle. But only 70 men had rallied to the lieutenant-colonel, and by 0215hrs they were at 40% of his battalion strength. Only a few containers carrying the mortars, machine-guns, and radios had been found The sound of Major Howard's whistle from the other side of the Orne river could be heard signifying the successful capture of the two bridges : Lieutenant Colonel Pine-Coffin could breathe a sigh of relief since his mission was now considerably simpler. 7th Battalion could abandon their heavy boat equipment and hurry at the double to reinforce Major Howard's men. Lieutenant Colonel Pine-Coffin decided to move off from the RV to the bridges without any further delay, leaving his second-in-command, Major Eric Steele Baume to collect any stragglers.

(1) In *Red Berets*, p. 161.

A little before 3.00 hours the bridges were crossed by the paras of the 7th battalion and the planned defensive positions prepared by the Oxs and Bucks were taken up, though the number of men available to do so was only half what it might have been. Major Taylor's A Company, once it had turned left after the bridge into Bénouville took up position in houses in the village to the south-west of the divisional bridgehead. Major Neale's B Company moved into positions in the wood and hamlet of Le Port indulging in some skirmishing with the Germans. C Company was held in reserve or patrolling the area with a platoon occupying a position north of Le Port on the bank of the canal.

The difficulties encountered by B Company are a good illustration of the problems caused by the dispersion of the drops. 2 platoons held the heights and a few houses in the hamlet of Le Port. The 3rd platoon had taken up position in a slight semi-circle around the entry to the canal bridge. But this platoon only had half of its men for while the first aircraft with Lieutenant Thomas aboard had dropped its stick right on target, the second had dropped the others 12 miles away and it would take days for the men to make their way through the German lines to rejoin their comrades. Major Howard and Lieutenant Colonel Pine-Coffin would altogether only have 270 men to defend the bridge, and without any heavy weaponry, machine-guns, or 3 inch mortars. The hours to come would be bitterly fought in repelling the German probing attacks !

12th Battalion

12th Parachute Battalion, Lieutenant-Colonel Johnny A.P.Johnson commanding, had the hamlet of Le Bas de Ranville as its objective, its RV being a quarry. The Stirlings bringing in the sticks had taken off at 2330hours the previous day and opened their hatches as they flew over the Normandy coast.

12th Battalion was dropped, together with the 13th, at 0050hours and was scattered. As with the 7th Battalion it was about three-quarters-of-an-hour before some of it began to assemble at the RV, a quarry near the hamlet of Ecarde, below the road between Ranville and Sallenelles near the river Orne. The first man to arrive at the RV of the Ecarde quarry was the Commanding Officer Lieutenant Colonel Johnny Johnson, who was accompanied by Major Gerald Richie who commanded A Company, and Captain Jerry Turnbull who was the second-in-command of B Company. The Regimental Sergeant Major was also with them. Most of the battalion had been dropped far east of the dropping zone in some woods and orchards, and it would take time to get back to the RV at Ecarde. The battalion's Intelligence Officer, the only HQ officer at the time in the right place, started to flash his torch as the signal for the RV to rally the scattered paratroops, but an enemy armoured vehicle opened fire every time he flashed his torch, interrupting the signal and holding up the whole procedure.

The second-in-command, Major Ken Darling, and the adjutant, Captain Paul Bernhard, had been dropped in error on one of the 3d Parachute Brigade's dropping zones, while the Headquarters Company Commander, Major George Winney had been dropped some distance away by a pilot who had mistaken the Dives for the Orne. All of them eventually rejoined the battalion a few days later !

Let us look at the example of Major Darling during his first moments on Norman soil. The Stirling that brought him to his fate was taking off from Keevil aerodrome when suddenly the aircraft veered sharply to the right and came to a grinding halt off the

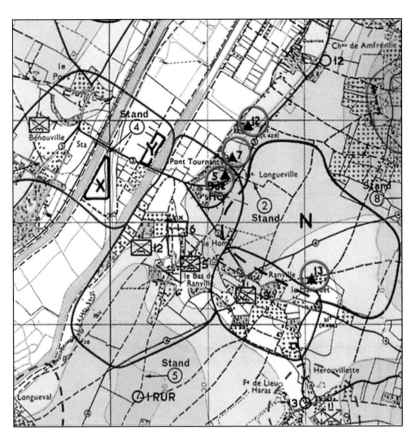

This map show 5th Brigade sectors around Ranville : 12 for 12th Battalion RV, the quarry, 7 for the 7th, 5 for 5th Brigade HQ, 13 for the 13th at Mariquet.

The various battalions were attributed different sectors also : 13th to the north, the 7th to the west, and the 12th to the south, near where it reads Stand. **(5).**

runway, stuck fast. Ken Darling thought for a moment he was going to miss the drop. The stick had to disembark, clamber into a spare truck and ten minutes later, emplane in a Stirling he had held in reserve. Everyone pushed and shoved to find any sort of place inside the aircraft, and they spent a great deal of the flight sorting themselves out, encumbered with kit in the lurching, vibrating gloom. Once over what they believed to be their objective, the men were dropped, scattered over an area 3 miles north-east of DZ N, in an orchard among tall poplar trees that were difficult to avoid before hitting the ground. Gunfire coming from the direction of the canal helped Major Darling and a few others to get their bearings, and once he had collected 6 men from his stick they set off across country, avoiding the roads. The close hedgerow country which they had never encountered before made the going hard and difficult in the dark. Quite by chance they stumbled onto the Biéville crossroads and a telephone line leading to a German position set up into the scrub. Darling could hear German being spoken but he restrained his men from lobbing a grenade into the shrubbery since their main task was to get back to their battalion RV without delay. A roadsign indicated the way to Le Bas de Ranville, so they took to the road and walked back to their battalion, by which time it was nearly daylight.

Meanwhile Lieutenant Colonel Johnson continued to rally his men now, 90 minutes after landing, having 60% of his men. He then led them off towards. Le Bas de Ranville, which they seized without difficulty, finding there many more of the battalion who had landed outside the dropping zone and recognising

Above : Frank Gleeson, a prisoner of war at Saint-Pierre sur Dives on D-Day.

- Frank Gleeson in 1993, wearing glasses... which he intended to wear on 7th June. (Heimdal)

where they were, had thought it best to repair at once to the objective rather than waste time looking for the l'Ecarde quarry which was the battalion RV. At **4.00 hours** the men of the battalion were already digging into their positions. A Company were astride the crossroads east of the Orne, between the quarry and the hamlet of Le Hom. B Company was in a forward position on the southernmost outskirts of Le Bas de Ranville. C Company was spread out on the rise to the south-west of the village, towards Caen and Colombelles, its right wing reaching as far as the west bank of the Orne.

Frank Gleeson, a young 19 year old para, suffering from bad eyesight but otherwise hale and hearty, formed part of this C Company. An hour after having left England, his tug began to come under heavy Flak before it was over its objective. Before this mortal danger some pilots mistook the Dives estuary for the Orne ; others gunned their engines to try and fly their way out of trouble, which was the response of Gleeson's Stirling. For Frank, as for so many of his comrades, it was his first operational jump. He dropped himself down the hatch and the parachute deployed with such violence he lost his rifle : it was far worse than any practice jump he had ever made ! After a safe landing – roughly where the Mariquet camp site is today – « *It was pitch dark. I looked north to get my bearings, thinking myself alone, and found I was standing nose to nose with a huge horse.* »

Lance Corporal **Gleeson** picked up C Company and took up his position to the south of Le Bas de Ranville. An old man peered out of his first floor window. When he got to where he thought he ought to be « *We stopped and started digging our pits, and then a couple of hours later along comes this officer and tells us that according to him we ought to be 200 yards further forward, by which time it was daylight and the German snipers were alert to the slightest noise or movement. In such conditions it was nigh on impossible to start digging into new positions.* » This would be a hedge near the crest of the rise shortly before the hamlet of Longueval. A road ran across this site to rejoin le Bas de Ranville behind them.

For Captain **J.A.N.Sim** of the York and Lancaster Regiment, his 'big day' had begun in the gloom of the

Stirling fuselage, lit by the row of dim lights in the ceiling. To try and help them relieve their sickness and anxiety, they shouted a few encouraging words to each other, trying to grin away that sickly feeling at the pit of the stomach – for young paras who had never experienced the reality of war, this was a real adventure, and they were quite incapable of conjuring up in their minds the true horrors of war. Sim nodded off, then the coast hove into view and Sim would be the first to jump. The despatcher asked him to help him open the double doors of the hatch and, leaning out, was conscious he was not hooked up ! (It was the same procedure in an Albermarle). « *Suddenly the monotonous greyness of the sea broke into parallel white lines. I saw the waves rolling towards the dirty yellow beach, then the cliffs forming a step from the beach and then the darker woods beyond. For some minutes I gazed down on the landscape clearly visible in the moonlight. The tracks of lanes, fields and hedgerows etched in various tones of grey and black.* » A moment later the red and then the green lights went on and – GO ! - he stepped through the hole.

« *There was a sudden stillness, the clean crisp rush of air behind the ears and round the body, the swelling of the chute above as it deployed, sensations quickly following the one after another, and I found myself floating lazily down, silently and, it seemed, alone...at any moment now I would land. As I watched the field beneath me see-sawing a wire fence flashed to one side ; the ground hit me and I rolled over. I was in Normandy...* ». With the help of a compass Sim repaired to the quarry RV, to the west of DZ N, picking up some of his men and other men misdropped from 7th and 12th Battallions ; shortly afterwards the bugler of the 7th and the hunting horn of the 12th sounded together from different directions to rally the men, adding to the racket and confusion and roar of the aircraft flying overhead. Once they got to the quarry he found Lieutenant Colonel A.P.Johnson who at that time only had about a quarter of his men with him. A para turned up with the heavy metal base plate of his 3-inch mortar, remarking,« *the f.....ing barrel had better turn up !* » Then they decided to set off towards Le Bas de Ranville to take up a forward position as dawn broke. His twelve-man patrol of N°4 Platoon dug in on the summit of the crest, 300 yards further south of the main defensive line of the company. He also had with him a Forward Observation officer with a wireless set engaged in ranging an offshore cruiser's guns onto likely targets. To beat off the determined efforts of the Germans to regain the village, N°4 Platoon was equipped with 2 Bren guns, 2 PIATs and a broken six-pounder anti-tank gun.

13th Battalion

Under the command of Lieutenant Colonel **Peter Luard,** just under half this battalion was dispersed, and when it too set off from its RV he only had about 60% of his men. Their mission was to seize and clear **Ranville** and cover the approaches to the Orne bridges from the south-east and between the Orne river and the Bois de Bavent. An advance party had dropped at 0020hours to seize the Ranville crossroads.

A Company, commanded by Major Cramphorn, together with a number of sappers of the 521st Parachute Squadron RE, cleared the landing grounds of 'Rommel's asparagus' for the gliders. These would start arriving at 0330 hours, bring in General Gale's forward HQ 4th Airlanding Anti-Tank Battery RA (photo p82), the 17-pounder troop (also p82), 3rd Airlanding Anti-Tank Battery RA, the Forward Artillery Observers (FOO and FOB parties) of 3rd Infantry Division, a platoon of 286th Field Park Company RE and ele-

This unusual colour photograph shows Major R.M. Tarrant, commander of a company of 13th battalion. Dropped to the north of Ranville at 0050 hours, he snitched the German HQ commanders flag out of his office set up in the Château Bruder (now N°6 Rue Général de Gaulle). Wounded on 19th August 1944 at Putot-en-Auge, he died of his wounds on 28th August. His rag doll Raggetty Ann, the Major's mascot, was with him when he jumped. (Coll Mairie de Ranville)

ments of the RASC (service company) would land at 0330 hours.

At **0150 hours**, with only 60% of his men, the various companies set off to carry out their mission. The Germans had started to react in the sector around 0130 hours, firing mortar and machine gun fire from Sallenelles, but their fire plan was thrown into confusion by the detonations demolishing glider poles, which had to be cleared by 3am.

Lieutenant Jack Watson commanded 36 paratroops that made up N°3 Platoon of A Company, the 2nd stick accompanied by Sergeant Farrell… In the evening of 5th June, these paras checked their equipment at Broadwell aerodrome and took off in 2 Dakotas at 2330hours. All the men in Watson's stick were quiet, thinking about what the enemy might have in store for them. His batman Gospel started singing a cockney song, which the men took up to try and blow away the cobwebs of anxiety that were beginning to settle, while below them, hundreds of ships of the allied armada were heading for the coast, some flashing an encouraging 'V' for Victory up at the aircraft.

Crossing the coast at 0100 hours the bombers dropped small 25kilo bombs before coming to DZ N. It seemed like an eternity to Jack Watson before he spied the green lamps signalling where they must drop : the paras were standing before the open hatch, and as Lieutenant Watson made to jump he heard his batman say « I'm right behind you Sir ! ». But as he parachuted down, the kit bag strapped to his leg would not detach itself and he dreaded the prospect of a leg fracture after coming all this way. But all went well, and he found himself in the middle of an orchard to the north of DZ N. All was very quiet, to a point where he felt he must have dropped way off course. He was relieved to pick up a machine-gunner of Sergeant Farrell's group – except the bad news was he'd lost his machine gun ! Jack Watson thought, « This is a real bugger's muddle !. » At 0115 hours he picked up a group headed for A Company's RV and gradually as they made their way forward he was able to rally their morale and the shrill calls of the hunting horns confirmed they were approaching the rallying point. There was another setback when he saw they were only 40 strong, so faced with this disappointment, they decided to wait a little longer. At 0145 hours the numbers were up to 60, but only 18 were from his platoon – a whole stick was missing. Despite their numbers he knew that they must now move to do what they had dress-rehearsed so often in the past at Bulford, the removal of « Rommel's asparagus ». It was a race against time - although the poles seemed lighter than expected, and the last ones north of Ranville church were being removed when the first gliders started to land at 0335 hours.

591st Parachute Squadron RE

This squadron, made up of engineers had been attached to the 5th Brigade, but Captain J. Lockey's mission was different. With his engineers company, his mission was to remove demolition charges under the bridges and consequently they must come in early. Emplaning at 2230hours into a Stirling, along with Lieutenant R and 14 sappers, he jumped last at 0015hours to arrive 300 yards to the west of his objective, the DZ N rallying point. His kitbag laden with 30 kilos of high explosive landed 10 yards away. The square field was overlooked by the tall church tower of Ranville (the spot is now occupied by the Commonwealth War Graves Commission Cemetery). All around, the sky was criss-crossed by probing spotlights and tracer bullets seeking out targets. Captain Lockey rejoined his RV immediately and found

the Captain Semple was in charge as there was no sign of Major Andy Wood, the unit's commander. The 36 sappers were to be put to work without delay to clear a Landing Zone (N) for the 5th Brigade.

Lockey had to get in touch with the sappers of the 249th Field company RE, attached to 6th Airlanding Brigade which had come in in Howard's gliders. Taking a country lane, with the dark sihouette of Ranville church behind them and the bridges ahead, they were surrounded by the shrill sounds of whistles and hunting horns.

At the river bridge Captain Lockey saw a German platoon debouch onto the road just a hundred yards in front of him, and turn off to the right towards Sallenelles. He went on alone to where the Oxs and Bucks were guarding the bridge, and after a brief investigation was amazed to see that no demolition charges had been laid to blow the old swing bridge. To left and right were scattered the dead and dying and the medics were hard at work in the scrub along the river bank. So he proceeded to the Bénouville cantilever bridge where he found another officer of engineers, Captain Bence : he had been with Major Howard in the N°1 glider that had careered into the barbed wire right by the bridge itself. (see p75). There too there were no demolition charges laid. The captain was just about to turn back to Ranville to make his report on the intact bridges when the sound of a German half-track going flat out slewed round the corner and rushed the bridge. A Piat bazooka slammed into it, and machine gun fire discouraged a platoon of Panzer grenadiers from approaching the bridge. Then the ammunition in the vehicle exploded – the sound picked up by Captain Webber of A Company as he walked towards the bridges.

Captain Lockey was now clear to return by the same road to Ranville. Before the junction with the Sallanelles road he met Brigadier Poett and his forward advance party, with some men of 7th Battalion. (see above). He told them what he knew ; beyond the road junction a German motorcyclist and side-car, with a staff car tried to roar past – a couple of grenades missed, but a burst of fire from 7th Battalion paras put paid to their presumption. So he came to his RV, where Captain Semple and his sappers had been doing good work : most of the poles in the field had been cleared, and indeed the poles had been a lot smaller than anticipated : 521st Squadron sappers and the paras of A Company of 13th Battalion had fulfilled their mission, and the 1000 yards of 'runway' was indcated with lights.

The 22nd Independent Parachute Compnay laid out rows of Halophern lamps 90 yards apart, the width of each landing strip for the gliders. It would soon be 0330hours, when they would start to come in.

The square belltower of Ranville church, separate from the nave, would prove a useful reference point for the many isolated paras lost in the dark night. (EG/Heimdal.)

Beret badge of the Royal Engineers. (Coll Ph. Wirton)

Lieutenant Jack Watson. (Coll. M. Guillou.)

Lieutenant Colonel Peter Luard.

Captain Lockey met Lieutenant Colonel F.H.Lowman, commander of all the engineering units. He left Harwell to the south of Oxford for RAF Fairford, emplaned a Stirling and crossed over with sappers of the 591st Parachute Squadron RE. Some of them enjoyed blackening up his face ! They took off at 2332hours, 20 paras on board with sixteen aircraft behind. As their objective approached, they were ordered to link up their safety strops to the static line and, standing, wait a further ten minutes. Red light – green light – go !– the line of men shuffled towards the rear of the Stirling, to the hatch that took them abruptly into a rush of cold air, silence, and a severe jolt as the parachute deployed. The other men in the stick were drifting out to the right as tracer bullets shot up from the ground. The fields spread out below him, and then Lowman found himself in the middle of a small garden. He released himself from his harness, stuck his head through the hedge, only to see barely 300 yards away the silhouette of a German light tank surrounded by soldiers. He had to

bide his time until the long shrill whistles rallying 591st Squadron pierced the night, a strange cacophony of noise that confused the Germans – fox-hunting bugles for the 7th, motorbike horns for the 12th, bicycle horns for 13th battalion. The way seemed clear, so he left his shelter, taking no notice of the panic-stricken German voices to right and left, and came to Mariquet to be greeted by a burst of machine-gun fire. They skirted round the crossroads at the double, weighed down by their heavy equipment, and avoiding the deadly bullets lobbed a few grenades into another German position before reaching the Ranville road. There they met another group from the 12th Battalion who had also to organise a LZ rallying point. It was 0230hours – 90 minutes late - when he reached the RV for the engineers by the Ranville church tower. There he found Captain Lockey, and his batman who told him that the officers and sappers were busy clearing the landing zone for gliders which would be landing shortly.

3rd Brigade

This was one of the strongest in the division, and would be given some of the hardest tasks of the operation. It was made up of two experienced battalions and the formidable Canadian battalion. Its commanding officer was Brigadier James Hill (see p7). Wounded in Algeria in 1942, he had been awarded the highest military decoration that can be bestowed by the French Army, the Legion d'Honneur. General Giraud came to his bedside – Hill had been seriously wounded in the neck, chest and arms – unpinned the decoration from his aide-de-camp's uniform, and pinned it to Hill's pyjama top. After seven weeks stuck in hospital, and not fully recovered from his injuries, Colonel Hill took command of 9th Battalion and then took over 3rd Parachute Brigade from Brigadier Lathbury. His first words were « I'm one of the oldest men in my brigade at the advanced age of 33 ! »

He was a man who with his quick intelligence and tall bearing required and won both respect and confidence : his men nicknamed him 'Speedy'.

He had been involved in the planning stage of the operation, most particularly the tough missions entrusted to his brigade, including the seizure of the Merville battery. No detail escaped him. While the Americans used 'crickets' to rally the men, the paras were issued with « ducks bakelite 1944 pattern », imitating the quack of a duck.

At 0050 hours Brigadier Hill would be dropped from a Dakota, and find himself among the men who were scattered widely owing to the loss of their DZ identification ground signal. Hill ended up over a mile too far east, south of Cabourg and floundering in 4 feet of the marshy waters of the Dives ! The many deep irrigation ditches hidden beneath the water surface and criss-crossing the sector made it very dangerous country to traverse. Brigadier Hill picked up 42 very wet stragglers eventually and headed off west to reach dry land and the Dropping Zone : what saved

them at this point was fastening themselves to one another by their toggle ropes.

« I was a highly sophisticated officer, so I thought, and had tea bags sewn into my battledress. It was maddening as Brigade Commander to spend four hours making cold tea. »

« Suddenly I heard a noise which I recognised and shouted to all the men to get down.... My party found itself in the middle of an attack by low flying aircraft coming in from the sea and using anti-personnel bombs... I looked around and knew I had been hit. The lane was covered in dust and the smell of cordite and death prevailed. In the middle of the track I saw a leg and thought it must be mine but then I realised it belonged to the officer on whom I was lying and who was now dead...there appeared to be only two survivors capable of getting to their feet, myself and my defence platoon commander... » (quoted in « Ready for Anything » p. 162 and « Go to It » Peter Harclerode p 69)

It took four hours to make it, leaving 3rd Brigade leaderless for that time (until 0545hours).

8th Battalion was also widely dispersed following from the errors in signalling out of DZK ; these first hours would be tough indeed for his unit.

8th Battalion

37 Dakotas brought in the battalion to DZ K, between Cuverville And Touffreville. Its redoubtable commander, Alastair Pearson had barely got over from the malaria he had caught in Sicily, before rejoining his 8th Battalion to see action again. General Gale had been delighted to have this experienced and highly professional soldier at his side, despite the crass way he had of speaking sometimes. Pearson had spelt out to Gale that he had no wish to be bothered by superior officers, and when Gale had asked what exactly he meant by that, he snapped back, « Anyone superior to me ! » Gale of course was one of them but he didn't make an issue of it. Pearson

Brigadier James Hill.

had taken great pains over the military training of his Midlands Counties battalion, Brummies for the most part. Training lasted 12 days with a 48-hour break every two weeks. The men would reach Birmingham on leave by train and would return to Lavington station, 4 miles from their base at Tilshead. There was no question of being picked up : walking back to base was all 'par for the course'. !

His pilots, two former sergeants of the Royal Canadian Air Force who said they had been bush pilots before the war, they pointed out to Pearson with so many aircraft about, there could be no second chance to try and spot the precise place where they were to jump and that to attempt to do so would be suicidal ! His Intelligence Officer stood by the open door as the Dakota crossed the coast, shouted they were on the right course, and then it was - red light - green light – go ! Pearson would be one of the last to jump, about 11th or 12th in his stick. Quite apart from the bout of malaria in Sicily, he had been victim of a misdrop in Sicily which had done in his knees. H.M.Government had therefore taken the trouble to fit him out with a wider than usual parachute to allow him a gentler descent. Hanging from his rigging he had a little more time than the other men to realise that things were not going as planned – instead of hunrdeds of paras, only his own stick was visible, yet theirs would be among the few coming in at the right place, DZ K. Pearson, almost as soon as he touched ground, was sprayed by a trigger-happy para and shot in the hand.

8th Battalion had suffered a serious setback in being the most widely scattered unit of the whole division, due in part, as we have seen, to the Pathfinder jumping out of the Albermarle and setting up their lamps and homing beacons for DZK in DZN. Most of the sticks jumped blindly into the dark, to be scattered over many square miles, and 13 sticks of 3rd Brigade fell into 5th Brigade area, thereby missing their roll-call.

Pearson reached the battalion RV at a track junction near Tourffreville at 0120hours, to find only thirty men plus a jeep and trailer belonging to the engineer squadron. Two and a half hours later this number increased to eleven officers and 145 other ranks, including

6 sappers. The units were all mixed together and he was only able to raise 2 full platoons. His equipment amounted to a light machine gun, 2 PIAT bazookas, 2 jeeps and 4 radios. Moreover there was as yet no news of Major Roaseveare and his squadron of sappers who were supposed to blow the Traorn bridge. Pearson was reduced to ordering a junior NCO, Lance Corporal Stevenson, his most senior engineer at this point, to take off all the plastic explosive the men carried and despatched the few sappers he had, together with one of his 2 platoons, to try and inflict as much damage as possible on the two bridges at Bures. Then the men fell back to wait at the crossroads

A mile north of Troarn and at 0400hours his group moved off to the crossroads which were in heavily-wooded terrain east of the main road between Troarn and Le Mesnil. On the way Pearson set up an anti-tank ambush which comprised three men armed with their only two PIATs, led by Stevenson, to cover the battalion's rear from the road, should the Germans counter-attack from there However Major **Roseveare** and his 3rd Para Squadron had landed a little further away. Once on the ground the men rushed to open the containers marked by 'Thomas' lamps attached to them. The light collapsible tubular canvas trolleys were unfolded and loaded with munitions and high explosive from the containers. The Horsa that had brought in the heavy equipment proved them with a medical unit's jeep and a trailer which was put to immediate use. They roared off in it, and met Lieutenant Thompson and A Company on the way to blow the bridge.

Although the confusion was widespread throughout 8th battalion, everyone was doing whatever was humanly possible to carry out their missions. Further north again, 9th battalion was to suffer an equally pitiless fate.

9th Battalion

The plan of attack was going to be extremely complicated and demanding : to take out the Merville battery. Led by Lieutenant Colonel **Terence Otway,** who had rehearsed his men down to battle phases

Lieutenant Colonel Alastair Pearson.

On this map, the encircled n° 8 signifies the RV of N° 8 battalion ; 'K' their Drop Zone. They, together with sappers of 3rd Parachute Squasron advanced on Troarn and Bures, to destroy 3 bridges, to pull back thereafter to Le Mesnil, to the east of Bures.

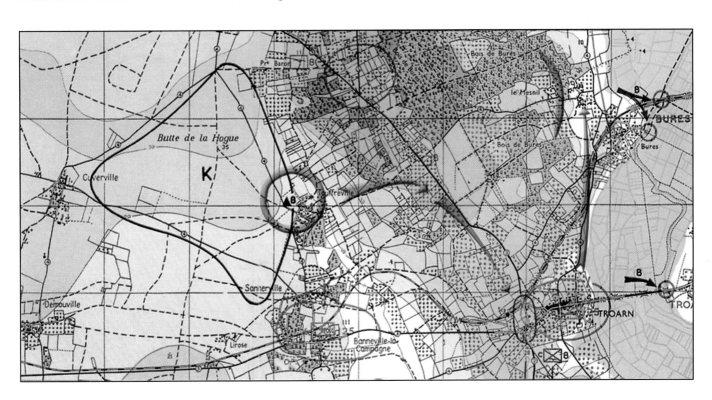

Lieutenant Colonel Terence Otway in 1944 and, below, in June 2000. (Ph. Wirton)

To the west of DZ V, near Varaville, we can make out 3rd Brigade HQ RV, the RV of Ist Canadian Battalion (1CA) and that of 9th Battalion (9). On the right, the Canadian's objective, the château and bridge at Varaville. Across the map, the trail to Merville and split off to Hauger and Le Plein d'Amfreville.

lasting a mere thirty seconds, the plan would involve first of all a massive bombing raid by 46/100 Lancasters (p180 Red Beret) bombers dropping four-thousand-pound bombs onto the battery, the equivalent in weight of an entire night-time raid by the Luftwaffe on London. This alone might have left the soldiers with nothing to do, except that, as we have seen (see chapter 2 pages 19-22) the gun battery had already undergone several bombing raids to little effect. It would, however, certainly have raised the morale of the men about to conduct the assault. This involved landing 3 gliders right on or among the concrete casemates. A coup de main party of 60 paras from A Company and 8 Sappers would immediately exit and engage the enemy, while most of the battalion, which would have landed on Dropping Zone V some 2200 yards away would be swarming through three breaches in the wire, clear paths over the minefield and join up with the paras. The Germans were to be killed or taken prisoner, the guns immobilised by 15 sappers (half a troop) with explosive charges. This audacious plan did not exclude the very real possibility that the men might end up firing on each other.

A farm near Inkpen, in Berkshire, had been selected to reconstitute the site of the battery for the purposes of training. For 5 days and 4 nights the battalion had battled there using live ammunition.

After that the men were to go on and secure the village of Le Plein, and the German HQ at Sallenelles.

At **0020hours** the first drop took place, bringing in the signals company of the 9th Parachute Battalion in 4 Albermarles to lay the ground for the coup de main party. 2 other Albermarles deployed the Pathfinders to mark out Drop Zone V, near Varaville. At **0050 hours** C-47 Dakotas of 47 Group dropped the para ; however as they flew over the coast, some anti-aircraft fire was encountered and in taking evasive action they lost their bearings and spread the men over fifty square miles. Most of the Pathfinders'

Eureka sets were so badly damaged as to be unusable and few lamps would be available in the right places at the right time to guide in the aircraft. The smoke triggered off by the bombing and blowing across the zone also contributed to so many men being dropped miles from their DZ, as far away as Cabourg and Dozulé, into the Dives marshes and even into the sea.

On the ground however the battery reconnaissance and rendezvous parties had dropped correctly. Major Allen Parry and his men set about clearing ways through the minefields, while Major George Smith and Company Sergeant Majors Harold and Miller moved up in the darkness past Gonneville-sur-Merville towards the battery, about a mile away – narrowly escaping elimination from the shower of bombs slamming down way off target.

With the sticks so widely scattered, it was going to be no easy matter to assemble a coherent force. Lieutenant Colonel Otway himself as he stood ready at the door of his Dakota, had been flung prematurely out as it was taking evasive action, and had landed 2 km from the RV. His knowledge of the area, gained by the study of maps and photographs, enabled him to recognise the spot where the west wind was pushing him, a German battalion headquarters. He and two men fell into the garden beside it, and were at once fired at by the Germans inside who fortunately seem to have been armed with nothing more lethal than pistols. One of the parachutists (Joe Wilson) silenced this fusillade by throwing a brick through the window, which the Germans mistook for a grenade. Otway took his bearings and set out for the RV which he reached at 0300 hours. The state of affairs was grim : only 150 men that could be organised into five 30-man companies. None of the 11 gliders bearing equipment had made it, so there were no jeeps or trailers, no anti-tank guns, no mortars, (therefore not possible to signal their position with yellow magnesium flares).

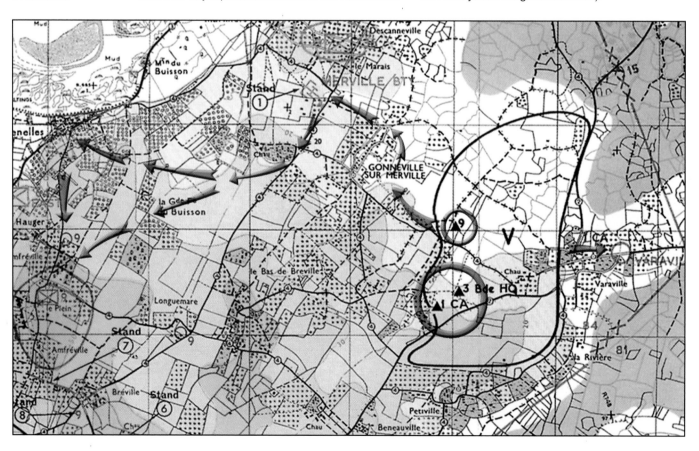

(Otway reported « Enough signals to carry on… p183 Red Beret and no sappers ; no medical stores (but six unit medical orderlies), no mine detectors or radio to link up with the cruiser HMS Arethusa (ordered to open fire on the battery at 0530hours in the event of the operation failing). There were only 20 lengths of Bangalore torpedo for the opening of gaps in the barbed wire, and one Vickers machine gun to silence all the enemy's machine guns.

The Merville Battery

Lesser men might have been daunted as such odds, but after a momentary sinking of the stomach, he pulled himself together, knowing that only determination and training would carry the day.

They set off towards their objective, and after following a route skirting the northern edge of the village of Gonneville-sur-Merville, Otway and his men, now 90 minutes late, made their way to a crossroads south of Descanneville (see map) where they met Major George Smith who explained that Captain Paul Greenway and his demining team, for want of mine detectors, had successfully cleared and marked four lanes through the minefields by crawling forward on their hands and knees, feeling for trip wires and marking the lanes by scratching heelmarks in the dust in lieu of the white tapes that normally did the job.

Otway split his force into four assault groups but decided to use only two of the breaches in the wire, two groups for each. It was now 0430am. Major Dyer being absent, Major Parry led one of the assault groups, Lieutenant Jefferson, Company Sergeant Major Ross and Colour Sergeant Harold Long the other three. The assault plan had to be changed slightly : Parry would take casemate N°1, originally Jefferson's objective. Otway would be in position 200 yards from the battery.

At this crucial moment two of the three gliders due to land among the batteries arrived. Since there were no shells or mortars to fire the star shells to illuminate the battery, one of the gliders flew right over the position and disappeared into the night; piloted by Sergeant Bone the Horsa landed two miles to the south. The second, flown by Sergeant Kerr and bearing Lieutenant Hugh Pond and his assault group of 20 men came in lower than the first, anti-aircraft fire poured into it, wounding four men inside. The tail began to smoulder and it landed in a large field two hundred yards from where the Bangalore torpedoes had been lain to blow the wire. As the battalion was deploying, six enemy machine guns from outside the battery position opened fire, three from either flank. Sergeant Mac Geever's Vickers machine gun engaged the enemy gun on the left and took out three. The group was immediately attacked by a reserve company of 736th Infantry Regiment of 711th Division The ensuing fight in the orchards to the southeast of the battery lasted nearly one hour thirty, thereby blocking the Germans' attempts to take Otway's flank. As for the third glider, its tow rope had parted early, and it had had to land in England, to the chagrin of its occupants.

The Bangalore torpedoes blew open gaps in the barbed wire and Parry blew his whistle to launch the attack. After that, as there were no radios, « it was every platoon for itself. », as Parry later remarked. Mines started going off, causing more casualties and once through the wire they were being shot at from the three remaining machine guns.

Major Parry was shot in the leg and used the cord on his whistle as a tourniquet ; he then hobbled into a crater. He was going to have to destroy the N°1

gun, and without sappers or explosives he contemplated how to set about silencing it ; while so doing he received a second wound, this time from shrapnel and in the wrist. The gun was not the calibre he expected – 100mm instead of 155mm – but his Gammon bomb seemed hardly sufficient to do the job, and grenades would not be much use against the massive concrete structures. The tobruk hole set in the top of casemate N°1 was also particularly troublesome, continually sweeping the site with its machine gun until successfully taken out.

Nevertheless as OC of the assault party, Major Parry was also responsible for neutralising the other three guns. Lieutenant Slade, in the N°2 casemate, was mindful of the fact that without a radio warning, HMS Arethusa would open fire on the battery. Meanwhile violent hand-to-hand fighting raged outside ; some Germans managed to escape into underground passages and get away : the rest were killed or wounded and 22 prisoners taken. The guns were all immobilised by 0500hours, but at a very heavy cost. Out of the force which had attacked the battery 5 officers and 65 paras were killed wounded or missing, leaving only about 80 unscathed. At 0600hours Otway decided to move off with his men, taking his wounded and the prisoners. After being mistakenly bombed by high flying RAF bombers, they reached a crossroads between the villages of Le Plein and Hauger on the approach to the high ground they intended to seize.

The assault on the Merville Battery. Notice the barbed wire fencing, the outlying minefields, the two routes taken by Lieutenant Colonel Otway and his men, and their fall-back positions. (RAF-Heimdal)

A tobruk hole used for a machine gun built into the top of casemate N°7 and effective against the paras attack. (E.G./ Heimdal.)

along the pre-arranged route towards the Merville Battery. On the way, Clancy's small force met no enemy but had to take rapid evasive action from the heavy bombing of Gonnevile-sur-Merville by the RAF.

After clearing a château of some enemy who had been firing on 9th Parachute Battalion, which by then had completed its task of destroying the Merville Battery, and after acting as a rearguard for the battalion's withdrawal, Clancy and his men finally reached 1st Canadian Parachute Battalion's positions at Le Mesnil at 1530hours.

B Company had also been dropped over a wide area, two platoons landing in marshy floodland terrain two miles from the drop zone. ....Five sticks landed in the flooded areas near Robehomme which were criss-crossed wihth large drainage ditches, many of which were up to seven feet in depth. Several men were forced to jettison their equipment to avoid drowning, whilst others were unable to free themselves of their heavy loads and were drowned.

A Frenchman appeared and warned them that Hauger was held by 200 Russian volunteers of 642 Ost-Batallion. The leading company, B Company duly came under fire from their mortars, rifle and automatic fire. Major George Smith led a company attack on the village, forcing a platoon of German troops back into Le Plein and into the church, killing about 15 of them in the process. As the battalion was clearing and securing a number of houses at the north end of the village, an enemy platoon counter-attacked but met the battalion's one and only Vickers machine gun which proceeded to wreak havoc at close range, killing twelve enemy and forcing the remainder to withdraw.

The battalion was by now very weak, with under a hundred men 'combat fit' left. Lieutenant-Colonel Otway decided to set up defensive positions in the Château d'Amfreville and await the arrival of the commandos of 1st Special Service Brigade led by The Lord Lovat.

1st Canadian Parachute Battalion

Their mission, with 3rd Parachute Squadron Royal Engineers was to blow the bridges at Robehomme and Varaville. They too were dropped over a wide area, most landing far from Dropping Zone V. At 0020hours the first men to be dropped were C Company, part of the Advance party of the forward HQ, together with 22nd Independent Parachute Company and a stick of 9th Battalion. Captain John Hanson, second-in-command of C Company landed ten miles off target ! Lieutenant Jon Madden, one of the platoon leaders, with his stick landed on the western bank of the Orne. only 1200 yards from the landing beaches ! Those paras who successfully landed in the Dropping Zone headed off to Varaville (see below) where they had to attack and neutralise the garrison, while the pathfinders marked out the area.

At 0050hours, with the rest of the battalion arrived, A Company was dropped over a wide area and some of its men linked up with elements of C Company who were preparing for the assault on Varaville. The rest of A Company were covering the withdrawal of Lieutenant Colonel Otway's 9th Battalion. When Llieutenant Jack Clancy reached A Company's RV, he found only two or three men waiting there. When no one else arrived, he decided to reconnoitre the nearby village of Gonneville-sur-Merville but found no signs of the enemy. On returning to his RV, he met one officer and twenty other ranks who had arrived in his absence. Taking them under command, he led them

Shoulder cloth badge, beret badge and parachutist qualifying badge, given by Norman Toseland to the Pegasus Memorial Museum.

Lieutenant Norman Toseland, the commander of N°5 Platoon in B Company, was one of the few to land on firm ground. After joining up with another member of his platoon, he met Sergeant Joe LaCasse who had a small number of men with him and together they headed for the Robehomme bridge which was one of the battalion's objectives. With the assistance of a French girl who acted as a guide, they made their way to the bridge, encountering a number of men from other units. As he headed for the objective, Toseland collected some ten men from his own platoon and others from the 8th and 9th Parachute Battalions, as well as some engineers. When they reached the Robehomme bridge, they met Major Clayton Fuller who had landed in the River Dives nearby.

Meanwhile, the Commanding Officer Lieutenant Colonel George Bradbrooke landed in a marsh west of the River Dives. However, he quickly headed for the Battalion's RV which was beside the drop zone. When he arrived, he met his second-in-command, Major

Jeff Nicklin, together with Lieutenant R. Weathersbee who was the Intelligence Officer and Lieutenant John Simpson, the Signals Officer. Also at the RV were a number of men from 8th and 9th Parachute Battalions and an anti-tank detachment of 2nd Battalion The Oxfordshire and Buckinghamshire Light Infantry whose glider had landed on the wrong location. Shortly afterwards, a small number of men from Headquarter Company and a section of 224th Parachute Field Ambulance also appeared. Deciding he needed information as to C Company's progress with its task at Varaville, Lieutenant Colonel Bradbrooke sent Lieutenant Weathersbee and two men to find out and report back on the situation. » (« Go To It ! « Peter Harclerode Caxton editions p. 71-72)

We will see later in this account the fate awaiting this company in the section devoted to the destruction of the bridges.

The gliders arrive, and General Gale

At 0315 hours, all the obstacles were destroyed and the gliders could land. « Major General Gale was travelling in glider N°70 flown by Major Billy Griffiths, and was accompanied by his ADC, Captain Tom Haughton, Major David Baird his GSO2, his signaller, his personal escort, his driver and Rifleman Grey who was Captain Haughton's batman. The party numbered twelve in all. Also in the glider was the General's radio-equipped jeep and two motorcycles.

Major General Gale described his flight to Normandy and the subsequent landing :

« In the glider we all wore Mae Wests, and taking our places we all fastened ourselves in and waited for the jerk as the tug took the strain on the tow-rope. Soon it came and we could feel ourselves hurtling down the smooth tarmac. Then we were airborne and once again we heard the familiar whistle as the air rushed by and we glided higher and highter into the dark night. I suppose all men have different reactions on these occasion. I went to sleep and slept soundly for the best part of an hour. I was woken up by a considerable bumping. We had run into a small local storm in the channel. Griffiths was having a ticklish time and the glider was all over the place. Between the glider and tug there is an intercommmunication line, so that the two pilots can talk to one another. In this bumping we received, the intercommunication line broke ; the only means of speech contact from the tug to the glider or vice versa was lost. The problem of cast-off would have to be solved by judgement. Griffiths merely said, 'the intercom has bust. »

Only a few minutes after that he said, « We will be crossing the French coast shortly. » We were flying at about five thousand feet and we soon knew the coast was under us, for we were met by a stream of flak. It was weird to see this roaring up in great golden chains past the windows of the glider, some of it being apparently between us and the tug aircraft. Looking out I could see the canal and the river through the clouds ; for the moon was fairly well overcast and the clear moonlight we had hoped for was not there. Nevertheless here we were.

In a few moments Griffiths said, « We are over the landing zone now and will be cast off at any moment. » Almost as soon as he had said this we were. The whistling sound and the roar of the engines suddenly died down ; no longer were we bumping about but gliding along on a gloriously steady course. Away went the tug aircraft with Crawford in it back to England. Round we turned, circling lower and lower ; soon the pilot turned round to tell us to link up as we were about to land. We all linked up by

putting our arms round the man next to us. We were also, as I have said, strapped in. In case of a crash this procedure would help us to take the shock.

I shall never forget the sound as we rushed down in our final steep dive, then we suddenly flattened out, and soon with a bump, bump, bump, we landed on an extremely rough stubble field.

Over the field we sped and then with a bang we hit a low embankment. The forward undercarriage wheel stove up through the floor, the glider spun round on its nose in a small circle and, as one wing hit on of those infernal stakes, we drew up to a standstill. We opened the door. Outside all was quiet. » (*Op. cit.,* pp74-75). Above them other gliders were coming in on their final approach. For those on the ground it presented a curious spectacle to see gliders not pointing south as might be expected, but higgledy-piggledy, in all directions ; it was a nightmare and extremely frightening.

Some landed well, others crashed into each other with the grotesque sound of splintering plywood and the yells of distressed occupants was like a scene from hell ! (Quoted in « Ready for anything » p156)

72 gliders had taken off from England, 68 Horsas and 4 huge Hamilcars towed by Albermarles, Halifaxes and Stirlings of 38 Group. They were bringing in the divisional advance headquarters, the heavy equipment, including the anti-tank guns of 4th Airlanding Antitank Battery. The weather began to deteriorate shortly after takeoff, resulting in 4 towropes snapping over the Normandy coast. Seven other Horsas were shot down or lost during the flight. 25 were crippled by Flak. Collisions on landing were frequent owing to the gusts of wind and the anti-glider posts. Of the 72 for 5th Parachute Brigade, 50 (48 Horsas and 2 Hamilcars) made it to Landing Zone N. In Operation 'Tonga' lost 7 aircraft and 22 gliders, but 74 gliders got through safely. 125 of the 196 glider pilots made it unscathed (2 per aircraft), the others being lost or captured.

By 0520 hours 4310 men, 44 jeeps (of 59), 15 sixpounder guns (of 17), 2 17-pounder guns (of 4) and 1214 containers had been landed in Normandy. The attempted disembarkation of a light Tetrarch tank had ended in failure, but a D4 bulldozer was at work clearing the ground in DZ N. Major General Richard N Gale : « *In the distance from the direction of the bridges we could now hear bursts of machine gun fire. Except for the arrival of more and more gliders around us, all seemed to be still. It was eerie. Had Ranville been cleared of the enemy ? Were the bridges taken ? Were they intact and safely in our hands ? How was Terence Otway and his gallant battalion faring at the Merville Battery ? We could still hear intermittent fire from the direction of the bridges. Whilst they were attempting to unload the glider the passing moments seemed like hours. It was still dark and this unloading was proving to be more difficult than we had anticipated. The crash we had had, though not serious, resulted in the nose being really well dug into the ground and the problem of getting the jeep out was defeating us. Eventually we had to give it up ; and so on foot we set out for Ranville. »* (Op Cit p 75).

Before leaving the field, General Gale made a point of greeting and thanking the glider pilots. On the way he made an unusual find. « A strange sound came from the other side of the road. Was it Germans ? We held our breath, waited, and in the end it turned out to be a horse peacefullly grazing and taking no notice of the warlike scenes going on around him. I took off the rope from around my waist and used it to lead the horse to my HQ. I had no idea what I was going to do with the beast and the soldiers burst out

This gas mask belonged to Arthur Shillemore, a soldier in the 1st Canadian Parachute Battalion who landed with his buddies at Gonneville-sur-Mer, near the 'Briquetterie', on the night of the 5th-6th June 1944. Shillemore was captured in the afternoon of 7th June by the Germans, and it was found in a house near there afterwards. (Musée Mémorial Pegasus - Photo E.G./Heimdal.)

Corporal Wagstaff looks with some surprise at a glider that has crashed into a house on the perimeter of LZ N. The house belonged to the Tanguy family who looked petrified from their beds into the cockpit of the glider filling the remains of their bedroom, the dead pilot lolling at the controls and a soldier catapulted out of the side door hanging in agony from a roof beam. A little further away, a luckier glider had slithered into the wall of a property. (IWM)

laughing ; it was rather funny. Unfortunately the Germans killed it the next day with a mortar shell. » (General Gale, quoted by Major Charles Strafford)

He found Le Bas de Ranville quiet and cleared of the enemy by 12th Battalion. Half a dozen German and Italian bodies were in evidence. French voices could be heard declaring, 'Les anglais ! les anglais ! » Captain Lickey and his men were conducting a house search when a German staff car suddenly tore through the village, was shot off the road with a burst of machine-gun fire and crashed into a wall. 2 men were killed and two wounded.

« Shortly afterwards as dawn was breaking, General Gale met Brigadier Poett who informed him that the bridges had been captured by the coup de main operation which had worked perfectly and that 7th Parachute Battalion was now on the west bank. He also told him that 13th Parachute Battalion was in Ranville whilst 12th Parachute Battalion was holding Le Bas de Ranville.

Meanwhile the rest of divisional headquarters had deployed from the twenty gliders in which it had arrived. By 0430 hours it was moving off the LZ in its jeeps and trailers and by 0600 hours was set up oin the Chateau de Heaume in Le Bas de Ranville. One key member of the headquarters who was missing, however, was Lieutenant Colonel Bobby Bray, the GSO 1 Operations. Together with an officer from the 6th Airborne Divisional Signals, he had landed in his glider near Varaville. Whilst heading west to rejoin the headquarters, the two men had a lucky escape when fired upon by a lost section of 9th Parachute Battalion.

The headquarters itself was set up with the operations staff and signals element in the stables, whilst the CRE, Lieutenant-Colonel Frank Plowman, shared a copse behind the main house with the ADMS, Colonel McEwan, and the AA & QMG, Lieutenant-Colonel Shamus Hickie. Meanwhile the CRA, Colo-

nel Jack Norris, and his gunner dug themselves into positiions in a nearby orchard. The headquarters was guarded by military policemen of the 6th Airborne Division Provost Company and the headquarters defence platoon.

At 0700 hours the Allied air and sea bombardment of the assault beaches began. This was the signal for radio silence to be broken and the signallers immediately busied themselves with establishing communications. » (Go to it p75)

Blowing the bridges

The Bures bridges

At 0400 hours, Lieutenant Colonel Pearson moved off with a group of roughly a hundred paras, across the heavily-wooded terrain east of the main road between Troarn and Le Mesnil. On the way he set up an anti-tank ambush mentioned above, led by Lance-Corporal Stevenson. He waited at the crossroads on the Touffreville – Le Mesnil road, and dispatched a patrol to reconnoitre the two bridges at Bures, one of which was a steel girder railway bridge, and the other a similar but shorter one carrying a trackway.

These two bridges crossed the Dives north-east of Bures, the railway bridge the further north of the two. At 0630 hours, N°2 Troop of 3rd Parachute Squadron RE, under the command of Captain Jim Juckes, reached the bridges. »

After a brief skirmish to the south, N°3 section, led by Lieutenant Shave, got to farm and road bridge, laid demolition charges, while shortly afterwards, the other group led by Lieutenant Forester, reached the railway bridge and also laid charges. At 0915 there was a huge explosion as the two bridges were blown and the central sections collapsed into the river bed of the Dives. With the mission accomplished, Captain Juckes' N°2 Troop laid mines around Bures and this rejoined 8th Battalion, dug in at Le Mesnil.

The crash of Horsa CN35 at Saint-Vaast-en-Auge on D-Day

On page 61 we saw three signalmen receiving their invasion currency. Ludovic Louis has discovered the fate of the two soldiers on the left (1), fatal for one. Signalman John Easby, on the left of the photo, was a motorcyclist courier for K section, Signal Platoon, HQ 5th Para Brigade. He fought right through the Normandy campaign, the battle of the Ardennes, to be taken prisoner during Operation Varsity on 24th March 1945 and liberated in May. On the right Signalman Douglas Davis (N° 6144046), part of the same HQ signals of the 5th Brigade. Unmarried, he came from Barnes in Surrey, but was judged unfit for the parachute jump of Operation Tonga and so was transferred to a glider at Brize Norton. The glider, with its two pilots and two other passengers of the 13th Battalion would crash, killing four on board. John Easby returns every year for the landing commemorations, and rediscovered his friend's tomb in 1999 and with Ludovic Louis' help has pieced together this tragic story.

On 6th June, at 0110hours Horsa glider LH324 (the number 35 chalked on the side for this mission) took off from Brize Norton, towed by an Albermarle (1823 Mark V) flown by F/O E.D.Halpin. Their Drop Zone was DZ N. (Ranville). On board were S/Sgt Colin Hopgood (Ist pilot 1892740), Sgt Daniel Phillipps (co-pilot, 6406473), both belonging to the 1st Wing of B Squadron, and their passengers Captain S. Daisley (Quartermaster of the 13th Parachute Battalion), Private John Aldred, (his captain's batman), Signalman Douglas Davis and two other soldiers as yet unidentified. A jeep and trailer carrying equipment for the 13th Parachute Battalion and Davis' motorbike were also on board. Once they reached the coast S/Sgt Colin Hopgood informed the tug to release the tow-rope, and following a navigational error the glider crashed into the 'wood of the manor farm' at Saint-Vaast, 15 km to the north-east of Ranville. Daisley, Aldred and Davis were all killed ; Monsieur Lefort owned the farm and his daughter saw the bodies inside the glider ; a villager, Monsieur Borel, found some food for the two surviving soldiers who had taken refuge in the 'lavoir' or village wash-house.

They had hidden the jeep under the bridge but would be taken prisoner by the Germans on the 8th June. It wasn't until the 10th June that the 5 victims of the crash would be buried, for the Germans feared to go into the wood with so many British soldiers about. They were buried in the cemetery near the church of Saint-Vaast-en-Auge, in tombs N° 8,9,10,11 and 12. Two of the men should never have been in the glider in the first place, Signalman Douglas Davis – because of his fitness problem, and Private John Aldred, who wasn't Captain Daisley's batman but had been picked out at the last moment for the role. Such is fate. For his part, Signalman John Easby, taking off from Fairford, had been landed safely onto DZ N. The small wood into which the glider crashed was cut down eight years ago.

(Investigation carried out by Ludovic Louis)

1. Taken at RAF Fairford on Saturday 3rd June, Signalman John Easby is showing his banknotes to Signalman Douglas Davis on his right. His name unusually figures on his shirt. When this picture was released to the London press on 7th June, Easby's parents were very surprised ! (IWM)

2. S/Sgt Colin Hopgood Ist pilot of Horsa CN35, killed 6th June. (Coll. L. Louis.)

3... Sgt Daniel Phillipps co-pilot, killed 6th June. (L.L.)

4. Captain S. Daisley, Quartermaster of the 13th Parachute Battalion, killed 6th June. (L.L.)

5. Private John Aldred, his captain's batman, killed 6th June. (L.L.)

6. The first row of temporary wooden crosses mark the graves of the 5 men killed at Saint-Vaast-en-Auge. (L.L.)

7. John Easby stands by the tomb of his best friend at Saint-Vaast-en-Auge. (L.L.)

The Troarn Bridge

Major Tim Roseveare commanding 3rd Parachute Squadron Royal Engineers attached to 8th Battalion had the task of blowing the Troarn bridge. With no news of Lieutenant Thompson, he led off his paras and sappers on the Troarn road, the sappers taking in turns to push the heavily laden trolleys fill with high explosive. At 0400hours they were joined by paras of 8th battalion, including Lieutenant Thomson and 50 or so men of A Company and other platoons with machine guns and 3-inch mortars.

« Roseveare had ordered Lieutenant Thompson to set a firm base at the crossroads to the west of Troarn to cover that flank with mortars while he went forward to deal with the bridge. Thompson had done so but made contact with the PIAT ambush party whilst personally reconnoitring the local area, and thus learned of the battalion's whereabouts. Not long afterwards, six enemy vehicles drove into the PIAT ambush and were destroyed. » (Go to it p71)

The Germans were identified as being from 21st Panzer Division. For his part, Major Roseveare began to set up his raid on the Troarn bridge. He only had a medical jeep and a trailer carrying 900 kilos of plastic and 45 detonators. Radio communications were established with the battalion through transmitters N° 68 and N°18, 30 paras and 40 sappers crept silently along the road with Major Roseveare. The jeeps were unloaded, the explosives put into the trailer, and Major Roseveare, a Lieutenant and 7 men perched on the high explosive and hitched to even more, set off slowly through the woods and at a level-crossing near the town they drove over a barbed-wire knife-rest. A sentry spotted them, but was shot dead. It took them twenty minutes to cut themselves and their vehicle free. At last the jeep squeezed through and they sent off two men to scout ahead at the next crossroads. Shooting a German on a bike rather than knifing him proved a mistake since this time the garrison sounded the general alert in Troarn, and flares were set off in the village. So, with the windscreen down and bristling with weaponry (they had Bren guns and 5 Sten guns) the 2-ton load of 8 men and high explosive tore down the High Street at top speed – 50 kph - Sapper Peachey, sat on the explosive charges in the trailer, acted as a rear-gunner and sprayed the town with his Sten, emptying clip after clip into his pursuers. The German dived into the doorways, shop fronts shattered, and they returned fire from every window – or so it seemed. As the jeep sped down the hill towards the bridge, the trailer lurching from side to side, it took a hail of machine gun bullets, none of them fortunately hitting the explosives ! The bridge was reached, the charges laid, and five minutes later a gap twenty feet wide had been blown in it. Where was Peachey ? Unfortunately in the crazed zig-zagging of the trailer, he'd been thrown out, wounded, and taken prisoner.

With the men piled back in, the jeep got bogged down on a track heading north, so it was ditched and Roseveare 's party proceeded on foot towards Bures, which they reached about 0500hours. They spotted a German patrol so changed course, skirted the area and reached Le Mesnil at 1300 hours.

« For his part, Pearson sent out patrols to reconnoitre the areas to the north and west of Troarn. He had received no confirmation of the Troarn bridge having been blown, so he dispatched Captain Tim Juckes and his sappers, together with N°9 Platoon of B Company under the command of Lieutenant Brown, to check whether the bridge had been destroyed, and if so, to further increase the damage if possible. » (Go to it p71)

They were equipped with a jeep and trailer, with about 40 kilos of explosives. 500 yards outside the village, the locals warned them that the Germans could be attempting to cut off their rear. Captain Juckes conducted probing patrols to cover this eventuality, and went forward towards the bridge. Sergeant Shrubbery burst onto the main road to draw the German light arms fire coming from houses near the church. Lieutenant Brown fulfilled his mission with only two men wounded. They captured 5 men, shot another dead as they pulled back : these were men from a reconnaissance patrol of 21st Panzer. Juckes and his sappers went forward and inspected the stone bridge in which they found a gap had been blown.... the work of Major Roseveare. Seeing the bridge superstructure between the central pillar and the embankment to be still intact, he placed further charges and increased the gap to a width of seventy feet. (over 23 metres). It was 1500 hours. With the mission accomplished, and having been plied with food and wine by local townspeople, the small force laid a few mines and the returned to Le Mesnil by 1630 hours.

The Robehomme bridge

When Lieutenant Toseland met Major Fuller it was 0300hours, and the sappers tasked with blowing the bridge had not arrived ; they were going to have to improvise.

« However, Sergeant Bill Poole of N°3 Troop of 3rd Parachute squadron RE, who was one of the sappers who had joined up with Lieutenant Toseland, collected all the plastic explosive carried by the infantrymen for making Gammon bombs. This amounted to some thirty pounds in all. Sergeant Poole attempted to blow the bridge but, with the limited amount of explosive available to him, only managed to weaken it. At about 0600 hours however, Lieutenant Jack Inman and five sappers of N°3 Troop arrived with two hundred pounds of explosive charges and the bridge was duly destroyed. » (Go to it p72)

The chateau and bridge at Varaville

« C Company had been undertaking the four tasks allocated to it with a fraction of its normal strength of over one hundred men. The company had been tasked with clearing the enemy garrison from Varaville, neutralising a 75mm gun emplacement at a road junction near the Chateau de Varaville just east of the town, the demolition of the bridge over the River Divette and the destruction of a radio transmitter station which was also near Varaville. Even for a full strength copmany this was a formidable task. As it was, when the company commander, Major Murray

McLeod, arrived at his company RV at 0030 hours, he found only a small number of his men. He himself, along with several others, had been on the drop zone when the RAF Lancasters bombing Merville battery had flown over the DZ on to which some of them had emptied their bomb loads. McLeod, along with everyone else on the DZ at the time, had been left badly shaken. By 0030 hours McLeod's group numbered only fifteen men and could muster only one PIAT, three Sten guns, eight rifles and his own pistol. Nevertheless, he led his small force off to take on the enemy at Varaville. As he did so, he met a small group from N° 9 Platoon, led by Private Rudko who had survived the RAF's bombing of the Drop Zone. Despite the fact that they were still somewhat badly shocked, they were unhurt and were in possession of all their equipment. With just twenty-five minutes left before the drop of 3rd Parachute Brigade's main force was due to take place, McLeod and his men made their way in the dark to Varaville. Passing through the village without being detected, they came to the château gatehouse which was some distance from the château itself and which overlooked the enemy defensive positions. McLeod could see that these consisted of a long trench fortified with concrete and earthworks, with machine gun positions located at intervals. At each end of the trench was a bunker. Unbeknownst to McLeod, a 75mm gun was located in a concrete emplacement to the rear of the trench.

Entering the gatehouse, some of McLeod's men searched it and found it was being used as a barracks housing a total of 96 men. McLeod positioned his men around the gatehouse. His one other officer, Lieutenant 'Chug' Walker, placed twelve men in a shallow ditch which would have been the position for the machine guns giving covering fire if all had gone according to plan. McLeod, accompanied by Private Thompson, went up to the second floor of the gatehouse where, shortly afterwards, they came under fire from the 75mm gun. An attempt was made to neutralise the gun with the group's one and only PIAT but this failed. Before a second attempt could be made, the gun opened fire on the gatehouse, setting off the bombs beside the PIAT operator, Corporal Oikle, and killing Lieutenant Walker. McLeod himself was mortally wounded.

At this point the company's second-in-command, Captain John Hanson, arrived with two more men which brought the total in the force to some thirty. Although the PIAT had been lost, there was now a machine gun. This was augmented shortly afterwards when Corporal Hartigan, accompanied by Private

Mallon, arrived with a 2-inch mortar. They both managed to reach cover just in time as enemy machine guns opened fire on the road. At 0830 hours the enemy showed a white flag and requested that they be permitted to send out their wounded. Captain Hanson, who had assumed command after McLeod had died in his lap shorlty after his arrival, gave permission. Shortly afterwards, a massive explosion was heard away to the south-east and Hanson and his men realised that other members of the company, under Sergeant Davies, had succeeded in demolishing the Varaville bridge and thus had achieved one of their objectives. » (Go to it p 73)

These three pictures show the three gliders of Major Howard's coup de main party. Picture **(1)** shows Howard's N°1 glider, the smashed nose broken away, **(2)** the three gliders, N°2 in the foreground, N°3 in the middle, and N°1 beyond that, with the Café Gondrée on the other side of the canal. Picture **(3)** shows glider N°2 with its nose torn off on the edge of the marsh. (IWM.)

The Road Bridge at Bures

The concrete structure we see today replaced a metallic structure after the war. N°2 Troop of 3rd Parachute Squadron RE, under the command of Captain Jim Juckes, reached the bridge at 0630hrs. The N°3 section, led by Lieutenant Shave, placed demolition charges on the bridge, and, in the same way as the other bridge, blew it into the river Dives at 0915hrs. A commemorative plaque recalls the action. (Photo E.G. Heimdal.)

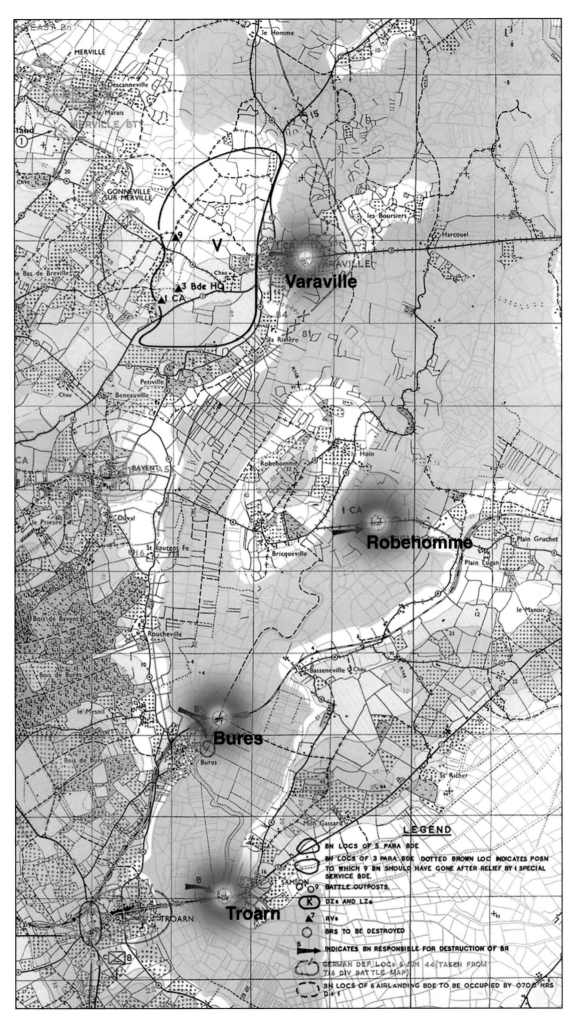

Detail of the map shown on page 41, showing where the 5 bridges were blown : reading from north to south, the Troarn bridge, the road and the railway bridges at Bures, the Robehomme bridge and the Varaville bridge.

Varaville

Robehomme

Bures

Troarn

LEGEND

BN LOCS OF 5 PARA BDE

BN LOCS OF 3 PARA BDE DOTTED BROWN LOC INDICATES POSN TO WHICH 9 BN SHOULD HAVE GONE AFTER RELIEF BY 1 SPECIAL SERVICE BDE.

BATTLE OUTPOSTS.

K DZs AND LZs

RVs

BRS TO BE DESTROYED

INDICATES BN RESPONSIBLE FOR DESTRUCTION OF BR

GERMAN DEF LOCs 6 JUN 44 (TAKEN FROM 716 DIV BATTLE MAP)

BN LOCS OF 6 AIRLANDING BDE TO BE OCCUPIED BY 0700 HRS D + 1

The railway bridge at Bures.

This bridge was destroyed at 0915hrs on 6th June 1944 by Captain Tim Juckes.

1. The railway keeper's lodge shattered by the shelling in a photograph taken after the fighting here. (CA via Ph. Wirton)

2. Aerial photograph taken from the north by the RAF showing the bridge still intact.

3 and **4.** The existence of this former railway cottage and this bridge abutment testify to its railway past. (EG/Heimdal)

5

9

8

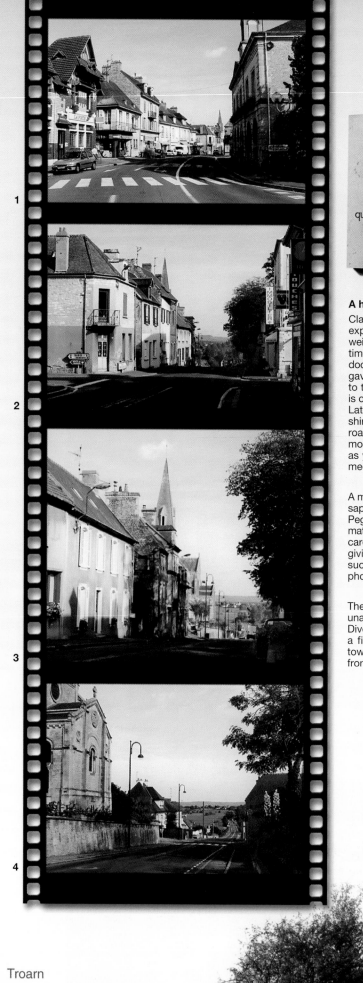

Erigé par la Population de TROARN
en l'honneur des Officiers et des Hommes du
"3rd Parachute Squadron Royal Engineers"
qui, sur des renseignements obtenus de la Résistance,
ont détruit les ponts de la Dives
pour protéger le flanc gauche du Débarquement
à l'aube du 6 JUIN 1944

5

A hell-for-leather ride through Troarn

Clambering into a jeep hitched to a trailer stuffed with high explosives, Major Tim Roseveare and 8 paras, despite the weight, hurtled down the High Street at 50 kph. It was night-time and the Germans fired at random from the shelter of doorways along the road. Bristling with weaponry, the paras gave a good account of themselves on their headlong rush to the bridge. **Pictures 1 to 4** follow the ride ; the church is on the left as you come out of town towards the bridge. Later in the day, Lieutenant Brown returned to put the finishing touches to Major Roseveare's work, taking the same road and getting into a skirmish by the church. A commemorative plaque **(5)** recalls this action. Nearby, on the right as you go down to the bridge you can see the wonderful medieval remains of Troarn abbey. **(6)** (EG/Heimdal)

A model of the stone bridge at Troarn **(7)** was made by the sappers of 3rd Parachute Squadron RE and is kept in the Pegasus Memorial Museum. It was made possible by information obtained from the local resistance, such as this postcard of the bridge at the beginning of the 20th century **(8),** giving some idea of how difficult it would be to demolish such as substantial stone structure. (Model and archive photo : MP film sequence EG/Heimdal)

The beautiful old stone bridge has been replaced by this unappealing concrete object **(9 and 10)** which spans the Dives at this point. From the middle of the bridge there is a fine view to the west and north –west, downstream towards the Bures bridges. This river would represent the front line for 6th Airborne until August. (EG/H)

bridge of
Saint-Samson Troarn

bridge of
Saint-Samson

old abbey

6

7

8

9   10

Dives river

Bures
railway bridge

bridge

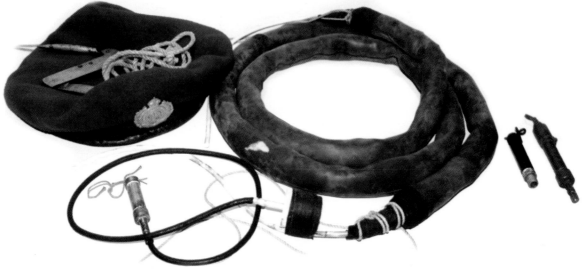

The Robehomme bridge

1st Canadian Battalion had the task of destroying this bridge. These photos show the bridge today. The bridge was blown at 0600 hrs on 6th June 1944 by Lieutenant Jack Inman and 5 sappers of the N°3 Troop of 3rd Parachute Squadron RE, using 200 pounds of explosive. (PH) Above, some of the explosive charges and fuses on the right used by the sappers of 591st Parachute Squadron RE led by Captain Semple to destroy the antiglider poles in Landing Zone N. (see page 89)

The Varaville Bridge
As important as the Troarn bridge, the Varaville road (above) leads straight to Cabourg and Deauville, from which could come reinforcements of the 711st Infantry Division. (Photos E.G./Heimdal.)

This bridge was destroyed at 0830hours on 6th June by Sergeant Davies of C Company of 1st Canadian Parachute Battalion and sappers of 3rd Parachute Squadron RE. A concrete structure replaces it. (Photos EG/Heimdal.)

Bénouville Church and the port area.

B Company held this sector in the northern part of the bridgehead at Bénouville. German sniper fire was very troublesome from the church tower overlooking the old village of Bénouville, so Corporal Kilean smacked it with a PIAT bazooka shell around 1000 hours. The firing stopped – only to take up again when the brigade of commandos was held up and took several casualties. A light tank sufficed to silence the snipers, leaving a great crater in the bell tower Here we see the church **(1)** with a detail **(2)** of the damage caused by the PIAT and tank shell. **(3)**, the church today, with the tower restored. The commandos cleared out the bell tower of Germans and in **(4)** we see one of the bodies. Some of the combatants were buried in the nearby church cemetery, including Corporal H Knox of the Oxs and Bucks, and driver G Dransfield o fthe Royal Engineers, both killed on 6 June **(5 and 6)**. Traces of shrapnel marks can still be seen on the wall of the church, **(7)** overlooking the canal **(8).** (Photos IWM 12,4 and EG/Heimdal)

5

6

7

8

111

1. and **2.** Paratrooper's helmet in the state in which it was found in 1975 in a Ranville cellar : its camouflage strips are original. The name R Watson and « Pret. Amcorp » is written on the chinstrap.

1

2

3

4

5

3. and **4.** The second pattern of the first model in the state it was found.

5. Despatch rider's helmet. Note the unusual divisional insignia painted on the helmet.

6. Oxs and Bucks helmet, first pattern of the first model : unlike 3 and 4 the chin straps were stitched and not rivetted. The regimental colours painted on this helmet found near Ranville were blue, pale yellow, red, and blue.

6

112

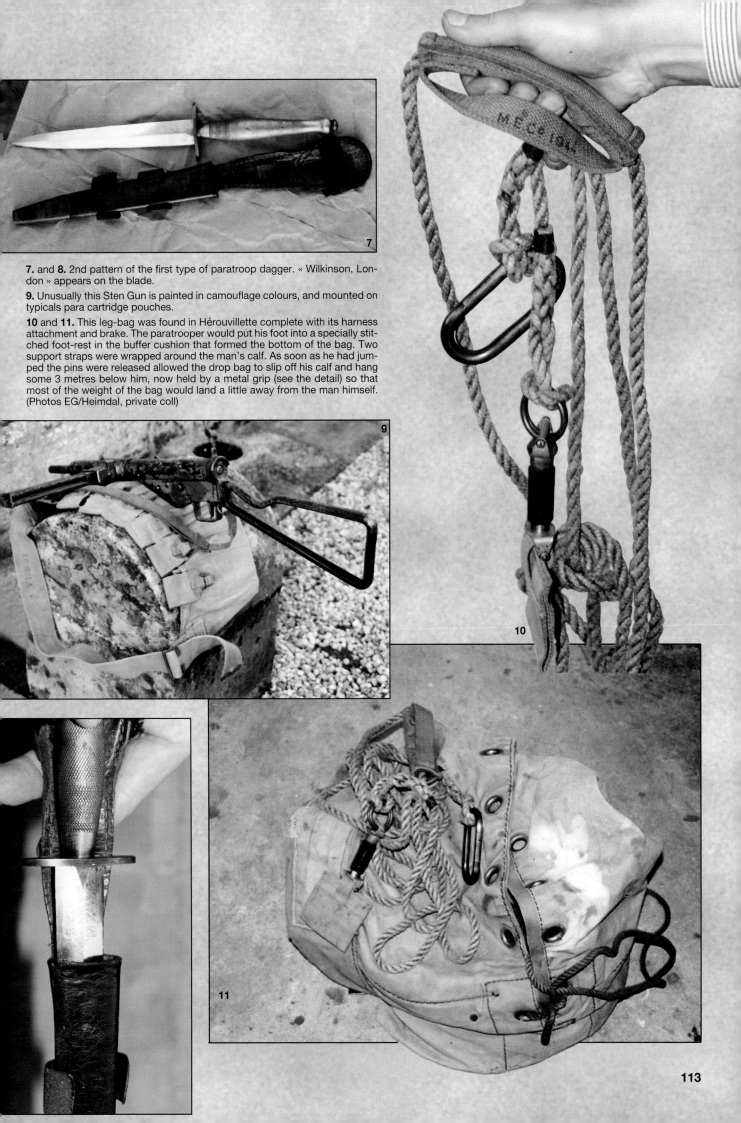

7. and **8.** 2nd pattern of the first type of paratroop dagger. « Wilkinson, London » appears on the blade.

9. Unusually this Sten Gun is painted in camouflage colours, and mounted on typicals para cartridge pouches.

10 and **11.** This leg-bag was found in Hérouvillette complete with its harness attachment and brake. The paratrooper would put his foot into a specially stitched foot-rest in the buffer cushion that formed the bottom of the bag. Two support straps were wrapped around the man's calf. As soon as he had jumped the pins were released allowed the drop bag to slip off his calf and hang some 3 metres below him, now held by a metal grip (see the detail) so that most of the weight of the bag would land a little away from the man himself. (Photos EG/Heimdal, private coll)

Right : A 10cwt trailer, specially designed for airborne troops, allowed for the transport of loads up to 500kgs, making a total weight of 750kgs. It was 2.7m long, 1.3 metres wide so it could be transported in a Horsa. A hook at the back allowed it to tow a second trailer. This diaroma shows one fully loaded with containers, the other under cover. (Made by V. Wirton)

Below : A jeep and trailer being unloaded out of Horsa « Charlie's Aunt » during Operation Mallard. (IWM)

Left : A Royal Engineers jeep with the number 49 of the Parachute Squadron displayed – recreating the jeep type used by Major Tim Roseveare*and his sappers. (Model made by V. Wirton)

Below : A Signals Corps jeep. The radio unit N°22, set up in the back with its aerial was the commonest type used in Normandy. It broadcast on a 2 to 8 MHz waveband with a range of 10 miles when used as a radio telephone, or 20 miles in morse. On the bonnet we can see rolls of telephone wire, on the wings spare batteries and sticking out of the front of the bonnet the bobbin for unrolling wire. (Model by V. Wirton)

Transport Methods for 6th Airborne Division

As we have seen (pp35-38) the Division had a wide variety of transport light enough to be carried by glider such as the folding bicycle and lightweight motorcycles (the 38kg Wellbike and the 65kg Royal Enfield). Jeeps would prove of particular value right from the first hours of D-Day, most especially for the transport of high explosives, as Major Roseveare so spectacularly demonstrated.

Over a thousand specially adapted transportable jeeps were used by 6th Airborne Division. These adaptations included :

- the windscreen was removed and the steering wheel could be taken off.

- the rear bumpers were removed and replaced by a tow bar.

- Handles and running boards were removed and the indicator lights displaced on the wings.

Period jeep on display at Beltring in 2001. (Photo Patrick Gibeau)

- Working tools such as picks and spades were often placed on the front bumper

- Jerrycans were moved to a slot behind the seats.

- The spare wheel for the jeep or the trailer was jammed between the front bumper and the radiator.

- A triangular towbar arrangement at the rear allowed two jeeps to pull a 17-pounder gun for example.

- Metal frames were added to the bonnet, the rear of the jeep, over each wing

in order to carry various items such as boxes of ammunition and spare batteries, etc

- Fixed clips to allow weapons to be attached to the vehicle (Bren guns, Lee Enfields etc)

- Specific modifications for a wide variety of functions were carried out :

- Special mounts for stretchers for the jeeps of Royal Army Medical Corps, specifically 195th Airlanding Field Ambulance, 224th and 225th Field Ambulance.

- Personnel working for the Headquarters Staff, 3rd Parachute Squadron RE, the 591st Parachute Squadron RE, the 249th and 289th Field Companies. The Royal Engineers' jeeps could carry up to 500kgs of material, demolition charges, electricity generators, compressors etc. ;

- The Royal Corps of Signals had specially adapted jeep as we have seen.

- The Recce Regiment had sturdy, self-reliant vehicles fitted with a Vickers machine gun.

- The Royal Artillery Regiment had their own jeep also.

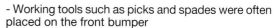

1. The jeeps of the Royal Army Medical Corps, specifically 195th Airlanding Field Ambulance, (77) 224th (75) and 225th Field Ambulance (76). This latter unit had the tactical number 76 painted against a black background under the windscreen, as we see recreated in this model. Also note the specific adaptation made to this vehicle : the folding metal framework at the back to carry two stretcher cases, the white star and red cross and the loaded weight plaque. (model VW)

2. This picture show most of the divisional adaptations made to the jeep : the cut-back front bumper and running boards, the spare wheel covering the radiator, munitions canisters strapped to the bonnet, metal frames for spare batteries welded onto the wings, a bobbin of telephone wire (for the signals version of the jeep) attached to the right front of the bonnet, etc (Photo Patrick Gibeau, Beltring 2001)

3. 65kg Royal Enfield motorbikes strapped into a Horsa glider prior to landing. (IWM)

Right : Tactical insignia to identify units in the division and painted onto vehicles. (Heimdal.)

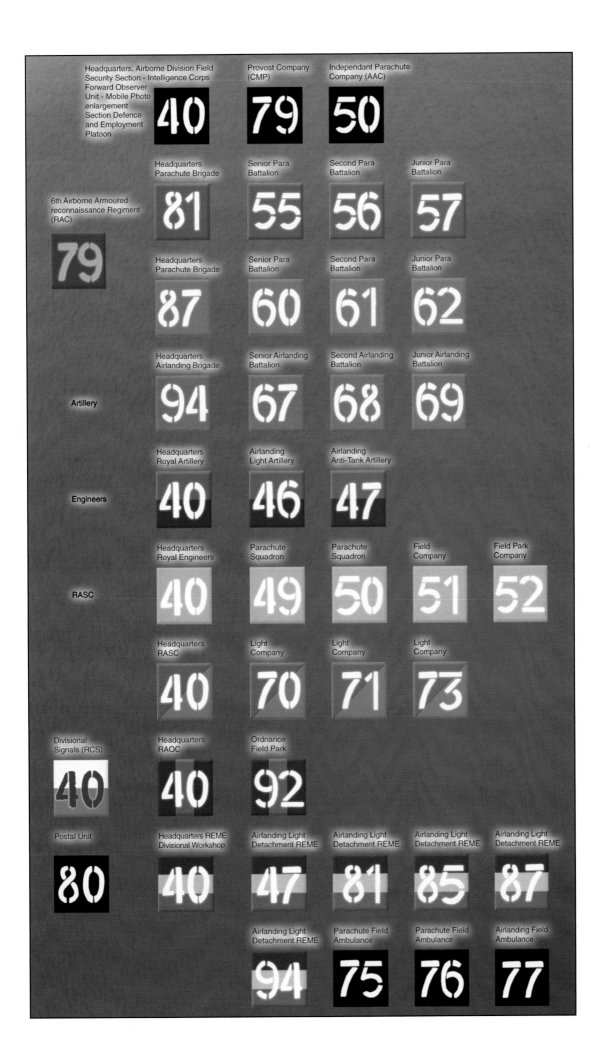

Headquarters, Airborne Division Field Security Section - Intelligence Corps Forward Observer Unit - Mobile Photo enlargement Section Defence and Employment Platoon
40

Provost Company (CMP)
79

Independant Parachute Company (AAC)
50

6th Airborne Armoured reconnaissance Regiment (RAC)
79

Headquarters Parachute Brigade
81

Senior Para Battalion
55

Second Para Battalion
56

Junior Para Battalion
57

Headquarters Parachute Brigade
87

Senior Para Battalion
60

Second Para Battalion
61

Junior Para Battalion
62

Artillery

Headquarters Airlanding Brigade
94

Senior Airlanding Battalion
67

Second Airlanding Battalion
68

Junior Airlanding Battalion
69

Engineers

Headquarters Royal Artillery
40

Airlanding Light Artillery
46

Airlanding Anti-Tank Artillery
47

RASC

Headquarters Royal Engineers
40

Parachute Squadron
49

Parachute Squadron
50

Field Company
51

Field Park Company
52

Headquarters RASC
40

Light Company
70

Light Company
71

Light Company
73

Divisional Signals (RCS)
40

Headquarters RAOC
40

Ordnance Field Park
92

Postal Unit
80

Headquarters REME Divisional Workshop
40

Airlanding Light Detachment REME
47

Airlanding Light Detachment REME
81

Airlanding Light Detachment REME
85

Airlanding Light Detachment REME
87

Airlanding Light Detachment REME
94

Parachute Field Ambulance
75

Parachute Field Ambulance
76

Airlanding Field Ambulance
77

The second pattern folding bicycle for paratroops, handy for getting about the dense network of country lanes within 6th Airborne bridgehead between the Orne and the Dives. This particular bicycle was found in good condition near Ranville and is complete with its period lamp and tyres. (Private coll)

The German counter-attack

East of the Orne

Towards midnight Major Hans von Luck heard the rumble of aircraft and put it own to just another raid on the defenses of the Atlantic Wall, or perhaps another raid heading for Germany. Yet these aircraft seemed to be flying unusually low : could this be due to the foul weather ? Then suddenly flares began shooting up, the phone rang, it was his N°2, Lieutenant Liebeskind. « *Major, paratroops have been dropped in our sector, and some gliders. I'll try and get in touch with 2nd Battalion and call right back when I have some news.* » Major von Luck immediately ordered : « *All units to go on red alert and inform Divisional Command. 2nd Battalion must engage the enemy wherever it can and wherever necessary. Try and get hold of some prisoners and bring them here.* »

At about **0030am** Oberleutenant Brandenburger's report was followed by others, all immediately forwarded to the HQ of 21st Panzer Division at Saint-Pierre-sur-Dives. The 1st and 5th platoon of 7/125 as well as 6/125 near Barneville, and 8/125 near Colombelles were taken completely by surprise by the attack. The Kommandeur of 2nd Battalion, Hauptmann Kuron, immediately counterattacked towards Troarn where 5th Company would manage to pull back. Contact was reestablished with this battalion : they captured a paramedic. But once through to 21st Panzer HQ, von Luck found General Feuchtinger absent, and his aide-de-camp, Oberleutnant Messner took his report in his place. Von Luck requested he be informed as soon as the General was back from Paris, in order to transmit the authority he needed in order to deliver a night attack. Already, captured paratroops were being brought in to von Luck before being sent on to divisional HQ at Saint-Pierre-sur-Dives on his advice. Hans von Luck now knew it was 6th Airborne Division which had made the night jump. Once he'd passed on this information Hans von Luck began to feel a rising tide of anger swell up in him at the thought of having to wait hour after hour for some reaction from Heeresgruppe B : Rommel, it appeared, was also absent. The 125th Panzer Grenadier Regiment was stuck fast, unable to move forward without the orders to do so. Heeresgruppe B assessed this assault to be a mere diversionary attack, and with each passing hour the chances of successsfully counter-attacking were diminished. But Hans von Luck remained calm. « *My experience in other theatres of war had taught me that the more critical and alarming the situation that one faces is, the calmer an experienced officer has to be in reacting to it.* »

Even so, with the first news coming in, at about 0200 hours Hauptmann Wagemann put the 21st Panzer Division on high alert, requiring the mobilisation of motorised units within 90 minutes. Generalmajor Feuchtinger was informed and made arrangments for his immediate return. But not only was the General absent but his Chief of Staff Oberstleutnant von Berlichingen was as well, so that the remaining officers at the Saint-Pierre-sur-Dives HQ were simply not up to taking the kind of decisions that need to be made at this critical hour. They would just have to wait for General Feuchtinger to turn up. Meanwhile, at 0130 hours the 15th Army had also raised the alarm (Alarmstufe II) in its sector and had informed Heeresgruppe B 10 minutes later.

While elements of II/125 were engaged with isolated groups of paratroops to the north of highway RN13, 1/125, (Major Schenk zu Schweinsburg) to the south of the road was getting its act together. Leutnant Gerhard Bandomir commanding 3rd Company of Grenadiers said to me : « *Our companies were relatively well prepared ; all the vehicles were well dug in for defence against a full-scale attack. We slept in our battledress. Night-time invasion exercises had been organised almost every night, including the night of 5th-6th June when a motorcyclist messenger roared up to our HQ at about 2 or 3 in the morning and this time it did look like the real thing. I had been woken up by the throb of aircraft engines out to sea, and then the bombs started falling on Caen. The sky was all lit up by flares suspended beneath parachutes, which made it clear to me that the invasion was starting. I put my men on alert. The motorcyclist held out a written order to rejoin my Regimental HQ without delay and keep my Company ready for deployment under the orders of my second-in-command, and to maintain a defensive position straddling the Sannerville-Troarn crossroads. At HQ I was joined by our Kommandeur, Major von Luck, in a huge room where I saw 3 prisoners of war sat in a corner.*

I was told the news and learnt that the paras had landed near the coast and two companies were already engaged. Unfortunately we had lost contact with them. Von Luck feared they might be surrounded. I was ordered to link up with one of the two companies fighting outside Troarn and fight with it into Hérouvillette and Ranville to relieve the other.

6 of 10 assault guns fitted with 75mm anti-tank guns or 105mm guns of our Sturmgeschütz-Abteilung 200 were affected to our operations. I took my orders and set off, only to shortly afterwards find myself at a crossroads where the lead group took the company

Lieutenant Bandomir.

Leutnant Bandomir launched a counter-attack against Escoville with his grenadiers of 3/125 at dawn on 6/6, backed by a mobile assault artillery of Sturmgeschütz-Abteilung 200. Below, we can see one of their powerful 105mm guns. (BA)

in the wrong direction, into the brush and I did my best to take what was left towards where we were supposed to go. By this time dawn was breaking and we later learnt that the road we were supposed to have taken had been heavily strafed and bombed by fighter-bombers. So our mission seemed to have started off with some signs of good luck. Then we advanced on Escoville from the east and there we were ordered to attack Hérouvillette and Ranville where the paratroops had been spotted. We managed to relieve 2nd Company of 2nd Battalion (2/125) without any difficulty and after talking it over with the officers of this company and those of the half-tracks (SPW) we decided to attack on foot with 2nd company on the right and mine on the left, with the anti-tank guns on their half-tracks backing us up. My company had to cross a field bordered by hedgerows and unfortunately the SPW followed us too closely when we came up against stiff resistance. Two assault guns were hit by PIATs and brewed up, four self-propelled anti-tank guns were struck by a single shell before we had even fired a shot. The second Company made slow headway in the undergrowth, so much so that my Company's attack also failed. The first platoon commander was killed and his men took heavy casualties, some 15 to 20 men. After this attack failed (in the grounds of the Escoville château) my company began preparing defensive positions in the rear. All this took place between 0700 hours and midday on 6 June (8am and 1pm Double British Summer Time) ».

Leutnant Hoeller had his photograph taken on 6th June before the British lines south of Bénouville : a rare picture. (Coll JCP)

Below : Major von Luck observing the British lines through his binoculars.His second-in-command, Helmut Liebeskind (right) would be a general in the Bundeswehr. (BA)

To the west of the Orne

Alongside 716th Infantrie-Division the 1st Panzerjaeger-Kompanie 716 moved up out of Biéville at 0205 hours tasked to sort out the Orne Canal situation. They came up against 7th Battalion paratroopers at 0230 hours (0130 hours British Double Summer Time) at the fork of the Caen-Ouistrham road off to the Bénouville birdge. The tank was taken out by a PIAT and the commander killed ; the unit then pulled back.

But to the west of the Orne, another Panzergrenadier Regiment (192) of 21st Division was also sent in to counterattack Bénouville. This was 8/192 led by

Oberleutnant Braatz. The II/192 under Major Zippe had been alerted at 0200 hours and sent in its heavily armed company, 8./(schwere)Pz.Gren.-Kompanie 192. It set out at 0310 hours to reinforce elements of 716th Division, 3/176 fighting the British paratroops near the Bénouville bridge. Corporal Weber had managed to get away and alert the garrison commander whose office was in Bénouville.

Groping through the dark, this column of substantial reinforcements for 716th Infantry crossed Biéville and Blainville heading for Bénouville, armed with 3 mobile 75mm Pak 40s at the head, loaded with explosive shells, Granatwerfer (Sfl), half-tracks carrying mortars, and three self-propelled 20mm anti-aircraft Flak, all formidable weapons in infantry support owing to their rapid rate of fire. The Company commander gave out a warning as they approached the paratroopers' positions at Bénouville, and the men spread out through the villages as they passed, in case of ambushes, and likely sources of trouble, like isolated farms, walls and hedges were covered by their anti-tank guns and Flak. The narrow roads slowed their progress and the local population peered from their shutters and windows down at this curious procession of men and hardware heading north. After Biéville, the grey day began to break. Another 500 yards and the motorised column, on the road parallel to the canal, found itself on the southern outskirts of Bénouville. They were tasked to clear the area and they would be expected to contact the paratroopers by surprises. But their vehicles were noisy and the paras had excellent road maps with them, showing all the particularities of the local area and the German positions in the sector.

One of the officers of the company, Leutnant Hoeller, received an order to send forward two signalmen along the ditch that ran along the left-hand side of the road, by a hedge behind which was an open field. On the right-hand side was the wall of grounds of the Château of Bénouville two metres high.

As the 3 grenadiers of 8/192nd came to the end of the wall they found themselves in the village. On the right, the keeper's lodge marked the end of the wall around the château grounds. Leutnant Hoeller came on a body of a British para, probably killed in a shootout with soldiers of 3/716th. 300 yards back they had 75mm and 20mm guns to cover them, but on their left a 3-foot high hedge afforded little protection. For a few minutes they took in the lay of the land : nothing moved. Leutnant Hoeller, wishing to keep a souvenir of this first reconnaissance at dawn on 6th June, took a camera out of his pocket, handed it to Corporal Atteneder, took off his helmet, and within a few yards of where the paras of A Company of the 7th Battalion were in position, had his photo taken ! Leutnant Hoeller and Oberleutnant Braatz returned to submit their reports to the commander of the battalion, Major Zippe. The roads were narrow, and the open tops of the armoured half-tracks made them vulnerable to grenades being lobbed into them from the houses on either side. It was therefore too risky to push on further without infantry support. So while they waited, the armoured vehicles of 8/192nd took up position across a broad front to the south of Bénouville. (Leutnant Hoeller's first-hand account can be seen in full in the book by J.C.Perrigault, devoted to 21st Panzer Division, Editions Heimdal, at the end of 2002).

At 0400 hours Heeresgruppe B finally gave out the alert to 21st Panzer Division but at 0520 hours Major General Feuchtinger, who had made it to his HQ at Saint-Pierre-sur Dives, told Major General Pemsel, 7th Army Chief of Staff, that paras had been seen south of Bretteville-sur-Laize and to the south-west of Mezidon ! He declared he would concentrate his counter-attack east of the Orne. At 0600 hours Feuchtinger and his Chief of Staff von Berlichingen called Heeresgruppe B to announce that these night-time operations were definitely a preliminary to the landings themselves. The O.B.West declared 'the beginning of the invasion' at 0625 hours. After so many setbacks and delays the two battalions of the Tank regiment of 21st Panzer were able to move off – but only at 0800 hours, by which time it was broad daylight and they were still short of Falaise. This provided a precious breathing space for 6th Airborne paras. The absence of generals at the crucial moment, Rommel for Heeresgruppe B, and Feuchtinger for 21st Panzer, as well as many others, put off vital decisions. In addition, quite apart from the fake airborne drops set up by the Allies, the widely scattered nature of so many of the drops added to the confusion and caused the Germans to hesitate even further as to what measures to best take : paradoxically it was this very confusion that proved an added bonus to the paras.

The 12th Battalion

Company C of 12th Parachute Battalion bore the full brunt of Major von Luck's counterattack. As dawn broke, Captain J.A.N.Sim was still in his forward position with a 12-man standing patrol of N°4 Platoon and an artillery forward observation officer who was glued to his radio and giving out rangefinding coordinates to an offshore cruiser. Suddenly Sim spotted a group of about 50 soldiers in camouflaged smocks and steel helmets similar to their own, and realised they were Germans. They must have outnumbered his own men by at least 20 to 1 and were 300 yards away and advancing steadily in line on their positions.

« I asked the Forward Bombardment Observer to direct the cruiser's guns on them and then to switch to the woods behind. A little while later he informed me that this could not be done as they were firing on a priority target.

Meanwhile the enemy continued to advance, knee deep in long grass. Only my sniper was active, further down the hedgerow, as our plan was not to open fire until the enemy had come to within fifty yards of us where there was a barbed wire cattle fence. We watched and waited as the enemy came closer and closer. When they had reached the fence, I fired a Verey light straight at them and my men opened fire. The enemy went to ground in the long grass. Simultaneously two self-propelled guns (probably from the Sturmgeschütz-Abteilung 200 : Ed) lumbered up from behind the ridge to our front and opened fire while on the move. They stopped seventy yards away from us, a sitting target for our 6-pounder anti-tank gun, but no gun opened fire. Shortly after, a soldier crawled up to me on hands and knees and saluted ! He was sorry but the 6-pounder could not fire as the breechblock had slipped and must have been damaged in the glider landing… We were now suffering casulaties rather quickly. The man on my right was dead. Another of my men, while crawling up to me moaning and groaning, slumped before me and lay still. I noticed that the FOB had been badly wounded. Meanwhile the enemy, under the covering fire of the self-propelled guns, were crawling round to my right flank… As so often happen in action, all fire suddenly ceased and silence reigned for a bit. I felt fogged and mentally dulled, incapable of realising I was in danger… To my amazement I saw the hatch of one of the self-propelled guns open, and a German officer, splendidly arrayed in polished jackboots, stiff cap and Sam Browne, leisurely climb down and light a cigarette. He was allowed two puffs only. I

don't think we killed him as we did not find his body later.

Again we were subjected to fire but this time by mortars, the bombs airbursting in the hedgerow trees… Again that sudden silence. One of my Sergeants came to me and informed me that there were only four of us left alive (his batman, Sergeants Jones and Millburn, and himself) and asked me what we were to do. I decided that, rather than wait in the ditch to be killed, it was worth the risk to dash back to our company position and perhaps live to fight another day. We could do no more good where we were in my opinion.

The four of us made use of a shallow ditch which ran alongside a ditch into the main position… soon after we had evacuated the forward position, it was subjected to 3-inch mortar fire and was reoccupied by another section from C Company… » (quoted in « Go To It ! p66-67)

Lance Corporal Frank Gleeson also gave us a first-hand account of the dramatic events in this sector. His version has it that as the Germans approached Captain Sim's position at 0600 hours, from 400 yards Sergeant Frank Millburn – a veteran of the North African campaign - repeatedly gave the order to fire, but as the Germans advanced, every hundred yards Gleeson asked for more time (« Hang on, let'em come on a bit… ») restraining his machine gunner and friend, Andrew Gradwell, from letting loose. Millburn was amazed at Gleeson's 'sang-froid ', forgetting that his short-sight hardly allowed him to do otherwise… At 50 yards – and within the range of a lobbed grenade - the last shrill order « Fire ! ! » was given and a swathe of machine-gun fire cut through the Germans.

As the sun broke through that June morning, Gleeson and his men saw many exchanges of fire between snipers and isolated patrols seeking to weedle out the Germans in front of their position. He saw one German, looking through a parachuted container shot by snipers of N°4 Platoon. It was now 1000 hours. « Rudolf » set off towards the wooded copse, but a hand-grenade was lobbed into the group of men – the ruse had been discovered. Gleeson and Andrew Gradwell saw it coming and threw themselves flat on the ground – but Millin was a goner. The thicket twitched and parted and out stepped a German Feldwebel to inspect his handiwork : his cry of « Ho ! » was smothered by the impacting bullets sprayed from a Bren Gun which flung him back over two yards. Now the Germans knew there were paras in position : machine gun bullets together with heavy mortar and artillery fire began winging across and down onto the paras' heads. The silhouettes of the men of 125th Panzer Grenadier Regiment knee deep in the long grass, infiltrating between N°4 Platoon and C Company, has been evoked above in Captain Sim's account. When Sim had reluctantly pulled out and got back to base, his Company commander, Major Stevens, asked him where his men were, and Sim simply replied, « They're all dead ! » Stevens returned : « But I can hear a Bren Gun firing ! » This was the firefight being pursued by Gleeson and Gradwell. Nevertheless the order to lay down fire over their former position was given.

The situation was looking increasingly desperate for Gleeson and Gradwell who, pinned down by German machine-gun fire were now being fired on by the mortars of C Company itself. 2 German tanks were just 50 yards away. Gleeson recalled an order given by an officer shortly before he had moved off towards the lines of C Company. : « Stay here ! », to which he had replied, « Really ? » Once the officer had gone Gleeson saw that there were only the two

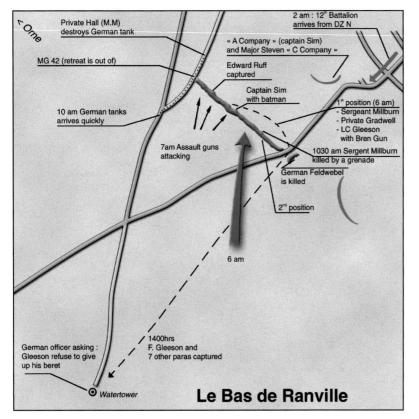

Private Hall (M.M) destroys German tank

MG 42 (retreat is out of)

10 am German tanks arrives quickly

7am Assault guns attacking

6 am

German officer asking : Gleeson refuse to give up his beret

1400hrs
F. Gleeson and
7 other paras captured

Watertower

2 am : 12th Battalion arrives from DZ N

« A Company » (captain Sim) and Major Steven « C Company »

Edward Ruff captured

Captain Sim with batman

1st position (6 am)
- Sergeant Millburn
- Private Gradwell
- LC Gleeson with Bren Gun

1030 am Sergent Millburn killed by a grenade

German Feldwebel is killed

2nd position

Le Bas de Ranville

This sketch based on Gleesons recollections shows the crossroads to the south of the Bas de Ranville (see Stand 5 sector on the map p. 87), and where Gleeson and his comrades took up their new positions around 6 am, with Captain Sim. It shows the German attacks at 6 and 7 am with assault guns. At 1000 hrs Private Hall destroyed a German tank and at 1030 hrs Sergeant Millburn died. Gleeson was captured at 1400 hrs, refusing to give up his beret (near the watertower). (Map Heimdal.)

of them left opposing the Germans. He turned to his 19 year old friend Andrew and gestured to him to get out. « Go, quick ! » « No, I'm staying with you. » « Go ! » « No, I'm staying here ! » More urgently this time Gleeson insisted « Go Go ! » Andrew picked up his Bren Gun and followed the same ditch taken shortly before by Sim. Once alone, Gleeson prepared to set off along the same ditch - but had the thought that third time might be unlucky. « This is not a good place to be ! ! » he decided to move off across the field hidden by the unharvested corn. But the sun was now high and pallid, making it difficult to work out where the British lines were. In crossing a road he jumped into a ditch already occupied by 6 Germans manning a MG42. He was taken prisoner. A Corporal bearing decorations from the Eastern Front disarmed and sat him down. When he saw the revolver which Andrew had given him when Gleeson had lost his rifle, the German grenadier believed he had captured the very paratrooper who had killed his own Sergeant at point-blank range. Rummaging deeper into his pockets he found chocolate, cigarettes and 300 rounds of rifle cartridges and all was spread out on the ground. Standing over him the Corporal seemed uncertain as to what fate he should meet out to his enemy, at which point a bullet struck one of his comrades between the eyes and Gleeson said to himself » That's it then, it's all over ». But as a reflex he brought out his first aid dressings and held them out for the man to be tended. The corporal thanked him but said the man was already dead. According to Gleeson this gesture probably saved his life. The Corporal declared : « For you the war is over – but not for me ! » And so Gleeson was sent to the German rear.

There, along with other 6th Airborne prisoners, he was loaded into a lorry and driven 20km to Saint-Pierre-sur-Dives. The journey passed off without incident, until a superb motor car coming from the other direction stopped the convoy and out stepped a German officer carrying a camera. He stiffly marched up to the lorries to take a photo of their prisoners of war,

but the British, most of them barely 20 years old, started calling names and making mock of his odd Germanic bearing. It hardly made for the type of photo he had in mind, so, flushed with indignation and without uttering a word, the officer got back into the car and swept off.

These three eyewitnesses, Leutnant Bandomir, Captain Sim and Lance Corporal Gleeson have each given us a first-hand account of the violent firefights that broke out to the south of Le Bas de Ranville during the morning of 6th June. Gleeson and Sims' accounts vary only in detail : for example Sim does not refer to the first attack and puts the death of Sergeant Millin towards the end of an action which Gerhardt Bandomir's account also recounts from a different perpective. From this we can say that the armoured half-tracks were self-propelled guns of the Sturngeschütz-Abteilung 200. Leutnant Bandomir's attack was halted in the grounds of the château of Escoville south-east of C Company's position. The grenadiers who swamped Captain Sim's position would have attacked on the left (to the west) of Leutnant Bandomir's, who recalls the 2 assault guns being taken out by the 2 Piats.

Bénouville : 7th Battalion

When dawn broke the battalion was still in position holding the western bank of the canal, and had put up stiff resistance against the weak and disorganised attempts by 716th Division to dislodge them. But during the early morning hours as the counterattack was being prepared, Lieutenant Colonel Pine-Coffin only had about 200 paras available and the 70 men under Major Howard – and no heavy weapons. B Company was in position north of Bénouville. C Company was in reserve near the bridge. To the south Major Nigel Taylor's A Company was well dug in. Facing south, on the outskirts of the village Sergeant Villis' platoon kept a watchful eye on the approach road from the houses on either side. Lieutenant David Hunter's platoon was set up in a farm ; 3rd Platoon led by Lieutenant Bill Bowyer until his untimely death in a night skirmish, was set up along the north – south road in some houses along the eastern side. Here A Company would face Oberleutnant Braatz's armour of the 8/192 shortly before dan.

The break of day would also bring in a flood of refugees, women and children for the most part, fleeing the combat zone and trying to get over the bridges. While they may have been delighted to see the British paratroops, it did not make the paras' task any easier.

The main threat seemed for the moment to come from the north of the village. Some German soldiers were esconced in the church bell-tower and were firing down on the British paras. Corporal Killean fired a well-aimed PIAT shell and blew a great hole in the tower, silencing the snipers. A little later, around 0700 hours, some light tanks of Ober leutnant Braatz's 8/192 appeared over the horizon, heading north towards C Compnay's position. They stopped, Leutnant Hoeller carried out some reconnaissance, and decided to pull back, as we have seen. Shortly after Sergeant Villis's platoon opened fire with light arms and hit some of the armoured crews who had got out of their vehicles and now promptly scuttled back. This, together with the directed naval bombardment of the Allied fleet off the coast broke up the German armoured columns heading for the coast.

All through the morning the counter-attack continued. Self-propelled guns were brought up to the outskirts of Bénouville and started firing on the village, forcing Sergeant Villis' platoon back towards the

Above : Bénouville château overlooks the canal and this view of it is from the bridge. (E.G./Heimdal)

Madame Vion, with her Free French armband (FFI) ran the maternity hospital and orphanage set up in Bénouville château. She won the high respect of the British paras. (IWM)

village centre. During this time, to the west, Lieutenant David Hunter's platoon was confronting a number of German snipers who were trying to get round his right flank. Later, riflemen and tanks managed to break into the southern end of Bénouville village, but their advance was blocked by A Company. Another attempt by Panzer IV to get through to the centre of the village was stopped in its tracks by Gammon grenades. It had been a close call.

Lieutenant Atkinson of C Company sent a probing patrol to the Bénouville château to the south-east of the village, overlooking the whole area from its extensive grounds. This huge château had been built at the end of the eighteenth century by Louis XVI. It sports a fine façade with fluted pilasters and Ionic columns in the classical style. It was being used as a maternity home and orphanage. It had a chapel dating from 1290 in the grounds and it was here that the orphans were baptised. Madame Vion, who ran the home, was 54 years of age and had been a nurse there during the Great War. Apart from her official responsibilities she was an active member of the resistance. She had sheltered men who refused compulsory labour service and was known to the English as a 'true Joan of Arc'.

As Lieutenant Atkinson's patrol reached the château, he crept into the cellar to see if any Germans were holding out there : there, by the light of the breaking day he took his first prisoner : it was the strange figure of Madame Vion in trousers ! In perfect French Lieutenant Atkinson told her they were soldiers of the British army of liberation. Madame Vion, somewhat flabbergasted to see the officer and nine paratroops, declared, « What, all of you ? » She then proceeded to show them 'what stuff she was made of' by guiding them to a German anti-tank gun set up in the vegetable garden. But the château was still outside the defensive perimeter of 7th Battalion. In the morning a German officer, with a Sergeant and Corporal, proceeded to set up a machine gun on the roof of the château. Madame Vion protested, declaring

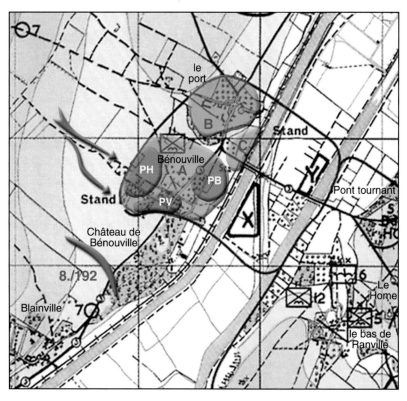

The 7th Battalion position around Bénouville : B Company was in position north ; C Company was in reserve in the east. PB : Sergeant Villis' platoon. PH : Lieutenant David Hunter's platoon ; PV : the 3rd Platoon led by Lieutenant Bill Bowyer, killed in a night skirmish.

that as a maternity hospital it was under the protection of the Red Cross. The German officer took no notice of her protests and ran up the vast staircase that led to a large empty room on the third floor. Peeping out of the window he noticed the German anti-tank gun down in the garden. An artillery shell crashed through the château and out the other side ! The officer withdrew and Madame Vion rushed out

General Gale and Brigadier Poett walked over Bénouville bridge, wearing the maroon beret and stick under the arm, dressed as you see here. (IWM)

Orne. These were General Gale, Brigadier Poett and Brigadier Hugh Kindersley, head of 6th Airlanding Brigade who had arrived with advance HQ in a glider and were coming to assess the situation. Wearing their maroon berets and battledress they were walking over the bridge, stick under their arms, when two Kriegsmarine gunboats set out to try and reach Caen from Ouistreham. Major Howard let them come up to within a hundred yards of the bridge before having his men open fire with PIAT and Bren guns. The PIAT bomb landed in the wheelhouse, and out of control, the boat ran into the east bank where the crew surrendered ; the other managed to turn round and flee back to Ouistreham, to be captured a few hours later by men of N°4 Commando.

A PIAT gun and bomb. (Photo Heimdal.)

to fetch Lieutenant Atkinson. He remained imperturbable, while she was outraged at the lack of offensive spirit She declared she had been following General de Gaulle's call to resistance since 1941. The château would remain in German lines all morning and for 51 days would come under German fire. The indomitable Madame Vion would remain in post, and deliver 18 babies - all girls - were born in the first 18 days after the invasion !

Towards 1000hours, three important 'top brass' headed for Bénouville from the opposite bank of the

The V.P. Boot 212 near Blainville one of the German boots destroyed after the attack on Bénouville. (Coll. P. Dalzel-Job.)

In England British paras are loading containers with Piat bombs prior to D-Day. These were precious items of ammunition, more often than not lost in the Dives marshes when parachuted into France with the paratroops : there would be a desperate shortage of them in the first hours of landing in France. (IWM)

Above and right : A group of paratroops taken prisoner in the morning of D-Day, and photographed the same day in the afternoon... (BA.)

Through the rest of the morning the battalion was sporadically attacked by Germans at company strength and backed by a few tanks. They also tried to infiltrate the paras positions, but were contained by probing patrols. Defence could not be coordinated for want of radios, and Major Howard's advice ' Hold until you're relieved ! » made more sense more than ever.

Lieutenant-Colonel Pine-Coffin and Major Howard were waiting for the seaborne troops landing at Sword

Midday : the Commandos arrive

1st Special Service Brigade commandos advance on Bénouville. (IWM.)

After a succession of German counterattacks against the bridgehead at Bénouville, casualties were piling up : all of the officers of 7th Battalion were either killed or wounded by the end of the afternoon. The coming of relief was long and eagerly awaited : the first elements of 3rd Infantry Division who landed at 0720 hours onto Sword Beach (0731 hours for the Commandos) was almost three miles away. The lead elements were 1st Special Service Brigade under the Lord Lovat, with his personal piper Bill Millin alongside him. This Brigade of Commandos was tasked to reinforce and hold the northern sector of 6th Airborne Division bridgehead. N°3 Troop of N°6 Commando was next in line. Advancing through Colleville and Saint Aubin d'Arquenay, they reached Bénouville around midday. N°4 Commando, setting out from Hermanville around 1300 hours took up the rear. The sound of bagpipes skirling over the hori-

zon boosted the morale of the paras : Lord Lovat of the Fraser clan, and Bill Millin, wearing the badge of the Lovat's Scouts on his green beret were hoving into view. As they approached Bénouville he was playing « Lochan Side » : then the sound of bullets and shrapnel was heard – probably mortars and machine gun fire together. Some Germans stood up with their hands on their heads in willing surrender and were sent unescorted to the rear. On entering the village where the road veers right, the head of their column came under more automatic fire. Bill Millin stopped playing and everyone took shelter behind a wall on the bend in the road. Several men were wounded : then a Churchill tank came up and they set off behind it, this time Millin playing « Blue Bonnets ». Despite the morning action with PIATs more fire was coming from the gutted church tower, so the tank opened fire on it and three commandos emerged with a wounded German prisoner. On the other side of the road three commandos fired at a house and two others lobbed a grenade over the garden wall of another to clear the sector. The the tank moved away, leaving the commandos without the cover that Providence had briefly provided. On the other side of the village the Lord Lovat took in the sight of the whole bridge and Orne sector, covered in a haze of smoke after almost 12 hours of battle. The few civilians about looked quite terrified, and the commandos were under stress and fearsome in their battle gear.

« Right, Piper, now we're going to set off and I want you to carry on playing as long as you can. We are not far from the Orne bridges and I want the chaps who are holding them to hear you and know that it's the Commando Brigade on its way. »

So to the sound of « the Blue Bonnets over the Border » and rattling mortar and artillery fire, they started off, following the road out of the church square and three hundred yards on, it curved round a large house on the right. Bill Millin was impressed by the sheer size of this building enclosed by a long, low wall topped by a cast-iron fence. He kept an eye out for the odd sniper who could be hiding behind a win-

Men of n° 45 Royal Marine Commando return fire with their Bren Guns as they advance on Bénouville. (IWM.)

Lord Lovat

A legend in his own lifetime, Simon Fraser Baron Lovat was born in 1911. He would often sign his first name « Shimi », in the Scottish manner. His ancestors came from Anjou, and accompanied the Norman barons at the conquest. Simon Frisel (later Fraser) was a Scottish baron in 1160. The future 17th Baron Lovat grew up in Beaufort Castle in Scotland, was commissioned into the Scots Guards in 1932, and became the 17th Baron, and 25th clan leader on the death of his father in 1933. When war broke out he was a captain and was eager to join the Lovat Scouts (raised by his father in 1899 for service in the Boer War). He first saw action with N°4 Commando in the successful raid in the Lofoten Islands off the coast of Norway in March 1941. In August 1942 he had been promoted to Lieutenant Colonel in charge of N°4 Commando raid at Dieppe, which was a disaster. For Operation Overlord Lovat was promoted to raise and command 1st Special Services Brigade, which covered Nos. 3, 4 and 6 Army Commandos, and N°45 Royal Marine Commando. « Shimi » Fraser, the Lord Lovat, died in Scotland on the 'bonny banks' of the Beauly, on 16th March 1995.

Bill Millin

Another legendary figure of the D-Day Landings, Bill Millin came from an old Scottish family near Fort William, by Ben Nevis. He was born in Regina, Canada, joined the Commandos in North Africa and the landings into Sicily, and was picked by Lord Lovat as his personal piper. Sword Beach would be his third landing. He would emerge unscathed from all the fighting around him, most of his comrades in the commando brigade being killed or wounded during the Battle of Normandy.

Bill Millin, Lord Lovat's Piper, playing for the commandos in England the day before D-Day. (IWM)

Lord Lovat and Bill Millin on Bénouville bridge as performed in « The Longest Day ».

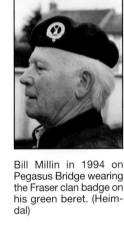

Bill Millin in 1994 on Pegasus Bridge wearing the Fraser clan badge on his green beret. (Heimdal)

dow. The sound of automatic fire swamped the bagpipes, but the Lord Lovat was still there. Just a hundred yards from the house on the grass where the road veers left (where the present roundabout and monument to 7th Battalion can be seen), he stopped playing to greet an old French friend of N°4 Commando, Maurice Chauvet. Then he ran off to rejoin Lord Lovat who was talking to a paratroop officer of 7th Battalion. It was now 1330 hours : the paras were now linked up to the main body of troops !

As the paratroop officer took his leave, Brigadier Lovat turned towards Bill Millin and gestured to him to move off across the bridge, a large, well-built metal structure straddling the canal. A veil of black smoke lay over the whole area ; the crackle of automatic small-arms fire filled the air, apparently from German positions somewhere over to the right, coming in fact from the Bénouville château to the south. Bullets were ricocheting off the bridge. The wounded were carried into a nearby café during a lull in the fighting. Bill Millin started to play, but someone said' « *For God's sake Piper hang on till we get to the other side before you start that !* » He stopped, and the commandos, ducking to avoid the bullets winging over the bridge, walked over to the other side. About two-thirds of the way over Brigadier Lovat nodded to Bill Millin that he could resume playing : the strains of « The March of Cameron » were heard, then they proceeded along the 200 yards of dusty road separating the two bridges, to stop 50 yards short on a signal from two paras dug in on the opposite bank : « *I looked across and I could see two airborne on the other side dug in a slit trench. I kept my eye on those two chaps. They were signalling, « Down, down », and pointing to the side of the river. They kept looking at Lovat. He was walking along there as if he was out for a walk on his estate... anyway I piped over that, playing « Blue Bonnets over the Border ».* The

This was the spot where Bill Millin took up playing on Bénouville Bridge : this 1994 view shows him on the original bridge, now in the care of the nearby museum. (Heimdal)

Bill Millin's commando dagger and sheath, on the tartan of his bagpipe bag. (Photo Heimdal)

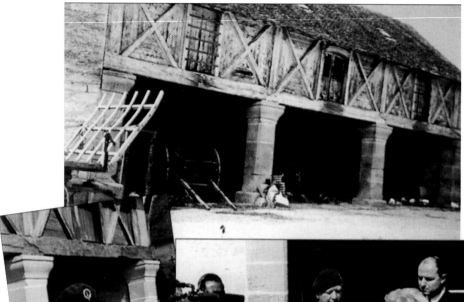

In the Ecarde farmyard in 1944, and in 1994. With George Bernage, TF1 filmed Bill Millin meeting up once again with Josette and playing the same tune before her that he played on D-Day. (Photos Heimdal)

Bottom : Bill Millin's bagpipes now in the Mémorial Pegasus Museum. (Photos Heimdal)

Josette on the left, sitting with her sister shortly before D-Day. (Coll. J.G.)

two airborne chaps thought we were crazy... » (Bill Millin).

The fire was continuing to come from the roof of the Bénouville château to the south-west. Once he had reached the opposite bank, he shook hands with a tall airborne officer – Brigadier Nigel Poett – and apologised for being late. Meanwhile his men ran across the bridge some carrying three wounded given to them by a medic.

To get clear of German fire the men filed off left just beyond the bridge to head towards the Ecarde farm. Josette, an eight year old girl lived there with her sis-

ter, her mother and stepfather, along with some labourers. What was on their mind was rather the condition of the animals, many of which had been killed, including some horses some distance off. The path taken by the column of men ran along the western side of the farm property, and at the sound of the approaching bagpipes the little girl felt an intense wave of emotion :

« The adults didn't utter a word as we came by but the children were intrigued by the bagpipes. They kept their distance but a little girl aged about 8 or 9 kept up with us for some way asking for « musique..musique.. ». I decided to play a popular Scottish air called « Nut brown maiden », which set the villagers off clapping. The little girl was as pretty as a picture with her red hair tumbling over her shoulders. She was wearing an old-fashioned dress and her bare feet were in wooden clogs. Further on I looked back and saw her waving at us. » (ex La Cornemuse du D-Day Ed Heimdal)

1st Special Service Brigade

This Commando Brigade commanded by The Lord Lovat, consisted of :

N°3 Commando (Lieutenant Colonel P. Young)

N°4 Commando (Lieutenant Colonel R.W.F. Dawson)

N°6 Commando (Lieutenant Colonel D. Mills Roberts)

N°45 Royal Marines Commando (Lieutenant Colonel N.C.Ries)

An Army Commando unit was made up of an HQ (administration, signal, intelligence, transport, about 90 men in all), Troops with heavy equipment such as three 3-inch mortars, 3 Vickers machine-guns, about 40 men all ranks, and 5 assault Troops (about 60 men all ranks in each). The total Commando group would consist of roughly 460 men.

N°4 Commando also included 177 French commandos under the orders of Commandant Philippe Kieffer.

1

Bill Millin met up with Josette once again on 25th August 1994 to play the same tune : her russet hair reminded him of the 'lassies' back in Scotland.

After a ten-minute march the column passed by the Ecarde quarry, but not before taking more casualties from a mortar barrage near the crossroads. The Commando Brigade certainly was a much appreciated reinforcement to 6th Airborne positions. Elements of N°3 Commando (N°3 Troop) assisted 12th Parachute Battalion to seize the Plein d'Amfreville in the afternoon, while the remainder of the unit helped to reinforce the HQ at Ranville. N°45 Royal Marine Commando marched on Merville-Franceville, but had to dig in before Sallenelles. N°6 Commando took up position between Bréville and le Plein while N°4 Commando dug in around Hauger around 2000 hours. Brigade HQ was set up in the Saulnier's farmhouse in Le Plein.

7th Battalion

In the face of German counter-attacks coming from the south during the late afternoon, where they were solidly entrenched in the Bénouville château overlooking the whole sector, A Company was cut off from the rest of the battalion and stiff, close fighting broke out. Major Nigel Taylor, who had been wounded in the hip during the morning, directed the battle from the window of a house, until, in the middle of the afternoon, he had to pass over the command to his second-in-command, Captain Jim Webber. By this time there were barely more than 20 men still able to fight ! They stood their ground for 17 hours together, and when relief came, all the officers had been killed or wounded. At 2115hours, as the gliders were landing (see next chapter) 2nd Battalion the Royal Warwickshire Regiment, one of 3rd Infantry Division battalions landed on Sword beach fought their way to the bridges. It was 0300hours on 7th June before they met up with 7th Battalion.

Other battalions of 5th Brigade

After Captain Sim moved off, towards the Bas de Ranville, 2 German tanks were knocked out by a six-pounder anti-tank gun of 12th Battalion's B Company. Apart from some skirmishes with forward patrols, until 1700 hours things quietened down. So Lieutenant Colonel Johnson decided to try out a counter-attack, backed by artillery from 3rd Division, but would be pushed back after a violent exchange. At 2100 hours a rumbling grinding noise from 4 German self-propelled cannon advanced from Hérouvillette, only to be destroyed by six-pounder artillery. Another counter-attack would be launched in the afternoon in the Ranville sector only to be also thrown

back. 3rd Division reinforcements, and airborne reinforcements would start coming in at 2100 hours

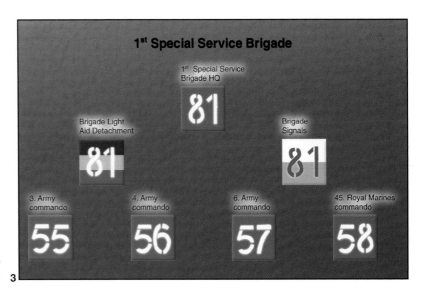

1. Commandant Philippe Kieffer commanded the French N°4 Commandos. (IWM)

2. The commandos of 1st Special Brigade have just crossed Ranville bridge on D-Day and are using a requisitioned horse and cart to carry their material. (IWM)

3. Tactical signposts used by 1st Special Service Brigade. (H après JB)

3

1st Special Service Brigade

1st Special Service Brigade HQ		
	81	

Brigade Light Aid Detachment		Brigade Signals
81		**81**

3. Army commando	4. Army commando	6. Army commando	45. Royal Marines commando
55	**56**	**57**	**58**

Operation Mallard

Landing Zone Z to the north of Ranville, as it is today… (Heimdal)

… and in 1944 (IWM)

Orientation table at LZ N north of Ranville. (Heimdal.)

At 2100 hours, just as the counterattack led by 21st Panzer Division had reached the coast, the sky began to fill with the sound of hundreds of aircraft engines : 246 tugs towing 216 Horsas and 30 Hamilcars to reinforce the airborne bridgehead were pouring over the coastline : Operation Mallard was under way, and it would prove an immense morale-booster to 1st British Corps.

The sight of this immense aerial armada puzzled the 21st Panzer-Division commander : was it a ploy to cut off his rear ? He immediately ordered a withdrawal, and the threat to the landing beaches was lifted.

For the paras of 6th Airborne, the slackening of the German stranglehold and the slowdown in the ever-mounting casualty lists before this fresh air bridgehead raised their spirits considerably.

The air armada was divided into two groups. 142 planes towing 112 Horsas and 30 Hamilcars were to land on Landing Zone N at Ranville. 74 aircraft were from 46 Group and 72 from 38 Group (including the 30 Halifaxes towing the 30 Hamilcars.) Precious heavy material reinforcement was aboard these aircraft : Tetrarch tanks from the reconnaissance regiments, 17-pounder anti-tank guns in the Hamilcars, jeeps and trailers, guns and other material in the Horsas.

Over a hundred aircraft brought 104 Horsa gliders onto Landing Zone W, between Saint-Aubin-d'Arque-

nay and Bénouville, on the western bank of the Orne, with men of 6th Airlanding Brigade on their flanks. The Brigade HQ, 1st Battalion the Royal Ulster Rifles (RUR), 2nd Battalion the Oxfordshire and Buckinghamshire Light Infantry (Oxs and Bucks), less the six platoons holding the Orne and canal bridges, and A Company of 12th Battalion of the Devonshire Regiment, the rest of that company arriving by boat. Also there were 6th Airborne Armoured Reconnaissance Regiment, 211th Airlanding Light Battery R.A., 249th Field Company, R.E., and two sections of 195th Airlanding Field Ambulance, one per battalion. The Brigade HQ and the RUR took off from Brize Norton on 6 June at 1840 hours and had a smooth flight. 110 gliders were used, towed by Stirlings and Albermarles of 38 Group. One glider was lost at sea, one would get lost way east of his zone and two made emergency landings in England. The weather was far better than the night before and at 2100hours the Normandy coast, with the Orne estuary and Ouistreham hove into view. Visibility was ten miles and the wind 20-25 kph coming from bearing 320. 106 Horsas brought 2800 soldiers into landing Zone W between 2052 and 2120 hours. Apart from some light flak and a few accidents, all passed off smoothly. Major Napier Crookenden, the Brigade Major, saw smoke coming from one of the grounded gliders.

Lieutenant Geoffrey Sneezum, leader of N°9 Platoon of A Company of 12th Battalion, the Devons, was sat in N°3 seat of his Horsa taking him to Normandy. He took off at 1850hours from Brize Norton – his birthday ! N°1 and 2 seats were taken up by two Flight Sergeants responsible for the plane. Normally 28 men on board, but on this occasion the 29th passenger was a rather fat civilian carrying a bag, apparently a journalist. Having rather arrogantly demanded a N°3 seat he'd been stuck in the tail, causing the glider to run in at a lower altitude than the other planes.

Lieutenant Sneezum had been earlier briefed as to this man's mission, part of Parker Force., whose mission was to blow the Mézidon-Cagny railway line.

One glider snapped its towrope and dropped into the sea five miles short of the coast. On board were six men from the Devons, the two pilots, a jeep and two trailers. The weight of the equipment quickly dragged the wrecked glider into the sea, taking the pilots, killed on impact, and CQMS Dunphy with it. The 5 survivors managed to get into their inflatable dinghy drifted towards Merville where they were taken prisoner by the Germans.

As Sneezum's glider made its final approach, lining up with a petrol depot, conveniently on fire to guide them, the ground came up at them, they could see 'Rommel's asparagus', here wired together, suggesting minefields and then, contact ! the great glider careered into the poles in a hellish ripping and splintering sound. It was 2051hours. « Out, quick ! » Lieutenant Sneezum was the first out : a second glider slithered into the tail, wrenching it off the ground and flinging the men about inside. Charlie Land, who had to feed the ammunition into his Bren Gun, was slightly wounded in the shock : Lieutenant Sneezum had not to forget the trolley packed with explosives left in the glider : these were destined to blow the line. Then N°9 Platoon set off in the direction of Bénouville. On the way Lieutenant Sneezum noticed to his amusement the curious similarity beween a red circular sign on the gable of a house (now painted white) and the target they had used on exercise back in England. The platoon passed in front of Bénouville church, transformed into a field hospital where the Reverend GEM Parry was finding plenty to do : towards the end of the day he would be killed and his tomb would be added to the others lining up in the church cemetery. The sound of battle approached the château, where an attack was being halted in its tracks. On crossing Bénouville bridge Sneezum saw two infantrymen of the Warwick regiment, 3rd Infantry Division guarding the bridge taken earlier by Major Howard and his men. Apart from some activity coming out of the Café Gondrée, all was quiet. A little further on some wounded men were awaiting treatment in a ditch on the right. The medic had been called up to replace Major Maitland, General Gale's medic, who had been killed with Gunner A. Bick Nell whom he was tending at the time. Urgent need was on every side : the Ranville bridge stood unguarded. Lieutenant Sneezum reached le Mariquet around 2300hours, where Major J Roger, the company commander had set up his HQ. Lieutenant Sneezum had his men dig themselves in around Ranville church and set up a defensive position there – to the great annoyance of the locals, upset at the idea of war coming to their own back garden.

On Landing Zone N (Ranville) 142 gliders, including all 30 Hamilcars, made textbook landings over a period of 32 minutes, the last slithering to a stop at 2123hours. Losses were surprisingly light ; two gliders had snapped their tow-ropes and been forced to return to base ; one tug with its glider had accidentally crashed into the sea, and one glider was missing. The only problem now was the ground strewn with countless numbers of parachutes and the rigging would keep getting wrapped around the axles and tracks of disembarked vehicles. 11 Tetrarch tanks were out of action in 5 minutes in this way.

Operation Mallard was a complete success. The shortage of aircraft and pilots meant that the second wave could not take place in under 17 hours after the first, night-time operation. Daylight landings were a risk, but given the weakness of the Luftwaffe, and the danger of night-time landings, the way the operation was carried out had paid off.

At 2230hours, that is only 90 minutes after the first landings, Brigadier Kindersley was able to issue his orders to the units of 6th Airlanding Brigade : Lieutenant Colonel Jack Carson, with his 1st Battalion R.U.R. was to seize and hold the Longueval-Sainte-Honorine sector near the Orne river, and Lieutenant Colonel Michael Roberts with 2nd Oxs and Bucks to take Escoville.

In 3rd brigade sector....

Once on terra firma, Brigadier James Hill learnt of the success of the Canadian Battalion. Around 0600hours he set off for Sallenelles to get news of the assault on the Merville battery. It was then that he became a too-close-for-comfort witness to « the largest and noisiest firework party of all time », the aerial and naval bombardment in the run-up to the seaborne landings. As the bombs came crashing down onto him, he would be one of the few survivors, albeit wounded in the left buttock. « Doc » Watts, 9th Battalion medic tended his wounds as best he could. When Hill got to General Gale's headquarters in Ranville, he said « Well James, I am happy to tell you that your brigade has succeeded in all its objectives. » But Brigadier Hill had an emergency operation at midday and then returned to his HQ at le Mesnil, reaching it at 1600hours. Alastair Pearson had assumed command during his absence, but several other officers at HQ were missing.

The Canadian Battalion at Varaville had been firing 2-inch mortars onto the German positions in the château, and at 1000hours 43 Germans surrendered to Corporal Hartigan, thereby ending the battle there. The Canadians were relieved in the afternoon by 1st Special Service Brigade Commandos and were able to rejoin their Battalion at Le Mesnil which Captain Hanson and his men would be waiting at 1800 hours.

Operational Balance Sheet

By **midnight,** all 6th Airborne Division had been deployed except for the seaborne elements to arrive in the morning. To the west 5th Parachute Brigade held the Bas de Ranville and Ranville with 12th and 13th Battalions. 7th Battalion was held in reserve on the western fringes of DZ N. 3rd Parachute Brigade was spread out along a four-mile front with the Brigade HQ and 1st Canadian Parachute Battalion at le Mesnil in the centre, 8th Battalion to the south in the Bois de Bavent and Bures sector, and 9th Battalion to the north, at Le Plein. Two 6th Airlanding Brigade battalions available were ready for engagement to the south-west. 1st Special Service Brigade held the villages of Hauger, Le Plein and Amfreville, to the north and north-east of DZ N.

The Reverend G.E.M. Parry's grave in the churchyard at Bénouville. He was killed in the afternoon of D-Day. (Heimdal)

These camouflaged binoculars, belonging to Lieutenant D.S.Calin – his name is written on the broken strap (and since repaired) were found near where he was killed at 0700 hours on D-Day by 'friendly fire' coming at them from a low-flying RAF raid. Brigadier Hill was wounded in this attack also. (Private Coll)

250 gliders muster for Operation Mallard

In England over 250 gliders lined up on their airfields in southern England ; 142 of them – 112 Horsas and 30 Hamilcars were planned for Landing Zone N (Ranville), 104 Horsas for Landing Zone W (near Saint-Aubin-d'Arquenay, west of the canal), bringing in the bulk of 6th Airlanding Brigade – less Howard's Oxs and Bucks platoons who had landed in the night, and the seaborne Devons landing in the morning of 7th June. Only A Company of 12th Battalion of the Devonshire Regiment would fly in, out of Brize Norton on 6th June at 1850hours. With a length of 22 metres and a wing span of 29 metres, the rows of gliders were an impressive sight. Despite the flak and the Luftwaffe, which was largely absent from the skies, they made a smooth daytime landing. Night-time landings led to far more accidents. (IWM)

1. The airborne troops enjoying a brew-up before their night-time departure to LZ N in a couple of hours. The paratroops here are probably from 12th and 13th Battalions of 5th Brigade Headquarters. There are also some signallers, and some are wearing life-belts around their waists. The trooper far left has his fighting knife slipped into a sheath held by tabs sewn to the legs of his Denison Smock. The Corporal on the left is wearing the parachutists qualifying badge introduced on 17th June 1942 for all those who were not part of a paratroop unit. (IWM)

2. With the weather improving, some men are enjoying a few rays of sun before emplaning. (IWM)

3. Some medical personnel are climbing on board a huge Horsa for the Big Day. (IWM)

1. No Mickey Mouse operation this, despite the chalked graffiti on the planes ! The name 'Anna Catharina' can be made out.

2. « The Channel stopped you, but not us. Now it's our turn, you've had your time you German Schweinhunds »

3. The « angels with dirty faces » have scrawled the names of their sweethearts on the fuselage : Margaret, Joyce, Margie, Kath, Olive and Elsie.

4. At around 1850 hours an Albermarle lifts the Horsa gently off the runway at the end of its towrope.

5. Glider Pilot Crossland's logbook details his flight for Operation Mallard. (Mémorial Pégasus)

3

4

5

246 gliders tugged by as many aircraft brought in the bulk of 6th Airlanding Brigade and the heavier equipment 6th Airborne Division so urgently needed. The take-off began around 1850hours, by which time the weather was making a definite improvement. The flights passed off smoothly, although one of the gliders, carrying Lieutenant Geoffrey Sneezum of A Company, the Devonshires, was a little overloaded by a portly war correspondent...

Opposite : Two giant Hamilcars are coming into land on Landing Zone N. 30 such gliders arrived around 21 hours, bring in precious heavy equipment like the 17-pounder anti-tank gun, and light Tetrarch tanks. (IWM)

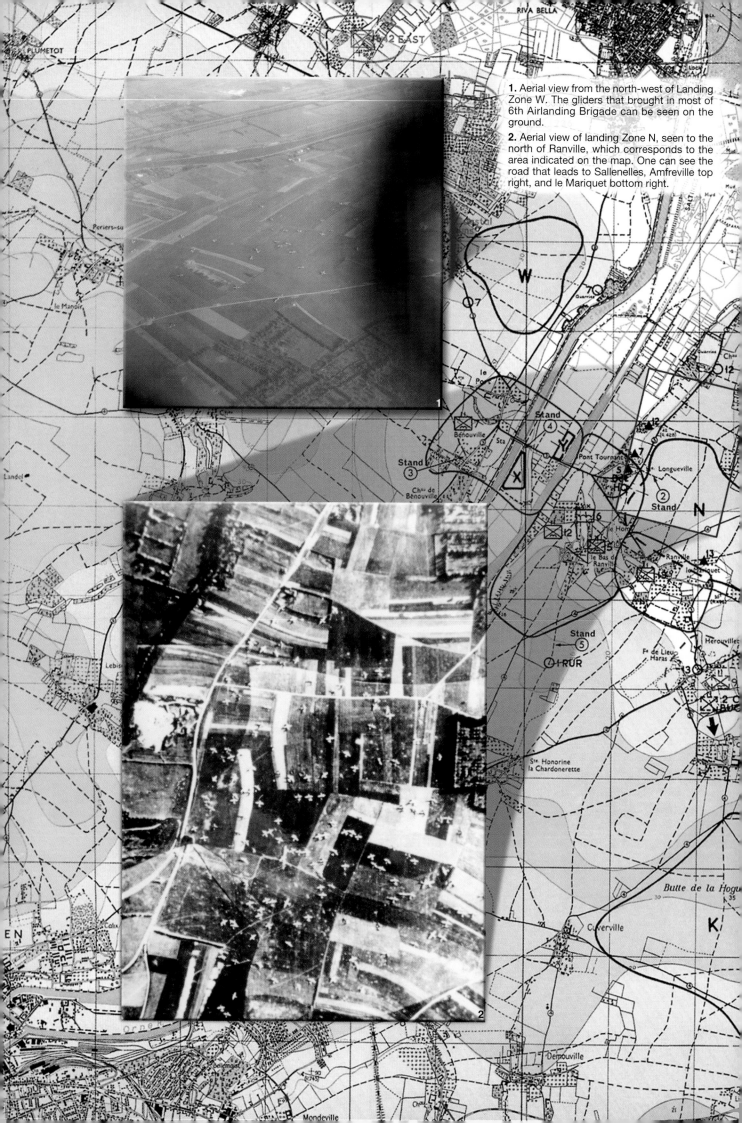

1. Aerial view from the north-west of Landing Zone W. The gliders that brought in most of 6th Airlanding Brigade can be seen on the ground.

2. Aerial view of landing Zone N, seen to the north of Ranville, which corresponds to the area indicated on the map. One can see the road that leads to Sallenelles, Amfreville top right, and le Mariquet bottom right.

3 and 4. Landing Zone N. On these details we can see the collapsed parachutes whose rigging caused so many problems by wrapping themselves round the tracks and wheels of exiting vehicles.

LEGEND

BN LOCS OF 5 PARA BDE

BN LOCS OF 3 PARA BDE. DOTTED BROWN LOC INDICATES POSN TO WHICH 9 BN SHOULD HAVE GONE AFTER RELIEF BY 1 SPECIAL SERVICE BDE.

BATTLE OUTPOSTS.

DZs AND LZs

RVs

BRs TO BE DESTROYED

INDICATES BN RESPONSIBLE FOR DESTRUCTION OF BR

Some views of Landing Zones N and W. Notice how explosive bolts in the fuselage can break off the rear of the glider to allow vehicles to exit quickly. Notice also the crudely brushed « invasion stripes ». The top and bottom pictures show some of « Rommel's asparagus » still in place, forcing incoming gliders to veer on landing. (IWM)

These pictures were taken by German war correspondents to show the remains of crashed gliders in « enemy territory ». Some of these aircraft had a tragic end, such as CN35 that crashed into the small wood of Saint-Vaast-en-Auge. Here we can see N°221 piloted by Staff Sergeant K.A.Evans which came down at 0330 hours in the south of Landing Zone N bearing a bulldozer, war correspondent David Woodward and a guardsman Both were injured. The unusual colour photo below was taken off a war correspondent attached to the « Hitlerjugend ». (Heimdal Coll. except bottom right, BA)

belltower of Ouistreham

lighthouse of Ouistreham

Merville

A panoramic view of Landing Zone W seen from the high ground at Saint-Aubin d'Arquenay, looking east. The Orne valley cuts through the country, and beyond extends the airborne bridgehead to the north (left) and south (right). (Heimdal)

Le Plein

Amfréville

Bréville

Landing Zone N

Cabourg

Bavent
wood

l'Ecarde

Ranville

Bénouville

Pegasus Bridge

Bénouville Bridge

1. Towards 2100 hours the airborne bridgehead would receive two significant reinforcements from two directions : Operation Mallard, bringing in part of 6th Airborne by glider, and the seaborne troops of 3rd Infantry Division. Men of the Warwickshire Regiment can be seen here coming out of Bénouville past the garage opposite the Café Gondrée before crossing Bénouville canal bridge to take over the sector from the paras of 7th Battalion. (IWM)

2. The same spot today. (EG/Heimdal)

3. The small building today which the soldiers are seen to be passing in front of below.

(EG./Heimdal)

4. Here the café Gondrée is on the left on the opposite, western bank of the canal. Traffic was already intense over the Bénouville bridge. (IWM)

5. The same spot today, although from a slightly different angle : we have crossed the road to where a 50mm German gun is still in its housing. (E.G./Heimdal)

Several Dakotas crashed in 6th Airborne Division sector.

These two photos were taken shortly after the war. Top : a C-47 of 48 Squadron, code UV, matriculation N° KG426, based at Down Ampney, was reported missing on D-Day, and had in fact crashed near Merville as we see here. Opposite the three photos show another C-47, matriculation N° KG329, belonging to 233 Squadron based at Blakehill Farm, shot down by Flak while dropping equipment over Ranville on 7th June and crashlanding onto the dunes at Merville.

(Photos C.A. via P.W., identification Joël Huard - photo actuelle des dunes de Merville : EG/Heimdal.)

7th June 1944 : 6th Airborne Division now turned on to the offensive and counter-attacked against the principal threat, south against 21st Panzer Division. 6th Airlanding Brigade with two front-line battalions, 1st Battalion, the Royal Ulster Rifles (RUR) in the west, and 2nd Battalion of the Oxs and Bucks in the east were tasked with taking the high ground south. At 0900 hours the Ulstermen of 1st RUR, led by Lieutenant Colonel Carson, advanced 1500 yards south towards Longueval which they were to seize and hold from high ground. C Company, led by Major Bob Hynds, with Lieutenant Harry Morgan's machine gun platoon behind them. Longueval turned out to be clear of the enemy so Carson pressed on, D Company HQ under Major Dyball stayed in Longueval while A Company under Major Charles Vickery and B Company under Major Gerald Rickord continued attacking south, C Company in the vanguard. However they came up against German mortar fire and assault artillery, and their own artilery, 76th Field Artillery Regiment (3rd Infantry Division) was wanting, as was long range fire support from HMS Arethusa. All they had were 7 3-inch mortars and 8 Vickers machine guns to press home their attack to Hill 30 at 1100hours. By the time companies A and B had belatedly reached Company C, they had run out of ammunition and had to advance through self-generated smoke. The Germans were well dug in before Sainte Honorine and they took heavy casualties in the attack of 1215 hours. The battalion had to fall back with 143 casualties : Companies A and B took 6 killed, one an officer, 70 wounded (6 officers), and 67 taken prisoner (although twenty would manage to escape and get back through the enemy lines).

On the left (eastern) flank 2nd Oxs and Bucks under the orders of Lieutenant Colonel Michael Roberts, also set off to attack Hérouvillette at 0430hours. Major Johnny Granville's C Company led the attack and the Germans pulled back to Escoville. At 0830 the battalion invested Hérouvillette and prepared its assault on Escoville. Companies A and B sent out probing patrols into hedgerow country. Finding no Germans in Escoville they moved into the village, leaving C Company in Hérouvillette. Despite some sniper activity by 1100 hours they could dig in, with A

1. 7th June 1944. Military Police of the Provost Company, Lance Corporal A Burton in the foreground, and Lance Corporal L. Barnett guard the Ranville crossroads from their trench. The Sten MkV was reserved for paratrooops. Number 46 indicates 20th Anti-Tank Regiment of the neighboring 3rd Division. The German signposts are still in place. (IWM)

2. Major General Gale in his HQ on 11th June is seen talking to Leonard Mosley, a journalist for Kensley Press who had been dropped in the first wave to prepare a feature on the battle. (IWM)

3. Ranville, le Hom, the château used for 5th Brigade HQ. (G.B./Heimdal)

4. To the east of that lies this other château used as a HQ for 5th Brigade. (G.B./Heimdal)

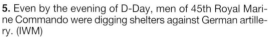

5

6

5. Even by the evening of D-Day, men of 45th Marine Commando were digging shelters against German artillery. (IWM)

6. 1st Special Service Brigade Commandos preparing a shelter a few hours after their arrival, near their HQ. (IWM)

7. « Apple Sammy », a Tetrarch tank taken out in the battle, perhaps in the 7th June morning attack.

8. A wrecked Hamilcar, taken after the battle. CA via PW)

9. A Devons beret (6th Airlanding Brigade), small dagger and rope. (Private coll)

10. These ropes were worn around the neck or waist, and when tied together could form a ladder. (Private coll)

7

8

Company (Major Gilbert Rahr) to the west and D Company (Major John Howard) to the south. Lieutenant Colonel Michael Roberts had hoped to set up his HQ in the château at Escoville but had to give up when it became the target for a self-propelled gun. From the south and east German shells and mortars were pouring into the village and a counter-attack began at 1500 ; shells starting impacting into the church bell-tower, fired from Panzer IV's of the 4/Panzer-Regiment 22. Then light armoured half-tracks of the Panzer-Aufklärungs-Abteilung 21 commanded by Major Waldow (who had just returned from his wedding in Berlin) started probing attacks on their positions. Grappling with British forces in the grounds of Escoville château, these elements of 21st Panzer took heavy losses. But without their 6-pounder anti-tank guns, the Oxs and Bucks was forced to withdraw from their position, covered by C Company from Hérouvillette where three other companies would back off. Lieutenant Colonel Michael Roberts had been injured in the landing ; he was evacuated and replaced by his second-in-command, Major Darell Brown.

But the counterattacking elements of 21st Panzer Division had also taken serious losses. At around 0900hours a light Tetrarch tank attacking out of Bavent towards positions held by 4/22 broke down after ramming a tree and its crew were taken prisoner.

A general assault launched on Ranville by Major von Luck made up of Panzer IV tanks of 4/22, assault artillery of the Stug. Abt.200 and grenadiers of 11/125 attacked across the open plain opposite Saint Honorine and veered towards Escoville. A storm of anti-tank fire from the R.U.R in Ranville backed by the naval artillery of H.M.S.Arethusa and H.M.S. Mauri-

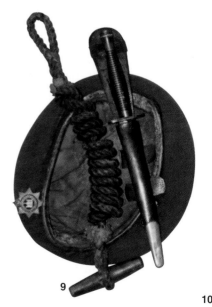

9

10

From left to right : Commando Laot, Commando Priez (Troop 1) who was wounded on 12th June, Mme Andrée Michèle and the little Danièle Michèle. (IWM)

French N°4 Commandos in Amfreville. From left to right : Commando Paoli, M. Guyard who volunteered on 8th June and was wounded on the 10th ; Commando Ziwolava, Mme Nicole Michèle, M. Potel (a solicitor's clerk), Mme Lefèvre, Commando Wavrault, Commando Gabriel (wounded on 11th June), and partially hidden, Commando Lanternier. (IWM)

Lieutenant Colonel R.W.E. Dawson commanded N°4 Commando. (IWM)

tius. Tank 431 was hit by a shell, and 4/22 pulled back to the west, between Sallenelles and Longueval. Tank 435 took a direct hit from 2 self-propelled 75mm M10s of 3rd Infantry Division. The driver and radioman in the Panzer burnt to death. The commander of 432 knocked out both these guns in the afternoon and seriously threatened the RUR HQ. In the evening German artillery started firing on the whole sector south of Ranville. The trenches of 6th Airlanding Brigade were attacked and the Devons' observation post took a direct hit. At 2030hours a German attack was launched under the cover of artificial smoke against A Company and the Devons, but it was repelled. The 13th Battalion HQ had been set up in the château Bruder in Ranville ; Following heavy casualties A Company, the Devons, was merged into the Battalion, Divisional HQ was only 500 yards behind the Devons' position and would suffer shelling. The commander of the Divisional artillery, Lieutenant Colonel Jack Norris had been severely wounded in the throat the previous evening while watching the incoming gliders land. Major General Gale was also wounded in his HQ.

In 3rd Brigade sector Brigadier Hill had withdrawn 9th Parachute Battalion which had suffered heavy casualties from Amfreville to the Bois du Mont between Bréville and Le Mesnil, hingeing on the villa of Bois du Mont (the summer residence of the Mayor of Bréville). The 1st Canadian Parachute Battalion HQ was just 1500 yards to the south of Le Mesnil. 8th Parachute Battalion held the Bois du Bavent, taking over the southern front of the bridgehead. The north front was now held by 1st Special Service Brigade which had taken up position with 9th Battalion at Le Plein and Amfreville.

The Commando Brigade HQ was set up in a large farmhouse belonging to the Saulnier family on the edge of the vast plain of Le Plein : henceforth this farm would be known as the « Commandos' Farm ». In the evening of D-Day Lieutenant-Colonel Mills-Roberts led his N°6 Commando to the farm and, framed by the great stone portal leading into the far-

myard, he spotted the large shambly figure of the farmer, M. Saulnier in corduroys and jacket watching them. He called out for them to use his farm as part of the British front line. M. said « Do you know what you might be letting yourself in for ? » and the farmer replied, « I was a former officer in the Hussars ! » Soon after the French commandos arrived and took up their positions on the north side of the village square. Men started digging trenches and manholes and a battle of position-taking and probing patrols ensued before an enemy as yet unknown. M. Saulnier's son, Bernard, aged 20, had been guiding the paras since dawn on D-Day ; now he was engaged in similar work for the commandos, guiding them through dangerous terrain.

Lord Lovat set up his HQ in the farmhouse dining room to the left of the farmyard porchway, and around the farmyard the troop created sleeping quarters, a kitchen, an infirmary and a morgue.

During the morning of 7th June 2 Troops of N°3 Commando set out to attack and destroy the Merville Battery after the setbacks of the night.

But lacking equipment, this operation did not obtain the hoped-for results and the commandos had to pull off after taking losses. The guns continued firing.

On 7th June 1st Canadian Parachute Battalion was supplied with mortar bombs which would prove their worth : the next day a PIAT gun would be deployed and take out a single Panzer IV which was causing havoc among the Canadian ranks : the mortars would wreak havoc among the Germans on 8th June, forcing them to pull back. On 9th June a patrol led by a platoon of C Company went forward to patrol Bavent village. Three men attracted German fire as they crossed the village to scout out the enemy's positions and strength. It was little short of miraculous that all three managed to pull back unscathed. On 10th June the Germans launched a major counter-attack out of Bréville, a weak point between the Commando and 3rd Brigade sectors. Once solidly in position they formed a wedge in the British line, threatening Ranville. The same day the Canadians had to face another attack towards LZ N to the northwest of the Le Mesnil crossroads where the Canadian and 9th Battalion sectors met. It was pushed back by a deluge of machine-gun and mortar fire. This tough firefight for Bréville lasted from 8th to 10th

1. French commandos on parade in Le Plein on 14th July. (IWM)

2. The same spot today. (G.B./Heimdal)

3. The same spot in Le Plein d'Amfreville ; Lieutenant Colonel Mills-Roberts of N°6 Commando, and Brigadier J. Slater (IWM)

4. The same spot today. (G.B./Heimdal)

June. Then on 12th June a violent artillery barrage fell on, the whole of 3rd Brigade sector. The 9th Battalion was now too reduced to be able to carry on fighting effectively. Brigadier Hill asked Lieutenant Colonel Bradbrooke to peel off some reinforcements to give Lieutenant Colonel Otway This consisted of Major Hanson and 40 Canadians of 3rd Battalion of 51st Division came to reinforce the paratroops, the Scottish Black Watch being here a precious reinforcement as the companies that had taken heavy casualties.

Further south conditions were no easier for the paras of 8th Battalion set up in the depths of the Bures wood, damp and dark where the trenches were muddy or clouds of mosquitoes, but morale held as men led patrols as far as Bures and Troarn.

A static front

In the afternoon of 12th June General Gale could begin to draw up a balance sheet of what had been achieved. Despite the heavy casualties and the more than 3000 men still unaccounted for, having been misdropped, captured or still struggling to return to their units, the front was holding. To the north the Amfreville sector they dominated the open high ground ; to the east the Bavent and Bures woods made their front almost impenetrable ; to the south the British positions formed an arc on the high ground

5. On the other side of the village square, the Saulnier farm, known as the 'Commandos' farm'. (G.B./Heimdal)

of Longueval and Hérouvillette facing the Caen plain. The front formed a kind of basin with raised sides, well conceived for defensive purposes. The first six days of combat had taken a heavy toll, but with the 6th Airlanding Brigade seaborne reinforcements bringing in the bulk of 12th Battalion the Devonshire Regiment on 7th June, the paras of 12th Battalion could go into reserve, along with 7th Battalion.

Reinforcements also consisted of elements of 3rd Infantry Division, including a squadron of 13/18th Hussars Sherman tanks and 3 Battalions of 51st Division, which had just landed. The 716th Infantry Division opposite had been wiped out on 6th June, and 711st Infantry Division was no great threat, being blocked by the flooded marshes of the Dives. As for 21st Division, it only had a few battalions deployed here, most of them being disposed around Caen : the few tactical units available could not make any decisive move against a well-dug-in defender. (the

6. The monument to N°6 Commando in Le Plein. (G.B./ Heimdal.)

6

RUR had already found this to be the case to their cost.) So the front became static in nature.

The 346th ID sent in to reinforce 711th Infantrie-Division threatened the eastern flank of the 6th Airborne Division : at 2200 hours on 12th June General Gale decided to launch an attack to relieve the exhausted 3rd Brigade towards Bréville, tasked to the 12th Parachute Battalion led by Lieutenant Colonel Johnny Johnson, and the Devons. On 13th June at 0200 hours a Troop of 13/18th Royal Hussars seized Bréville with heavy casualties amounting to 162 killed (9 of whom were officers) for 12th Parachute Battalion and D Company of the Devons. Of the 550 paras of 12th Battalion who had jumped on D-Day, barely a command company and a company of 50 men remained in line. 77 German bodies were found in the ruins of the village. Fortunately towards the end of the day fresh reinforcements of the 3 Battalions of 152nd Infantry Brigade and 51st Highland Division began feeding in, adding to the first elements of the division already in place. 6th Airborne Division was no longer alone in its bridgehead, and the static front began to take shape and would last until 16th August. Operation Goodwood, launched on 18th July, in the middle of this period, was a mass armoured and aerial attack which ground to a halt south-east of Caen. The battle ended with the dash for the Seine : the bridgehead had fulfilled its role and allowed the Allies to burst out on the German flank.

1. Paratroop R Watkins looks happy to be back with his mates after having been behind enemy lines until 10th June. (IWM)

2. These three men from Major Howard's Company did not get to return to their lines before 15th June. From left to right : Private Frank Gardner, Captain John Priday (second-in-commmand) and Lance Corporal B.H.Lambley, who wears the units insignia on his helmet. (IWM)

3. Also on 15th June, in Bénouville the paras pose with a young woman on a German motorbike. (IWM)

4. On 23rd June Stirling bombers resupplied the bridgehead on Landing Zone W at Saint-Aubin-d'Arquenay. Some of the anti-glider poles are still in place. The summer storm had created a crisis of supply, making this measure necessary. (IWM)

5. That day, some of RASC Company gathered up the supply drop of containers onto Landing Zone W. (IWM)

6. On the 12th July a signpost already refers to Bénouville Bridge as Pegasus Bridge : it has gone in to history under that name and this panel can be seen in the Museum : the bridge itself is on permanent exhibition in the grounds of « Mémorial Pégasus ». (IWM)

7. Until 1993 the site was still largely unchanged. (Heimdal)

7

6th Airborne had been tasked with a mission which presented some very difficult conditions. Scattered in the air drop, some of the first casualties of D-Day would be the men drowned in the Dives marshes or in crashed gliders. 1166 men were killed in Normandy, and most are buried in the Commonwealth War Grave at Ranville.

1 and **2.** A few tombs were dug by local civilians around the churchyard : here the graves of 3 British soldiers, Driver Dransfield of the Royal Engineers, and Private Ellmer and Lance Corporal A Haymond, both of 7th Parachute Battalion. They all still lie here. See page 111. (IWM)

3. Temporary wooden crosses marked the provisional graves while the battle raged : here 5 soldiers of the Royal Ulster Rifles, 4 of 12th Battalion and 2 unidentified soldiers. (Mémorial Pégasus)

4. Ranville cemetery in 1944. (Mémorial Pégasus)

5. Amfreville cemetery in June 1944. (IWM)

The main cemetery is in Ranville : here we can see the graves of men of 6th Airborne Division killed on D-Day, and representing various units in the division. A « German block » of graves also features in the cemetery, which is overlooked by the medieval church tower and the separate, nineteenth century Gothic Revival nave. (Photos E.G./ Heimdal.)

1. Brigadier James Hill, commander of 3rd Parachute Brigade at a ceremony in Merville in June 2001. He displays the Legion of Honour he had received from General Giraud in his hospital be in 1942.

2. Lieutenant Colonel Terence Otway commanded 9th Parachute Battalion. Like Howard, he was an officer from a working-class background, full of high spirits and energy and determined to show what he was made of in front of the public school officer class that prevailed. His reputation was his rigour and determination to carry out the impossible, which here was the capture of the Merville battery. The operation was prepared with clockwork precision. He would be deeply affected by the loss of so many of his men ; he was wounded a few days later and had to withdraw from the field. This photo was taken on 5th June 2001 at Merville, when he was awarded the Legion of Honour. (Ph. Wirton)

3. Some veterans of the 9th Parachute Battalion in Merville on 6th June 2001. (Ph Wirton)

4. Major John Howard led the other 'coup de main party'. This photograph was taken in 1993 in front of Pegasus Bridge. In the background is Hans von Luck, his enemy in 1944 who became his friend. They used to meet up every year. (Heimdal)

5. Hans von Luck and John Howard are looking at wartime photographs of 6th Airborne Division in the château at Damigny. Both men are now deceased. (Heimdal)

6. Their modern-day successors, British paras at Ranville in 1993. (Heimdal)

7. A fanfare heralds the arrival of the Parachute Regiment on the bridge in 1993, followed by paras in camouflaged battledress. (Heimdal)

10th AIR LANDING LAD REME

Name	Rank	Number	Date	Location
BARNARD J R	Cfn.	10540241	25/06/44	La Delivrande, V-G-5

12th AIR LANDING LAD REME

Name	Rank	Number	Date	Location
HALLIDAY A R	Cfn.	806064	12/08/44	Ranville, IVA-E-12
SLAUGHTER T D F	Cfn.	7590171	12/08/44	Ranville, VIA-B-21

6th AIRBORNE DIVISIONAL PROVOST COMPANY - CORPS OF ROYAL MILITARY POLICE

Name	Rank	Number	Date	Location
NIMMO T B	L/Cpl.	903274	06/06/44	Branville
DAVIES S A	L/Cpl.	7685953	07/06/44	Ranville, IVA-O-20
SCOTT A R	Sgt.	317153	08/06/44	Ranville, IAE-18
BUNTING C G	L/Cpl.	1870634	09/06/44	Ranville, IA-D-12
DRUMMOND A R	L/Cpl.	3325850	20/07/44	La Delivrande, VI-A-8

245th PROVOST COMPANY - CORPS OF ROYAL MILITARY POLICE

Name	Rank	Number	Date	Location
HENDERSON T J	Cpl.	3771465	07/06/44	Ranville Church, 20

SERVICEMEN OF DIFFERENT UNITS ATTACHED TO 6th AIRBORNE

Name	Rank	Number	Date	Location
BICKNELL A	Gnr.	1548697	06/06/44	Ranville Church, 47
POPE A A	Major	77672	06/06/44	Saint Vaast En Auge, 1
SCHOLES F C	Captain	245654	16/06/44	Ranville, IIA-C-13
McBRYDE J R	Captain	45069	18/07/44	Ranville, IVA-C-13

SERVICEMEN ATTACHED TO ARMY AIR CORPS

Name	Rank	Number	Date	Location
BREWER B M	Lieut.	258672	12/06/44	Ranville, IVA-B-11
CLINTON R A	Pte.	55113033	19/06/44	Ranville, IIA-L-2

325th AIRBORNE FIELD SECURITY SECTION INTELLIGENCE CORPS

Name	Rank	Number	Date	Location
JAGO H T	Sgt.	2345561	03/10/44	Bayeux, II-L-13

THE PARACHUTE REGIMENT AAC

Name	Rank	Number	Date	Location
MAX J H	Captain	137383	06/06/44	Ranville, IVA-H-20
GREENWOOD C E	Captain	240263	07/06/44	Ranville, VA-L-2
FITZGERALD PE	Lieut.	281130	19/08/44	Ranville, IIA-N-9
CRAMP E R	Major	174967	21/08/44	Ranville, IVA-K-14

3rd PARACHUTE BN AAC

Name	Rank	Number	Date	Location
DELAHUNT D	Pte.	277637	06/06/44	Ranville, VA-C-3
JOHNSON G	Pte.	3386281	06/06/44	M.I.A. Bayeux, P.18-C.1
WILKINSON A T	Captain	124287	08/06/44	Ranville, IAC-20
CALVER F R	Pte.	5828446	10/06/44	Ranville, IA-G-22

5th PARACHUTE BN AAC

Name	Rank	Number	Date	Location
DIMMICK W	Pte.	4030978	19/06/44	Ranville, IA-M-6
TROTTER J W	Pte.	7047440	07/07/44	M.I.A. Bayeux, P.18-C.2

1st BN THE BORDER REGIMENT

Name	Rank	Number	Date	Location
BULL E	Pte	3602499	06/06/44	Bayeux, X-E-18
OLIVER B	Lieut.	109526	17/08/44	Ranville, IAE-4

THE GLIDER PILOT REGIMENT AAC

Name	Rank	Number	Date	Location
BEVERIDGE H	Sgt.	2332874	06/06/44	Ranville, IA-C-1
BRABHAM J P	S/Sgt.	1950346	06/06/44	Saint Desir, Lisieux, VI-B-14
BROMLEY J L	Lieut.	137319	06/06/44	Ranville, IVA-G-20
CHADWICK R	Sgt.	1455316	06/06/44	Saint Desir, Lisieux, III-A-2
CODDINGTON J F S	S/Sgt.	6143799	06/06/44	Ranville, IIIA-E-8
FUELL J H	Sgt.	4620584	06/06/44	Saint Desir, Lisieux, III-A-7
GIBBONS J R M	Sgt.	860893	06/06/44	M.I.A. Bayeux, P.18-C.1
GOODCHILD E J	Sgt.	5119586	06/06/44	Ranville, IIIA-H-8
HAINES V	Sgt.	1888144	06/06/44	Abbeville, IAJ-2
HOPGOOD C H	Sgt.	1892740	06/06/44	Saint Vaast en Auge, 11
HOWE W R	S/Sgt.	913370	06/06/44	Ranville, IIA-J-5
LIGHTOWLER E J	S/Sgt.	4618546	06/06/44	Ranville, VA-E-6
LUFF R S	Sgt.	1462774	06/06/44	Ranville, IVA-M-20
MARFLEET W K	S/Sgt.	7537176	06/06/44	Bayeux, X-J-17
MARTIN E J	Lieut.	186684	06/06/44	Ranville, IIIA-F-8
NASH J H	Sgt.	5680493	06/06/44	Ranville Church, 44
NEW R G	S/Sgt.	7523696	06/06/44	Sainte Marie, Le Havre, 67-H-15
OCKWELL H V	Sgt.	8311885	06/06/44	Sainte Marie, Le Havre, 67-I-8
PERRY S W	Sgt.	5252214	06/06/44	Ranville, VA-H-4
PHILLIPS D F	S/Sgt.	6406473	06/06/44	Saint Vaast En Auge, 8
PHILPOT G E	S/Sgt.	6746290	06/06/44	M.I.A. Bayeux, P.18-C.1
POWELL B	Sgt.	5184835	06/06/44	Ranville, IVA-J-20
RIGG A	Sgt.	951367	06/06/44	Ranville Church, 3
ROBINSON C B	S/Sgt.	1881121	06/06/44	Ranville Church, 29
SAUNDERS V C	S/Sgt.	1427651	06/06/44	Saint Desir, Lisieux, III-A-6
SEPHTON A H	Sgt.	14430328	06/06/44	Hermanville, 1-G-21
STANLEY E	S/Sgt.	5251641	06/06/44	M.I.A. Bayeux, P.18-C.1
STEAR A T	S/Sgt.	1098498	06/06/44	Ranville Church, 10
STONEBANKS W H	Sgt.	981236	06/06/44	Brucourt, 4
TAYLOR E M	S/Sgt.	2036063	06/06/44	M.I.A. Bayeux, P.18-C.1
TURVEY P P	S/Sgt.	5252071	06/06/44	M.I.A. Bayeux, P.18-C.1
WRIGHT D P	S/Sgt.	1509818	06/06/44	Ranville, IIIA-B-2
RIDINGS L	S/Sgt.	1116413	07/06/44	Saint Vaast en Auge, 5
FLETCHER S W	S/Sgt.	410230	09/06/44	Manchester Southern, England, E-1081
HEBBERD L R	Sgt.	14309890	09/06/44	Twickenham, England, 676
FOSTER P	Sgt.	82488	18/06/44	La Delivrande, IX-A-6
SIMPSON F W	S/Sgt.	3249838	04/07/44	Cadder, Scotland, B-110
ANSELL H J	Sgt.	6897960	10/07/44	Longside, Scotland, 86
DOWDS H M	S/Sgt.	2986798	10/07/44	Grangemouth, Scotland, S.13-175

3rd PARACHUTE BRIGADE AAC
1st Canadian Parachute Bn

Name	Rank	Number	Date	Location
ADAMS L H	Lieut.	A 104589	06/06/44	Ranville, IA-E-7
ARCHIBALD A R	Pte.	D 138072	06/06/44	Ranville, IA-J-9
AUBIN J E	RSM	P 15392	06/06/44	Ranville, IIIA-B-8
CLARK W J	Pte.	C 94256	06/06/44	Ranville, VA-F-2
COBURN J C	Pte.	B 75489	06/06/44	Calais Leubringhen, 8-C-4
CONNAGHAN G C	Sgt.	G 12254	06/06/44	Ranville, IX-B-23
COSGROVE F D	Pte.	L 74035	06/06/44	Ranville, IIA-O-5
ELLEFSON O M	L/Cpl.	D 166551	06/06/44	Ranville, IVA-H-6
FLEXER A E	Capt. Rev.		06/06/44	Ranville, VA-C-6
HARRIS G	Sgt.	H17245	06/06/44	Saint Vaast En Auge, 3
LA CROIX G R	Pte.	F 31928	06/06/44	M.I.A. Bayeux, P.27 C-2
McINNIS A J	Major		06/06/44	Ranville, VA-B-1
McLEOD HM	Pte.	B 137923	06/06/44	Ranville, IVA-J-6
McPHERSON M A	A/Sgt	M 103553	06/06/44	Ranville, VA-B-8
MODDERMAN P J M	Pte.	B 135512	06/06/44	Ranville, VA-E-8
OXTOBY C M	Pte.	B 114490	06/06/44	Bayeux, XVI-B-15
REYNARD M H	Lieut.		06/06/44	Ranville, VA-G-8
ROUSSEAU J-Ph.	Lieut.		06/06/44	Ranville, VA-B-2
WALKER H M	Pte.	B 24351	06/06/44	Bretteville Sur Laize, VII-B-2
BISMUTKA P I	Pte.	B 135587	07/06/44	Ranville, IIA-M-5
BROADFOOT J G	Pte.	B 139066	07/06/44	Ranville, IA-D-7
LAPIERRE C D	Capt.		07/06/44	Bretteville Sur Laize, XIX-F-10
MacLEAN D S	Pte.	B 26879	07/06/44	Calais Leubringhen, 8-C-12
NIGH J S	A/Cpl.	F 96045	07/06/44	M.I.A. Bayeux, P.27 C2
OIKLE W E	Pte.	B 79949	07/06/44	Ranville, IIA-L-3
PLEDGER K M	A/Cpl.	A 54594	08/06/44	Ranville, VA-B-4
BASTIEN O M	Cpl.	P 28106	08/06/44	Hermanville, I-J-7
DRAY F A	A/Sgt	L 56826	08/06/44	Ranville, IA-D-9
HUARD C E	Sgt.	B101038	08/06/44	Hermanville, 1-N-1
LACASSE J A	Sgt.	M 50866	08/06/44	Ranville, IA-B-7
BLAIR A E W	Pte.	D 96420	09/06/44	Ranville, IIIA-J-2
LANTHIER M J	Pte.	M 102621	09/06/44	Ranville, IIIA-H-2
RACE D A	Pte.	B 138258	09/06/44	Ranville, IA-A-9
TURNER D G	Pte.	F 64797	10/06/44	Ranville, IA-F-7
COMEAU G A	Pte.	K 50501	10/06/44	Ranville, IA-C-7
DAVIDSON G H	Pte.	K 62733	10/06/44	Ranville, IA-J-7
EMBREE G W	Pte.	F 40775	10/06/44	Hermanville, I-K-1
HARDIMAN J K	CSM	L 74243	10/06/44	M.I.A. Bayeux, P.27 C2
NEUFIELD L A	Pte.	A 76154	10/06/44	M.I.A. Bayeux, P.27 C2
WILSON I G	Pte.	B 110359	11/06/44	M.I.A. Bayeux, P.27 C2
JOWETT J B	Pte.	A 37973	11/06/44	Ranville, IA-F-9
ROBERTS J H	Pte.	L 102427	12/06/44	Ranville, VA-K-8
BOARDMAN R M	Pte.	B 143410	13/06/44	Ranville, IA-H-9
SAUDER L	Pte.	K 66663	14/06/44	Ranville, IA-E-9
EVANS W J	Pte.		14/06/44	

Date	No.	Name	Rank	Burial / Location
14/06/44	B 68693	SACHRO J F A	Pte.	Ranville, IA-H-7
15/06/44	A 102477	ROSS L D	Pte.	Ranville, VA-J-8
16/06/44	B 133241	BOYD G R	L/Cpl.	Ranville, IA-B-9
17/06/44	H 9595	SHWALUK W M	Pte.	Ranville, VA-J-7
19/06/44	F 24322	DAVIES G	Sgt.	Hermanville, IA-K-15
19/06/44	B 3047	DUCKER, W S	Pte.	Ranville, IA-C-9
19/06/44	B 47149	JOHNSON C A	Pte.	Brookwood, England, 51-G-1
20/06/44	R 127013	CHADDOCK W J	Cpl.	Ranville, IA-G-9
22/06/44	B 77222	HALL R C	Pte.	La Delivrande, II-A-7
25/06/44	L 86734	DELAMERE E J	Pte.	Ranville, IA-A-7
27/06/44	A 43023	MOHRING H S	Pte.	Ranville, IA-G-7
28/06/44	F 30136	KING J H	Pte.	Ranville, IIIA-G-9
29/06/44	H 40668	MIDDLETON M C	L/Sgt.	Ranville, IIIA-M-7
29/06/44	K 62682	MILLER V W	Pte.	Ranville, VA-B-3
01/07/44	C 120203	WOODBECK M E	Pte.	Hermanville, II-A-23
02/07/44	F 52097	JENKIN W C	Pte.	Beny Sur Mer, IX-C-11
04/07/44	H 41482	TROUGHTON T B	Rfn.	Beny Sur Mer, II-F-13
06/07/44	G 32888	HANLON C E	Sgt.	Ranville, IIA-E-14
07/07/44	F 15271	LEECO M S	A/Sgt	
09/07/44	E 15248	OUELLET C H	Pte.	Brookwood, England, 54-C-2
01/08/44	H 1626	SCHROEDER E	Pte.	Ranville, IA-C-16
02/08/44	H 20387	BARTKO P	A/Cpl.	Ranville, IA-F-16
02/08/44	K 65593	BRIERLEY J T	Pte.	Ranville, IA-G-16
		GENEREAUX J W	Pte.	Beny Sur Mer, XIV-B-6
		CHRISTISON G M	Cpl.	Hottot Les Bagues, I-C-9
10/08/44	A 105185	FRITZ H E	Pte.	Beny Sur Mer, XII-G-6
17/08/44	K 46849	JESSON R E	Pte.	M.I.A. Bayeux, P.27 C2
17/08/44	M 8139	SYLVESTRE H P	Pte.	Verneuil Sur Avre, 26
17/08/44	K 1163	PEARSON A P	Sgt.	Ranville, IIA-C-14
18/08/44	B126264	SWANTON G A	Pte.	Ranville, VA-B-7
18/08/44	H 67598	ARMSTRONG L C	Pte.	Ranville, VA-E-8
20/08/44	C 120522	BENOIT J L	Pte.	Ranville, IVA-F-8
20/08/44	G 50443	COTE C A	Cpl.	Ranville, IIIA-B-9
20/08/44	U 1982	EVANS E G	Sgt.	Ranville, IVA-G-8
25/08/44	F 77984	McPHEE M C	Sgt.	Ranville, VA-O-8
26/08/44	F 50331	BLACK A	Pte.	Beny Sur Mer, XII-C-11
27/08/44	B 147225	BELL W N	Pte.	Bayeux, XVI-C20
30/08/44	B 133045	DEW M J	Pte.	Toronto Canada, Mil 1-457
24/09/44	F 65510	RUGGLES H C	Sgt.	Brookwood, England, 55-D-4
19/01/45	M 10865	KROESING G	Sgt.	Prague, Czech Republic, III-E-11

8th Parachute Bn

Date	No.	Name	Rank	Burial / Location
06/06/44	6354301	BILLINGTON T W	Pte.	M.I.A. Bayeux, P.18C.1
06/06/44	3252324	BOYLE J P	L/Cpl.	Ranville, V-B-1.22
06/06/44	14330657	CANTIN R F	Pte.	Troarn, 2
06/06/44	886971	CARTER H M	Pte.	Herouvillette, 12
06/06/44	4208750	COOPER C A P	Pte.	Ranville, V-B-1.22
06/06/44	14420679	COX S G	Pte.	Troarn, 1
06/06/44	5124711	DAVIES J P	Sgt.	Ranville, V-B-1.22
06/06/44	5107022	DOCKERILL A	Sgt.	Ranville, V-B-1.22
06/06/44	5121244	FEWINGS S R	Cpl.	Ranville Church, 18
06/06/44	14407958	FRYER A	Pte.	M.I.A. Bayeux, P.18C.1
06/06/44	14400579	HINDS D W	Pte.	Ranville, V-B-1.22
06/06/44	5120676	HIPKISS E G	Sgt.	Ranville, V-B-6
06/06/44	5125357	HOLLIS C F	Pte.	Ranville, V-B-1.22
06/06/44	14623429	HOPKINS T J	Sgt.	Ranville, VIA-C-26
06/06/44	5105574	HORNER J	Sgt.	Ranville, V-B-1.22
06/06/44	14414284	HUMPHRIES A	Pte.	Troarn, 3
06/06/44	4860760	ILIFFE J A	Sgt.	Herouvillette, 4
06/06/44	5097971	ISAACS J	CQMS	Ranville, V-B-1.22
06/06/44	14405715	JOHNSON D W	Pte.	Ranville, V-B-1.22
06/06/44	14630298	JONES E	Pte.	Ranville, V-B-1.22
06/06/44	881359	KENT R P	Pte.	Ranville, V-B-1.22
06/06/44	13807801	KUTTNER A R	Pte.	Banneville La Campagne, XVII-C-2
06/06/44	274820	LANGDON R W	Cpl.	Herouvillette, 2
06/06/44	14605779	LEVERSUCH A F	Pte.	Banneville La Campagne, VII-C-9
06/06/44	7344882	LONGMAN T R H	Cpl.	Ranville, V-B-1.22
06/06/44	14384224	MEIKLEJOHN M	Pte.	Herouvillette, 1
06/06/44	6103738	MILLS J A	Pte.	Ranville, V-B-1.22
06/06/44	5124499	MOIR J A	Sgt.	Ranville, V-B-1.22
06/06/44	14245520	PIGGOTT W	Pte.	Ranville, V-B-1.22
06/06/44	5384418	PLATT A	Pte.	Watchfield, England
06/06/44	3600656	RICHARDSON W	Pte.	Ranville, IIA-N-8
06/06/44	14629902	ROBINSON J	Pte.	Ranville, V-B-1.22
06/06/44	1437445	ROGERS J M	Cpl.	Banneville La Campagne, XVII-C-7
06/06/44	14654924	RUSSON D	Pte.	Herouvillette, 7
06/06/44	14520558	SCOTT R T	Cpl.	Banneville La Campagne, XVII-C-8
06/06/44	5118245	SMITH L F	Pte.	Ranville, V-B-1.22
06/06/44	7344953	THORPE W H R	Pte.	Ranville, V-B-1.22
06/06/44	3656971	WALTON S S	Pte.	Herouvillette, 3
06/06/44	14410209	WARNER A H	Pte.	Ranville, IIA-F-10
06/06/44	14422129	WATKINS J H	Pte.	Ranville, V-B-1.22
06/06/44	14340968	DOHERTY W H	Pte.	Ranville, IA-L-2
07/06/44	5121228	EVANS J W	L/Sgt.	Ranville, IA-C-3
07/06/44	150817	KAY J A	Rev.	Ranville, IA-M-2
07/06/44	14528074	LUKE D R	Pte.	Ranville, III-B-3
09/06/44	1428459	HARVEY J T	L/Cpl.	Ranville, IIA-D-10
10/06/44	14649703	RUFF F C	Pte.	Ranville, IIA-E-10
11/06/44	5114376	TISDALE M A	Sgt.	Ranville, IVA-G-5
11/06/44	5120614	WOODHOUSE J	Pte.	Ranville, IIA-C-10
13/06/44	4801292	KEIGHTLEY G W	Cpl.	M.I.A. Bayeux, P.18C.1
13/06/44	5121418	PYE G R	Pte.	M.I.A. Bayeux, P.18C.1
16/06/44	7949753	BONHAM C E	Pte.	Ranville, IIA-F-8
16/06/44	4123637	CHARTERS J	Pte.	Ranville, IIIA-L-8
16/06/44	3320414	COWAN D	Cpl.	Ranville, VIA-B-27
16/06/44	14401579	DAVIES J W	Pte.	Ranville, IIA-D-8
16/06/44	5110870	DUNCAN A H	Pte.	Ranville, IIA-G-8
16/06/44	14537124	KELLY A P	L/Cpl.	Ranville, IIA-B-8
16/06/44	5440047	MOUNCE E R	Sgt.	Hermanville, 1-S-12
16/06/44	14576337	NEIL G	Pte.	Ranville, IIA-C-8
16/06/44	5347414	RUSHTON D V	Pte.	Ranville, IIA-J-8
16/06/44	3244755	SCOTT J	Sgt.	Ranville, IIA-N-7
16/06/44	14217345	SIMMONS G P	Pte.	Hermanville, 1-U-14
16/06/44	5127076	VINE N A	Pte.	Ranville, IIA-L-8
17/06/44	14427738	HEYDEN R V	Pte.	Bayeux, XI-F-1
17/06/44	2825027	McINAW J	Pte.	Ranville, IIA-M-10
18/06/44	6204578	NOTLEY A W	Cpl.	Enfield(lavender Hill), England, 6907
27/06/44	5118032	IMPEY H R	Pte.	Ranville, IIIA-F-9
28/06/44	14538033	MILLER L C	Pte.	La Delivrande, V-K-8
30/06/44	2763132	CHURCHILL M C	Pte.	Deptford(Brockley), London, England, F-630
30/06/44	14552984	TAYLOR G H	Pte.	Ranville, VA-Q-8
01/07/44	2571722	FREEMAN G A	Pte.	Ranville, IIA-H-8
02/07/44	3602318	CASSON T	Pte.	Ranville, VA-Q-7
02/07/44	14556549	HODDINOTT J H	Pte.	Ranville, IIIA-E-8
19/07/44	5126287	RAYNER J	Pte.	Ranville, IVA-F-1
28/07/44	14577833	PANNELL J F	L/Cpl.	Ranville, IA-K-8
31/07/44	2064184	SMITHIES J	Pte.	Ranville, IA-A-12
02/08/44	3653462	LLEWELLYN A	Pte.	Ranville, VIA-B-25
05/08/44	14408893	BATES F J	Pte.	M.I.A. Bayeux, P.18C.1
09/08/44	14552789	CARTWRIGHT F E F	L/Cpl.	La Delivrande, III-B-9
17/08/44	5182800	COLLINS M	Pte.	Ranville, IVA-B-8
17/08/44	14409647	PORTER E	L/Cpl.	Ranville, IVA-C-8
18/08/44	6032150	SKEGGS A E	Pte.	Ranville, IVA-D-8
18/08/44	3065382	FALCONER J M	Pte.	Ranville, IIIA-M-7
18/08/44	5120965	ROBERTS W S	Sgt.	Ranville, IIA-M-6

Date	Service No.	Rank	Name	Location
06/06/44	14614437	Pte.	PHILPOTT N R	M.I.A. Bayeux, P.18C.1
06/06/44	6025170	Cpl.	PLEDGER R	Ranville, VA-F-6
06/06/44	14207046	L/Cpl.	PLESTED S J	Ranville, IA-B-17
06/06/44	6026870	L/Cpl.	ROBINSON P G	Ranville, VA-F-7
06/06/44	6012502	Pte.	SHARPLES P J	M.I.A. Bayeux, P.18C.1
06/06/44	5501056	Pte.	SHEAT F J	M.I.A. Bayeux, P.18C.1
06/06/44	4394622	Pte.	SMITH F J	Ranville, VA-K-6
06/06/44	14405378	Pte.	WALTER P F	Ranville, VA-E-2
06/06/44	6216556	Pte.	WHITE G V	Ranville, IA-A-5
06/06/44	6031294	Pte.	WILSON J T	M.I.A. Bayeux, P.18C.2
06/06/44	6216032	Pte.	WISE D W H	M.I.A. Bayeux, P.18C.3
06/06/44	7363459	Pte.	YORK G E	Ranville, IVA-N-6
06/06/44	6977467	Pte.	YOUNG J	Ranville, IIA-H-3
07/06/44	48003632	Pte.	YOUNGER J	Ranville, IA-G-3
07/06/44	14562115	Lieut.	BEDFORD G A	Ranville, IA-H-3
07/06/44	14400600	Pte.	DUNK H	Ranville Church, 6
07/06/44	189323	Lieut.	HALLIBURTON T C	Ranville, IA-M-3
07/06/44	14409489	Pte.	HURLEY D R	M.I.A. Bayeux, P.18C.1
07/06/44	6025566	L/Cpl.	ROLLINGSON J T	Ranville, IA-L-3
07/06/44	6410789	Pte.	TAYLOR B E	M.I.A. Bayeux, P.18C.1
08/06/44	4911764	Sgt.	ROSE J E	Ranville, IA-H-20
08/06/44	7365440	Pte.	TOWNSEND W V	M.I.A. Bayeux, P.18C.3
08/06/44	3961363	Pte.	WILLIAMS F J	M.I.A. Bayeux, P.18C.2
09/06/44	58172	Major	CHARLTON E G	Ranville, IA-B-19
09/06/44	189318	Lieut.	PARFITT G S	Ranville, IA-J-19
09/06/44	57482	Pte.	ROCHE T M	Ranville, I-A-E-3
10/06/44	14406165	Pte.	RAYNER E M	M.I.A. Bayeux, P.18C.1
10/06/44	7381528	Pte.	SPENCER W V	M.I.A. Bayeux, P.18C.3
11/06/44	14362477	Pte.	BLUCK H	M.I.A. Bayeux, P.18C.1
12/06/44	76551	Lieut.	CHRISTIE M W	Ranville, IA-J-15
12/06/44	5511515	Pte.	JEPP R S	Ranville, IA-G-15
12/06/44	1595047	Pte.	McSORLEY G F	Ranville, IA-F-20
12/06/44	14219502	Pte.	SANDERSON P	Ranville, IA-J-20
12/06/44	4972413	Pte.	TOPHAM W	Ranville, IA-H-19
12/06/44	14003053	Pte.	WILSON P	Ranville, I-A-E-20
12/06/44	5380052	Pte.	WINGROVE F W	Beaconsfield, England, 1531
17/06/44	7011364	WOI(RSM)	CUNNINGHAM W J	Ranville, IIA-B-12
17/06/44	6024551	Pte.	GIBSON H F	Ranville, IA-J-18
17/06/44	7589378	Sgt.	TARRANT R T	Ranville, IA-K-4
21/06/44	6216373	Pte.	PENSTONE D G	Tilly Sur Seulles, III-A-6
02/07/44	14402567	L/Cpl.	TAYLOR K M	Clichy, 16-16-13
05/07/44	2822443	Pte.	MUNRO G	Ranville, VIA-B-24
15/07/44	11003829	Pte.	LAING J	Banneville La Campagne, IVA-A-1
19/07/44	5346999	Pte.	EDE C	Ranville, IVA-F-3
23/07/44	1431738	Sgt.	ECOTT A D	Ranville, IVA-O-19
23/07/44	6031926	Pte.	TOWNES L V	Ranville, IVA-O-21
24/07/44	14406335	Pte.	SEBIRE C J H	Ranville, IVA-P-9
25/07/44	6025520	L/Sgt.	FOWLER R S N	Ranville, IVA-O-9
27/07/44	5384705	Pte.	PEDLER C E C	Ranville, IVA-P-7
27/07/44	5385856	Pte.	REVELL F J T	Ranville, IVA-O-7
08/08/44	3659827	Pte.	YARWOOD W S	Ranville, IVA-K-10
15/08/44	6027038	WOII(CSM)	SHERMAN W K	Ranville, IA-F-4
17/08/44	6009791	Pte.	BECKWITH W G	Ranville, VA-C-1
17/08/44	5111240	Pte.	SHEPPARD W	Ranville, IA-A-4
19/08/44	14202528	Pte.	CLARK T	Ranville, IIA-L-9
19/08/44	5338526	Sgt.	FRITH J H	Ranville, IIA-B-10
19/08/44	6011425	Pte.	HAMMOND J F	Ranville, IA-L-4
19/08/44	4193644	Pte.	JONES G	Ranville, IIA-K-4
19/08/44	14570651	Cpl.	MAYHEW W C	Ranville, IIA-O-4
19/08/44	14406258	Pte.	PARSONS R G	Ranville, IIA-C-9
19/08/44	14689319	Pte.	SPENN C F	Ranville, IIA-M-4
19/08/44	5387631	Pte.	STEWART A H	Ranville, IIA-E-9
19/08/44	14409626	Pte.	BROWNSWORD S A	Ranville, XIA-B-13
20/08/44	14439616	Pte.	KNIGHT R G	Ranville, IIA-D-4
20/08/44	4610600	Sgt.	RATTICAN J	Ranville, IIA-D-9
21/08/44	182869	Lieut.	RUDDICK J G	Ranville, IVA-B-2
21/08/44	11422417	Pte.	BAXTER N H	Ranville, IVA-E-14
21/08/44	5125299	Pte.	BROGAN J	Ranville, IVA-H-14
21/08/44	3597618	Pte.	CHAMBERLAIN C C H	Ranville, IVA-N-14
21/08/44	7363477	Pte.	COX C E A	Bayeux, II-H-15
21/08/44	5189699	Pte.	DAW C	Ranville, IVA-J-14
21/08/44	14218261	Pte.	EVANS H J C	Ranville, IVA-O-14
21/08/44	5125169	Pte.	GILBERT H	Ranville, IVA-F-14
21/08/44	4041970	Pte.	HILL E	Ranville, IVA-D-14
21/08/44	156645	2/Lt.	HORTON P C	Ranville, IVA-G-14
21/08/44	4800741	Pte.	JORDAN S	Bayeux, XII-C-15
21/08/44	3244239	Pte.	KILBRIDE P	Ranville, IIA-E-4
25/08/44	14407416	Cpl.	LANCASTER R S	Ranville, VA-L-4
25/08/44	5125793	Pte.	SHRIMPTON J D	Ranville, VA-L-3
25/08/44	36006902	Pte.	BOX R	Vatteville la rue
25/08/44	5192890	Pte.	CALDICOTT J K	Ranville, VA-L-5
25/08/44	14438005	Pte.	CLAYTON S	Ranville, VA-L-3
25/08/44	14591117	Pte.	COOPER S.	Ranville, VA-N-8
25/08/44	5189212	Cpl.	DEVONSHIRE G W	Ranville, VA-P-7
25/08/44	7888546	Pte.	GLOVER A	Ranville, VA-O-5
25/08/44	3051601	Pte.	HAMILTON J	Ranville, VA-L-6
25/08/44	5960619	Pte.	HOARE E L	Ranville, VA-O-2
25/08/44	14321426	Pte.	JONES E W J	Ranville, VA-O-3
25/08/44	14597979	Pte.	JONES T E	Ranville, VA-O-4
25/08/44	5112970	Sgt.	LITTLEWOOD W E M	Vatteville la rue
25/08/44	3244339	L/Sgt.	McILHARRGEY C R	Ranville, VA-O-7
25/08/44	14408447	Pte.	THOMPSON R J	Ranville, VA-M-7
25/08/44	3716837	Pte.	WARDLE E	Ranville, VA-O-6
25/08/44	14002935	Lieut.	WILLIAMS H B	Ranville, VA-M-8
26/08/44	224689	Lieut.	CLARKE J F	
10/09/44	14631269	Pte.	BROWN N	Sainte Marie, Le Havre, Div67-H-9

9th Parachute Bn

Date	Service No.	Rank	Name	Location
06/06/44	6410372	Pte.	ADSETT G D	M.I.A. Bayeux, P.18C.1
06/06/44	6408511	Pte.	ARMSTRONG A J	Ranville, IA-E-13
06/06/44	90840	Lieut.	CATLIN D S	Ranville, IVA-F-6
06/06/44	3244763	L/Cpl.	CLARKE E J	Ranville, IVA-M-6
06/06/44	14421641	Pte.	COPP B N	Hottot Les Bagues, III-A-1
06/06/44	14410713	Pte.	CORTEILE S	Ranville, IA-G-13
06/06/44	6008541	CQSM	DAVIES A M	Ranville, VA-K-2
06/06/44	14635646	Pte.	DOWLING M J	M.I.A. Bayeux, P.18C.1
06/06/44	237706	Lieut.	DURNEY L W	Ranville, IA-C-17
06/06/44	14653778	L/Cpl.	ECKERT S G T	Ranville, VIA-B-23
06/06/44	14404989	Sgt.	HALL R R	Hottot Les Bagues, III-A-2
06/06/44	6030996	Pte.	HANNEN T L	M.I.A. Bayeux, P.18C.1
06/06/44	14002721	Sgt.	HARDING S F	M.I.A. Bayeux, P.18C.1
06/06/44	14414817	Pte.	HARNESS D V	Ranville, VA-K-3
06/06/44	4801546	Lieut.	HUGHES A	Saint Vaast en Auge, 7
06/06/44	273622	L/Cpl.	HULL E T	Oxford, England, I-167
06/06/44	6465258	Pte.	LITTLE K R	Ranville, VA-K-7
06/06/44	14410471	Cpl.	MANDER J	Ranville, IA-D-13
06/06/44	6297299	Pte.	McGUIRK M J	Ranville, IVA-L-6
06/06/44	2718993	Pte.	McKEE R	Ranville, VA-D-1
06/06/44	6400094	Cpl.	NICHOLLS A	Ranville, VA-H-5.8
06/06/44	14409786	Pte.	PAINE H	M.I.A. Bayeux, P.18C.1
06/06/44	6204449	Cpl.	PARRIS M W	M.I.A. Bayeux, P.18C.1
06/06/44	6354232	Pte.	PECK N	Ranville, IA-C-13
06/06/44	14408977	Cpl.	PERRY R D	Pont Audemer, C-25
06/06/44	7516711	Lieut.	PETERS G F	Ranville, IVA-O-6

19/08/44	6025595	L/Cpl.	WARD A	Ranville, IIA-N-4
19/08/44	14546155	Pte.	WATTAM A	Ranville, IIA-K-9
20/08/44	6412488	Pte.	BOLINGBROKE S	La Delivrande, 1-H-2
22/08/44	6025593	Pte.	WRIGHT L V	Bayeux, V-A-10
25/08/44	1805781	Pte.	BANKS M R	Beuzeville, 5
Of HQ 3rd Parachute Bde AAC				
06/06/44	14410275	Pte.	ROSS J W	M.I.A. Bayeux, P.18C.2
08/06/44	14410877	Pte.	SUTTON E	M.I.A. Bayeux, P.18C.2
10/06/44	5828446	Pte.	CALVER F	Ranville, IA-G-22
15/06/44	5835418	Pte.	WRIGHT K G	M.I.A. Bayeux, P.18C.2
5th PARACHUTE BRIGADE AAC				
7th Parachute Bn				
06/06/44	14543706	Pte.	BARRETT P	Ranville, IIIA-C-9
06/06/44	5678355	L/Cpl.	BEARD A H J	La Delivrande, IV-K-4
06/06/44	5674103	Sgt.	BEECH J A	La Delivrande, III-K-5
06/06/44	176175	Captain	BOWYER W	Benouville, 20
06/06/44	14219916	Pte.	BROOKMAN H E R	Ranville, IA-B-18
06/06/44	2056538	Pte.	BURGESS K I H	Benouville, 14
06/06/44	3962078	Pte.	CAVEY J	La Delivrande, IV-K-6
06/06/44	5679083	L/Sgt.	CHAPPELL A E	Ranville, IIIA-G-8
06/06/44	14405006	Pte.	COPSON G	Ranville, VIA-C-1..25
06/06/44	5679243	Cpl.	DENHAM H	La Delivrande, III-K-8
06/06/44	5383220	Pte.	ELLMER A A	Benouville, 3
06/06/44	1475163	Sgt.	FIDDLER J E	Benouville, 15
06/06/44	4032616	Pte.	FINCH P S	La Delivrande, IV-K-5
06/06/44	14000182	L/Cpl.	FISHER C W	Benouville, 11
06/06/44	6354955	Pte.	FRANCIS R A E	Ranville, VIA-C-1..25
06/06/44	14420431	Pte.	FROST V P C	Ranville, VIA-C-1..25
06/06/44	4546638	Pte.	GARNETT F	La Delivrande, III-K-7
06/06/44	4343281	L/Cpl.	GASCOIGNE J	Ranville, VIA-C-1..25
06/06/44	14219260	Pte.	GEMMELL W	Benouville, 19
06/06/44	3782516	Cpl.	HARDING J P	Bayeux, X-A-4
06/06/44	5675290	L/Cpl.	HAYWARD S D	Benouville, 1
06/06/44	14210029	Pte.	HEK W	La Delivrande, IV-K-9
06/06/44	278546	Lieut.	HILL M R	Ranville, IIIA-N-7
06/06/44	14365155	Pte.	HOPGOOD W G A	Ranville Church, 17
06/06/44	5679931	Sgt.	HOUNSLOW E S	La Delivrande, IV-K-11
06/06/44	14403536	Pte.	HUGHES P	La Delivrande, III-K-10
06/06/44	5674214	Pte.	HUISH W L	Herouvillette, 17
06/06/44	4470319	Cfn	HUNT G W	Ranville, VIA-C-1..25
06/06/44	5674216	WOII(CSM)	HUTCHINGS J E P	Ranville, VIA-C-1..25
06/06/44	3253029	L/Cpl.	JACKSON F	Benouville, 13
06/06/44	5250009	Sgt.	JARVIS E W	La Delivrande, IV-K-3
06/06/44	14641426	Pte.	KEARNS J P	Ranville, IIA-O-2
06/06/44	5676360	Cpl.	KEMP A R	Ranville, VIA-C-1..25
06/06/44	3387613	Pte.	KERR D	La Delivrande, IV-K-2
06/06/44	6856578	Pte.	KINGSLEY R	La Delivrande, III-K-9
06/06/44	5675357	Cpl.	LEAMER G H	Ranville, VIA-C-1..25
06/06/44	5682680	Pte.	LEARY T C	Ranville Church, 46
06/06/44	14000090	Pte.	LOTHIAN A	Ranville, IA-C-8
06/06/44	3251685	Pte.	McARA J	Benouville, 5
06/06/44	14216814	Pte.	McGEE M J	Benouville, 12
06/06/44	14408742	Pte.	MILLS R H	Benouville, 16
06/06/44	3066484	L/Cpl.	MITCHELL R L	Ranville, VIA-C-1..25
06/06/44	1139320	Pte.	MORTIMORE J H	Ranville, IIIA-N-8
06/06/44	14381097	Pte.	PADLEY A	Ranville, IIIA-M-8
06/06/44	3252435	Cpl.	PANTON D	Benouville, 7
06/06/44	173033	RVD	PARRY G E M	Benouville, 21
06/06/44	5680060	Pte.	PHILLIPS L H	La Delivrande, IV-K-7
06/06/44	14327631	Pte.	RENNIE J R	Ranville, IX-C-34
06/06/44	3769861	Pte.	RILEY L H	Ranville, IIIA-D-9
06/06/44	5054158	Pte.	SAUNDERS A	Ranville, IIIA-O-8
06/06/44	14663800	Pte.	SCHWARTZ D R	M.I.A. Bayeux, P.18C.1
06/06/44	3251811	Pte.	SCOTT W	Ranville, VIA-C-1..25
06/06/44	14218485	Pte.	SHUTT D	Ranville, VIA-C-1..25
06/06/44	5434512	Pte.	SMITH F	Ranville, VA-G-2
06/06/44	4469397	Pte.	SMITH J W	La Delivrande, III-K-6
06/06/44	2026577	Pte.	STOBBART R W	Ranville, VIA-C-1..25
06/06/44	14407652	Pte.	STRINGER C K	La Delivrande, IV-K-11
06/06/44	14578482	Pte.	STUBBINS C C	La Delivrande, III-K-7
06/06/44	5498650	Pte.	SURMAN C J	La Delivrande, IV-K-8
06/06/44	5835746	Pte.	SUTTON C F	Ranville, IIIA-O-7
06/06/44	14430681	Pte.	THOMPSON S C	M.I.A. Bayeux, P.18C.2
06/06/44	14209955	Pte.	TRUEMAN M J	La Delivrande, IV-K-10
06/06/44	3244791	Pte.	TWIST R	Ranville, VIA-C-1..25
06/06/44	5676770	Cpl.	VAN RYNEN A	Ranville, VIA-C-1..25
06/06/44	4865382	Pte.	WALKER J	La Delivrande, III-K-8
06/06/44	5671819	Pte.	WEY L C	La Delivrande, IV-K-11
06/06/44	14301841	L/Cpl.	WHITTINGHAM P A	Benouville, 17
06/06/44	888352	Pte.	WHITTY A W	Benouville, 10
07/06/44	151578	Lieut.	BOWLER J A	M.I.A. Bayeux, P.18C.1
07/06/44	14401886	Pte.	TAPLIN H F	Ranville, IVA-K-12
07/06/44	5670432	Sgt.	VILLIS F R	Hermanville, 1-B-3
07/06/44	4469400	Pte.	VINCENT K I H	Hermanville, 1-B-12
09/06/44	5679154	Sgt.	BALDING L G	Ranville, IA-A-22
10/06/44	5679120	Pte.	BRANSON W	Ranville, IA-F-22
10/06/44	7620991	Pte.	GRATHAN A R	Ranville, IA-F-21
10/06/44	3191026	Pte.	JOHNSTON J B	Ranville, IA-G-18
10/06/44	14418286	Pte.	McCANN T K	Ranville, VA-F-3
10/06/44	5671017	Cpl.	METCALFE C E	Ranville, VA-F-4
10/06/44	5678261	Pte.	REED C W	Ranville, IA-E-21
10/06/44	5679544	Cpl.	SHELDON C H	M.I.A. Bayeux, P.18C.1
11/06/44	5339074	Pte.	ROBERTS G S	Ranville, VA-C-2
13/06/44	295223	Pte.	MUNDY E H	Walthamstow(St Mary), England, 2749
14/06/44	3244621	CQMS	SAVILL S C	Ranville, IIA-N-10
16/06/44	3976466	Pte.	DAVIES E G	Ranville, IA-K-8
16/06/44	14607558	Pte.	LEADBETTER R	Herouvillette, 10A
16/06/44	130115	Lieut.	TEMPLE W A B	Checkendon, England, 663
17/06/44	5250307	Pte.	JONES B	Mountain Ash,Wales, 8358
18/06/44	5674491	WOII(CSM)	DURBIN F E	M.I.A. Bayeux, P.18C.1
18/06/44	14540720	Pte.	FINDLAY J M	M.I.A. Bayeux, P.18C.1
18/06/44	3248506	Pte.	HAND G	M.I.A. Bayeux, P.18C.1
18/06/44	14000069	Pte.	SWAN J F M	Ranville, IVA-L-21
18/06/44	14204750	Pte.	TROTMAN H C	Ranville, IVA-D-21
19/06/44	3251502	Cpl.	McCULLOCH J A	La Delivrande, I-D-1
20/06/44	5679289	L/Cpl.	BLACKSHAW E E	Ranville, IVA-F-21
20/06/44	14406064	Pte.	PEGG W F	Ranville, IVA-E-21
20/06/44	5393694	Pte.	RAWLINGS E J C	Hermanville, 1-W-19
20/06/44	14000138	Pte.	WOODGATE D A	Ranville, IIIA-N-1
21/06/44	14203394	Pte.	COOLING H Q	La Delivrande, I-D-3
21/06/44	97003530	Pte.	LIDDELL D S	La Delivrande, V-F-7
23/06/44	14303815	Pte.	ROAST A E	Hermanville, 3-B-6
25/06/44	3254243	Pte.	BENNETT R D	Ranville, IVA-C-21
25/06/44	14436656	Pte.	GWILLIAM S S	Ranville, IIIA-K-9
29/06/44	278379	Lieut.	MacDONALD L G	Ranville, IIIA-B-9
07/07/44	228433	Lieut.	ATKINSON R N	Ranville, IIIA-L-1
07/07/44	4042722	Pte.	HODGES G F	Ranville, IIIA-K-1
07/07/44	14410593	Pte.	REID G	Ranville, IIIA-E-3
07/07/44	14275596	Pte.	TRAFFORD R H	Ranville, IIIA-M-1
10/07/44	6923991	L/Cpl.	COULTHARD A J	Ranville, IVA-H-21
10/07/44	53440704	L/Cpl.	PRICE S A	Ranville, IVA-K-21
10/07/44	5392732	Pte.	VARNEY A T	La Delivrande, III-H-9
10/07/44	6925114	Pte.	WILLIAMS D R B	Ranville, IVA-G-21

Date	Number	Rank	Name	Location
25/07/44	4035182	L/Cpl.	HINDLEY E	Hermanville, 2-G-4
10/08/44	2184150	Pte.	BURDEN A L	M.I.A. Bayeux, P.18C.1
10/08/44	14416229	Pte.	ELY P O W	M.I.A. Bayeux, P.18C.1
10/08/44	14421370	Pte.	WEBSTER J D	Ranville, IIA-B-18
19/08/44	14219568	Pte.	BALDWIN J	Ranville, IIA-D-14
19/08/44	5675267	Sgt.	FAY V C	Ranville, IIA-M-9
19/08/44	5436300	Sgt.	KEMPSTER F G	Ranville, IIA-D-13
20/08/44	6852353	Cpl.	WILSON W G A	Ranville, IIA-J-14
22/08/44	5439144	Cpl.	BALL F W	Ranville, IIIA-C-5
22/08/44	4033715	Pte.	DOWNES W E	Ranville, IIIA-B-5
22/08/44	14417638	L/Cpl.	THOMPSON B B	Ranville, IIIA-D-5
23/08/44	5387371	Sgt.	BLAKEWAY A V S	Ranville, IIIA-F-5
23/08/44	14412168	Pte.	O'BRIEN J R	Ranville, VA-Q-1
26/08/44	6020537	Cpl.	BUSHELL H R	Pont Audemer, C-28
26/08/44	4039307	Pte.	EVANS S H	Pont Audemer, A-27
26/08/44	14409029	Pte.	HOLDROYD G W	Ranville, VA-N-6
26/08/44	14514592	Pte.	KING M H	Pont Audemer, B-29

12th Parachute Bn

Date	Number	Rank	Name	Location
06/06/44	277469	Lieut.	AUSTIN A T W	M.I.A. Bayeux, P.18C.2
06/06/44	4392529	Pte.	BALDWIN G	M.I.A. Bayeux, P.18C.2
06/06/44	4387286	Sgt.	BELL F	Ranville, IIA-E-13
06/06/44	4394748	L/Cpl.	BERRY E W	Ranville, IIA-M-13
06/06/44	2567287	L/Sgt.	BLACK W J	Ranville, IIA-C-13
06/06/44	4279711	Cpl.	BRANDON S A	Ranville Church, 15
06/06/44	4693556	Pte.	BROADWELL C	Ranville, IVA-E-6
06/06/44	3321839	Cpl.	BURGESS E J	Herouvillette, 5
06/06/44	14385110	Pte.	CYSTER F N	Ranville Church, 35
06/06/44	4539727	Pte.	DOBSON W A	Ranville Church, 34
06/06/44	317547	Pte.	DRAPER P W	Ranville, IVA-L-5
06/06/44	14571341	L/Cpl.	HATELY R L	Ranville, IVA-P-5
06/06/44	6087896	Sgt.	HIGGINS S A	Herouvillette, 10
06/06/44	4621916	Pte.	HOWARD T	Herouvillette, 9
06/06/44	46227068	Pte.	HOWE R	Ranville, VA-H-3
06/06/44	1120624	Cpl.	JONES W	M.I.A. Bayeux, P.18C.2
06/06/44	14516037	Pte.	JOYCE D	Ranville Church, 32
06/06/44	14577989	Pte.	LOCKETT P J	Ranville, IIA-G-13
06/06/44	4347814	Pte.	LONSDALE T G	Ranville Church, 30
06/06/44	14382363	Sgt.	MASLIN R E	Ranville Church, 42
06/06/44	4343040	Sgt.	MILBURN F	Ranville, IIIA-H-5
06/06/44	14207546	Sgt.	NELSON G E	Herouvillette, 8
06/06/44	14583657	Sgt.	O'SULLIVAN D	Ranville Church, 33
06/06/44	4399320	Pte.	ROBSON R	Ranville, IA-D-21
06/06/44	14644483	Pte.	SKELLETT T A	Ranville Church, 28
06/06/44	6297727	Captain	TAYLOR R	Ranville, IVA-N-12
06/06/44	102005	Pte.	TURNBULL G	Ranville, VA-E-4
06/06/44	5621512	Pte.	VICARY H J	Ranville Church, 4
07/06/44	14554052	Pte.	BLACKBURNE E	M.I.A. Bayeux, P.18C.2
07/06/44	14417745	Pte.	DRAGE R T	Ranville Church, 40
07/06/44	4399270	Pte.	JOHNSON L	Ranville Church, 41
07/06/44	5127210	L/Cpl.	WILFORD P L	Ranville, IVA-H-8
09/06/44	949496	L/Cpl.	BEDALL W J	Ranville, IIIA-D-8
09/06/44	277634	Sgt.	BOWERMAN R G	Ranville, IIIA-D-5
09/06/44	7382424	Cpl.	CAIRNS D	Ranville, IIIA-D-4
09/06/44	14609669	Pte.	DERRY W A A	Ranville, IIA-E-5
09/06/44	10584940	Pte.	FRITH W	Ranville, IIA-G-15
09/06/44	6976155	Cpl.	HOLT L	Ranville, IIA-C-14
09/06/44	2981620	Cpl.	McGOWAN, S A	Ranville, IIIA-H-14
09/06/44	14216190	Cpl.	McKENNA S E	Ranville, IVA-P-8
09/06/44	102478	Pte.	PARR N	Ranville, IIIA-G-14
09/06/44	14416155	Pte.	PHILBURN H J	Ranville, IIA-B-22
09/06/44	176143	Pte.	POOLEY P H D	Ranville, IIIA-J-4
09/06/44		Captain	STEVENSON G H	
09/06/44	4755415	Pte.	TAYLOR H R	Ranville, IIIA-C-4
09/06/44	14427403	Cpl.	WALSH M K	Ranville, IIA-F-15
10/06/44	14580296	Pte.	WHITE A E	Ranville, IVA-D-4
10/06/44	14552227	Pte.	HULL D F	Ranville, IA-D-18
10/06/44	14217790	Pte.	MAYERS G H E	Ranville, IVA-N-5
10/06/44	14515843	Pte.	McKILLOP A	Ranville, IA-A-19
10/06/44	7905689	L/Cpl.	WINDER E	Ranville, IA-D-4
12/06/44	4446823	L/Sgt.	ARMSTRONG A	Ranville, IVA-D-11
12/06/44	5624359	Sgt.	BOWYER K J	Ranville, IA-F-18
12/06/44	4391532	L/Sgt.	CARTLIDGE H	Ranville, IVA-M-7
12/06/44	876958	Pte.	COLWELL W L	Ranville, IVA-F-18
12/06/44	14400841	Pte.	DUNN G	Ranville, IVA-F-11
12/06/44	14418285	Pte.	ELLIOT W L	Ranville, IVA-G-18
12/06/44	14000028	Pte.	FISHER E C	Ranville, IVA-O-17
12/06/44	4389954	Pte.	FRYER F W	Ranville, IVA-L-17
12/06/44	14528321	Pte.	GORDON R A	Ranville, IVA-B-18
12/06/44	4754197	L/Cpl.	GRAKAUSKAS J	Ranville, IVA-H-18
12/06/44	14410206	Pte.	HACKETT T H	Ranville, IVA-C-18
12/06/44	4394837	Sgt.	HARCOURT C W	Ranville, IVA-G-16
12/06/44	52653	Lt-Col.	JOHNSON A P	Ranville, IVA-C-10
12/06/44	4747561	Sgt.	KIRBY A W	Ranville, IVA-K-18
12/06/44	4387741	WOII(CSM)	MARWOOD J T	Ranville, IVA-H-11
12/06/44	5511915	Pte.	MASTERS C J B	Breville
12/06/44	14416049	Pte.	PRITCHETT A	Ranville, IVA-F-12
12/06/44	153174	Major	ROGERS H D	Ranville, IVA-J-17
12/06/44	1702085	Pte.	SPEAKMAN W	Ranville, IVA-N-6
12/06/44	14569146	Pte.	STONES W	Ranville, IA-B-8
12/06/44	14533126	Pte.	SUTTON R A	Ranville, IVA-K-7
12/06/44	6471659	L/Sgt.	TANNER J W	Ranville, IVA-J-11
12/06/44	160802	Pte.	THOMAS I	Ranville, IVA-K-11
12/06/44	3187693	Cpl.	THOMSON R	Ranville, IVA-E-11
12/06/44	2992681	Pte.	TOWERS J A	Ranville, IVA-N-17
12/06/44	14311628	Pte.	TRAYLEN F L	Ranville, IVA-G-11
12/06/44	1148194	Pte.	WHITE A R	Ranville, IVA-C-12
12/06/44	3054964	Sgt.	WILLIAMS G	Ranville, IA-H-1
13/06/44	11408291	Pte.	AUTY F	M.I.A. Bayeux, P.18C.2
13/06/44	287481	Lieut.	CAMPBELL J R D	Hermanville, 1-L-4
13/06/44	11411756	Pte.	SAUQUILLO L	Hermanville, 1-N-19
14/06/44	10579584	Pte.	HEYWOOD E F	Southampton (Hollybrook), England, M12-55
16/06/44	14612149	Pte.	WALKER K G	Ranville, IIA-D-12
17/06/44	14598287	Pte.	KIPLING H	Ranville, IIA-K-10
04/07/44	1448629	Sgt.	STEER W H E	Ranville, IIIA-D-7
07/07/44	14580317	Cpl.	FRIEDLANDER G E	Ranville, IIIA-F-3
08/07/44	4450333	Pte.	THOMPSON W J	Ranville, IIIA-B-3
10/07/44	14363980	Pte.	ALLAN W	Ranville, IIIA-F-1
10/07/44	253486	Captain	BLISS C L	Ranville, IA-B-1
10/07/44	14402404	L/Cpl.	BOYD W	Ranville, IIIA-E-1
10/07/44	14424514	Pte.	BULL J W	Ranville, IVA-E-18
10/07/44	14350096	Pte.	GILLON E	Ranville, IIIA-G-1
10/07/44	3602031	Sgt.	RICHARDSON T G	Ranville, IIIA-H-1
19/08/44	4395027	Pte.	BENNETT G G	Putot En Auge, A-5
19/08/44	6984191	Pte.	McCOMBE R H	Putot En Auge, C-1
19/08/44	5189351	Pte.	WINFIELD F H	Putot En Auge, A-6
19/08/44	4394965	S/Sgt.	WISE W H	Putot En Auge, A-4
20/08/44	4397622	Sgt.	WALKER E	Saint Desir, Lisieux, V-A-13
22/08/44	14415229	Pte.	ADAM-ACTON M	Ranville, VIA-B-14
22/08/44	288458	Lieut.	BERCOT J M	Ranville, VIA-B-16
22/08/44	3659654	Cpl.	CAMPBELL J H	Ranville, VA-M-6
22/08/44	3907450	L/Sgt.	DAVIES F C	Ranville, VIA-B-19
22/08/44	295963	Pte.	EVANS P T	Ranville, VA-N-2
22/08/44	3446130	Pte.	FRANCE H	Ranville, IIIA-E-5
22/08/44	5127890	Pte.	GILBERT W J	Ranville, VA-P-8

Date	Number	Name	Rank	Location
22/08/44	14513830	HAYES J J	L/Cpl.	Ranville, VIA-B-5
22/08/44	14506408	LANE H C	Pte.	Ranville, VA-N-4
22/08/44	6011198	LATHAM A	Pte.	Ranville, VA-M-1
22/08/44	2938479	McINNES W	Pte.	Ranville, VA-M-5
22/08/44	33115616	McKINLAY J	Sgt.	Ranville, VIA-B-1
22/08/44	4206287	McLEAN J	Pte.	Ranville, VA-N-5
22/08/44	14424353	RABBITTS A T	Pte.	Ranville, VA-P-8
22/08/44	14670703	WATTS K B	Pte.	Ranville, VIA-B-20
22/08/44	5253578	WILSON F E	Pte.	Ranville, VIA-B-3
01/12/44	822275	GILLARD L R	L/Cpl.	Wesbourne, England, 2-639

13th Parachute Bn

Date	Number	Name	Rank	Location
06/06/44	3656824	ALDRED J	Pte.	Saint Vaast En Auge, 12
06/06/44	133790	DAISLEY S	Captain	Saint Vaast En Auge, 10
06/06/44	5569086	DAY J	L/Sgt.	M.I.A. Bayeux, P.18C.1
06/06/44	14627663	FARMER R K	Pte.	M.I.A. Bayeux, P.18C.1
06/06/44	14202779	HALLAS J	Cpl.	M.I.A. Bayeux, P.18C.1
06/06/44	14422876	HARGREAVES A	Pte.	Ranville, IIIA-J-8
06/06/44	4696371	JOHNSON T H	Pte.	Ranville, IIA-L-10
06/06/44	14402094	MACKENZIE D J	Pte.	M.I.A. Bayeux, P.18C.1
06/06/44	249862	MIDDLETON G R	Pte.	M.I.A. Bayeux, P.18C.1
06/06/44	3866121	PIDDLESDEN R R	Cpl.	M.I.A. Bayeux, P.18C.1
06/06/44	3663288	POTTER E E	Pte.	Ranville, IIA-L-6
06/06/44	3961683	SHEPHERD C R	Pte.	M.I.A. Bayeux, P.18C.1
06/06/44	3663700	SUCKLEY H L	Pte.	M.I.A. Bayeux, P.18C.2
06/06/44	14654376	WAIN R S	Pte.	M.I.A. Bayeux, P.18C.2
07/06/44	14520557	DARBY C V	Pte.	Ranville, IIA-J-10
07/06/44	3651896	PARKER J W	Cpl.	Ranville Church, 24
08/06/44	117615	ELLISON F A N	Captain	Ranville, IA-E-12
08/06/44	154318	HARBET S	Pte.	Ranville, IA-H-18
09/06/44	408550	CLOUSTON W	Pte.	Ranville, IA-J-22
09/06/44	3782725	SWINDELL R E	Pte.	Ranville, IIA-K-22
10/06/44	4803038	BANKS J M	Sgt.	M.I.A. Bayeux, P.18C.1
10/06/44	4449027	BROWN A	L/Cpl.	Ranville, IA-E-8
10/06/44	14670118	BULL K F	Pte.	Ranville, IA-H-12
10/06/44	3663586	CLYNE F A N	Pte.	Ranville, IA-B-21
10/06/44	911708	COLLIER W C	Sgt.	Ranville, IIA-E-12
10/06/44	14417320	ORRELL A	Pte.	Ranville, IA-G-12
12/06/44	2047238	PRINCE W	Pte.	Hermanville, 1-K-8
12/06/44	3394124	WHITEHEAD F	Pte.	Ranville, IA-K-6
14/06/44	164968	COX A E	Pte.	Hermanville, 1-N-3
14/06/44	4387469	RAINE J T	Sgt.	Hermanville, 1-Q-8
16/06/44	7622507	GREEN H A	Cpl.	Ranville, IIA-K-11
16/06/44	3654790	MELBOURNE A	Pte.	Ranville, IIA-C-11
19/06/44	13117459	DENBY-DREYFUS P C	Pte.	Ranville, IVA-K-19
19/06/44	987069	MUIR J	Sgt.	Ranville, IIA-G-3
19/06/44	4928216	STANYON R H	Sgt.	Ranville, IVA-G-19
23/06/44	1091335	OSBOURNE S	L/Cpl.	Ranville, IA-D-1
25/06/44	4612433	LIGHTFOOT V A	Pte.	Ranville, IIA-B-1
25/06/44	5619755	PREW E R G	Pte.	Ranville, IIA-E-1
25/06/44	7952781	SMITH C	L/Cpl.	Ranville, IIA-C-2
28/06/44	4922337	WARE S L	Pte.	La Delivrande, V-A-3
28/06/44	14631805	BARKER L	Pte.	Biscot, England, E-5-5
-05/07/44	14210359	RICHARDS R D	Pte.	Ranville, IIIA-B-7
07/07/44	3658191	ARMITAGE J N	Pte.	Ranville, III-E-2
10/07/44	3714884	DIXON G H	Sgt.	Hermanville, 2-C-15
10/07/44	14438786	LORD D A	Pte.	Ranville, IVA-M-21
12/07/44	14660191	BRITLAND H F	Pte.	Ryes, Bazenville, V-G-3
12/07/44	109882	O'BRIEN-HITCHING G H	Lieut.	M.I.A. Bayeux, P.18C.1
12/07/44	14658563	SMITH G	Pte.	Ranville, IVA-L-19
15/07/44	3663790	DONNELY T J	L/Sgt.	Ranville, IVA-B-15
18/07/44	913145	LYSAGHT J J	Cpl.	Ranville, IVA-J-9
23/07/44	14434704	JOHNS R E	Pte.	Ranville, IVA-E-1
07/08/44	3655805	MEARS T	Pte.	Ranville, VIA-B-22
08/08/44	5185579	CRATES J E	Pte.	Ranville, IA-L-6
19/08/44	5044455	ASHFORD H	L/Cpl.	Putot En Auge, C-9
19/08/44	4038610	ATTRIDGE G A	Pte.	Putot En Auge, C-7
19/08/44	14289691	BARTON E D	Cpl.	Putot En Auge, C-10
19/08/44	242691	BIBBY E M	Lieut.	M.I.A. Bayeux, P.18C.1
19/08/44	6472489	BOTT F	Cpl.	Putot En Auge, A-3
19/08/44	4920167	BRASSINGTON R	Cpl.	Putot En Auge, C-12
19/08/44	4919420	CRUTCHLEY T H	Pte.	Putot En Auge, B-6
19/08/44	6985293	DUGGAN F	Pte.	Putot En Auge, C-3
19/08/44	978870	FUNNELL E W	Pte.	Putot En Auge, B-5
19/08/44	3606921	GLOVER C E	Pte.	Putot En Auge, B-1
19/08/44	6723301	HELLER A V	Pte.	Putot En Auge, C-14
19/08/44	14323799	HEWITT W G	Cpl.	Ranville, IIA-J-9
19/08/44	14314694	HUNTER W A	Pte.	Putot En Auge, C-4
19/08/44	14668927	JENKINSON S	Pte.	Putot En Auge, A-2
19/08/44	5618171	KNOWLES C W	L/Cpl.	Putot En Auge, B-4
19/08/44	3393994	LYONS A	Cpl.	Putot En Auge, C-15
19/08/44	3387610	McCRUDDEN W P	Pte.	Ranville, VA-P-2
19/08/44	3663313	McNALLY W	Pte.	Putot En Auge, C-13
19/08/44	7021780	MOLLOY T W	Pte.	Putot En Auge, B-3
19/08/44	2933690	MORRIS R	Pte.	Putot En Auge, C-6
19/08/44	4547111	PHILLIPS J	L/Cpl.	Putot En Auge, C-8
19/08/44	3769046	PROWSE A	Pte.	Putot En Auge, C-16
19/08/44	14414299	PYATT A W	Pte.	Putot En Auge, B-7
19/08/44	1462344	RENYARD R G	Pte.	Putot En Auge, C-11
19/08/44	6103112	RODWELL B V	Pte.	Putot En Auge, C-2
19/08/44	14370768	RUSDALE C R	Pte.	Putot En Auge, A-1
19/08/44	5735323	SANDS H	Pte.	Putot En Auge, B-2
19/08/44	3394129	SEDDON H	Pte.	Ranville, IIA-H-9
19/08/44	3606770	TONGUE H	Pte.	Putot En Auge, C-17
21/08/44	14337733	FREUDE W M	L/Cpl.	Ranville, VIA-B-15
22/08/44	321403	BEST J P	Pte.	Ranville, VA-B-6
22/08/44	14552474	GREGORY A F	Pte.	Ranville, VIA-B-10
22/08/44	3529525	KELLY G	Sgt.	Ranville, VIA-B-11
22/08/44	5825801	TURNER H F	Pte.	Ranville, VIA-B9
23/08/44	11263620	BINNS F	Pte.	Ranville, VIA-B-8
23/08/44	6103133	ECKERT C A J	Cpl.	Ranville, VIA-B-13
23/08/44	14202907	HINCHCLIFFE G	Pte.	Pont L'Eveque, 1
23/08/44	3649847	HUGHES E	Sgt.	Ranville, VIA-B-2
23/08/44	14209510	LOWTHER J	L/Cpl.	Ranville, VA-P-3
23/08/44	4388377	McKIRDY D	Sgt.	Ranville, VA-P-4
23/08/44	3656200	MEDLICOTT T W	L/Cpl.	Ranville, VA-P-4
23/08/44	1727073	MISSING J E S	Pte.	Ranville, VIA-B-7
26/08/44	14658854	WOOLHOUSE W T	Pte.	Saint Desir, Lisieux, III-D-4
28/08/44	58149	TARRANT R M	Major	La Delivrande, VI-B-10

HQ 5th PARACHUTE BRIGADE DEFENCE PLATOON AAC

Date	Number	Name	Rank	Location
23/08/44	3657106	WHITEHEAD R		Bayeux, II-H-24

6th AIR LANDING BRIGADE AAC
12th Bn The Devonshire Regiment

Date	Number	Name	Rank	Location
06/06/44	5615933	DUNPHY J J	CQMS	M.I.A. Bayeux, P.13C.2
06/06/44	5627686	NICHOLLS G D	Pte.	Sainte Marie, Le Havre, 67-O-16
06/06/44	5626689	PALMER W J	Pte.	Sainte Marie, Le Havre, 67-H-10
07/06/44	5621503	BICKLE G H	Pte.	Ranville Church, 27
07/06/44	5574643	CHUBB L H	L/Cpl.	Ranville Church, 25
08/06/44	5630633	FARLEY W J	Pte.	Ranville Church, 26
08/06/44	5773112	MORRISON J M	Pte.	Banneville La Campagne, XII-B-26
09/06/44	5630889	LEIGH C W	Pte.	Ranville, IVA-C-5
09/06/44	14418769	SMITH R B	Pte.	Ranville, IVA-K-5
10/06/44	5617609	CORBETT P J	Pte.	Ranville, IVA-J-15
10/06/44	14398179	GRIFFIN C W	Pte.	Ranville, IVA-D-5

[Regiment roll continued from previous page]

Service No.	Date	Rank	Name	Burial Location
5627968	10/06/44	Pte.	KOSTER J R	Ranville, IVA-H-5
5627125	10/06/44	Pte.	LAVENDER A G	Ranville, IVA-B-5
285352	11/06/44	Lieut.	GERMAIN A E	Ranville, IVA-E-5
5627538	11/06/44	Pte.	SALISBURY J	Ranville, IVA-M-5
5617603	11/06/44	Cpl.	SAYER D C	Ranville, IA-J-6
14570325	12/06/44	L/Cpl.	BAILEY F B	Ranville, IVA-B-16
50997	12/06/44	Major	BAMPFYLDE J A F W	Ranville, IVA-O-8
14584454	12/06/44	Pte.	BARRATT L A	Ranville, IVA-J-18
14579807	12/06/44	Pte.	FRY I L	Ranville, IVA-E-19
14579809	12/06/44	Pte.	GILMOUR R I	Ranville, IVA-N-18
14579817	12/06/44	Pte.	HOOPER L J	Ranville, IVA-J-6
14579821	12/06/44	Pte.	HYNAM F B	Ranville, IVA-H-6
184467	12/06/44	Lieut.	KITTOW J B E	Ranville, IA-G-6
14439727	12/06/44	Pte.	MINTER M D	Ranville, IVA-M-18
14618264	12/06/44	Pte.	MULLINS E C	Ranville, IVA-C-11
5616822	12/06/44	L/Sgt.	TAYLOR C A	Ranville, IVA-K-16
5627900	12/06/44	Sgt.	WALTERS H J	Ranville, IVA-D-18
5628427	12/06/44	Pte.	RUSSELL R A	Ranville, IA-J-2
14378537	13/06/44	Pte.	BENNING L A	Ranville, IA-M-9
5626557	16/06/44	Pte.	CLARKE A	Ranville, IA-L-9
14622549	16/06/44	Pte.	FOWLER W H	Ranville, IA-K-9
14391874	16/06/44	Pte.	PARROT G H A	La Delivrande, I-A-2
5627509	16/06/44	Pte.	VIANT J	Ranville, IA-L-5
5624950	21/06/44	Pte.	JEANPIERRE R J	Streatham Park, England, 24-33802
6471659	22/06/44	Pte.	TANNER A E	Ranville, IVA-J-11
5620654	23/06/44	Pte.	THORNE R C	Ranville, IIIA-M-9
14579828	28/06/44	Cpl.	JONES G A	La Delivrande, I-F-1A
14603957	02/07/44	Cpl.	HARRIS F J W	Ranville, VA-K-6
300339	02/07/44	Lieut.	LEWIS D E	Ranville, VA-K-5
14418684	03/07/44	L/Cpl.	GREENSLADE R R	Ranville, IIIA-E-7
14334221	05/07/44	Pte.	PUTTICK R H	Ranville, IA-G-20
5628387	11/07/44	L/Sgt.	COBDEN A F	Ranville, IVA-F-19
14610177	03/08/44	Pte.	BERRY E J	Ranville, IA-C-10
14610195	03/08/44	L/Cpl.	CHIVERS M W H	Ranville, IA-D-10
14579838	03/08/44	Pte.	LEACH W C	Ranville, IA-E-10
5626550	06/08/44	Pte.	YEOMAN T H	Ranville, IA-B-10
277585	08/08/44	Lieut.	GRANGE D C I	Ranville, IA-A-6
249194	13/08/44	Lieut.	TUCKER R L	Ranville, IVA-O-13
2568569	17/08/44	Pte.	WEIGHT M F W	Coryton (St Andrew), England
14622953	17/08/44	L/Cpl.	ARMES A	Ranville, IA-B-4
5628395	18/08/44	Cpl.	FOSTER K S	La Delivrande, V-D-6
5627650	19/08/44	Pte.	HAMMOND J A	Ranville, IIA-H-14
5627201	19/08/44	Pte.	PARSONS R H	Ranville, IIA-J-4
5682448	20/08/44	Pte.	LOCKETT I H	Bayeux, II-H-3
14603393	21/08/44	Pte.	TOVEY F S	Ranville, IIA-J-13
5628471	21/08/44	Cpl.	WOODCOCK E A S	Saint Desir, Lisieux, III-A-10
5620311	24/08/44	Pte.	DAVIES L E	Tourgeville, 4-G-1
5630596	24/08/44	Pte.	WEBB V L	Honfleur (St Leonard), 3-14-9
14618205	25/08/44	Pte.	AMIS K A	Honfleur (St Leonard), 3-14-10
5735137	25/08/44	L/Cpl.	MONTAGUE T H	Honfleur (St Leonard), 3-14-11
5624058	25/08/44	Cpl.	SMITH I	Fatouville Grestain
14625002	26/08/44	Pte.	PLUMRIDGE C R	Saint Desir, Lisieux, V-A-1
14563033	26/08/44	Cpl.	RUSSELL F A	Fatouville Grestain
5735366	28/08/44	Cpl.	BOYCOTT J H	
5620801	29/08/44	Pte.	LOCKYER E L	

2nd Bn The Oxfordshire & Buckinghamshire Light Infantry

Service No.	Date	Rank	Name	Burial Location
271185	05/06/44	Lieut.	DEACON T	Plymouth, England, P.2
237676	06/06/44	Lieut.	BROTHERIDGE H D	Ranville Church, 43
5387231	06/06/44	Cpl.	KNOX H D	Benouville, 9
5380843	06/06/44	Pte.	MILTON C	Ranville, IA-C-3
5383457	07/06/44	Sgt.	BARWICK C C	Herouvillette, 22
5384161	07/06/44	Pte.	BOWDEN P W	Ranville, IIIA-N-2
5380172	07/06/44	Pte.	ECKLE F J	Bayeux, X-K-2
6031906	07/06/44	Pte.	EVERETT E J	Ranville, IA-J-13
3449663	07/06/44	L/Cpl.	GREENHALGH F	La Delivrande, V-C-4
5381332	07/06/44	Pte.	HEDGES W P	Perriers En Auge
5569975	07/06/44	Pte.	HIGGINS L C	Bayeux, X-L-1
5784313	07/06/44	Pte.	KELLY E D	Ranville, IA-A-3
6014906	07/06/44	Pte.	MORROW T	Ranville, IA-A-2
5388641	07/06/44	Pte.	NEWELL E G	Herouvillette, 20
5835641	07/06/44	L/Cpl.	PARK J	Ranville, IA-A-15
5777847	07/06/44	Pte.	REEVE G E	Ranville, IA-A-13
5393423	07/06/44	Pte.	ROBERTS C L	Ranville, IA-C-2
6408421	07/06/44	Pte.	SEFTON F J D	Ranville, IIIA-K-8
5385699	07/06/44	L/Sgt.	SUMMERSBY A A L	Ranville, IIIA-O-1
5385976	07/06/44	Pte.	WHITE A D	Bayeux, X-K-22
5682457	07/06/44	Pte.	WILKINS W S	Escoville
6030351	07/06/44	Pte.	WILKS V	Herouvillette, 19
5682314	07/06/44	Pte.	WILLCOCKS C E	Ranville, IIA-N-1
164417	08/06/44	Lieut.	CHICKEN G C	Ranville, IA-H-4
5392120	08/06/44	Cpl.	JOHNSON K F	Ranville, IA-H-22
5672399	09/06/44	L/Cpl.	FROST S	Herouvillette, 14
14406961	09/06/44	Pte.	HIGGINS C H	Ranville, IA-J-8
14301159	09/06/44	L/Cpl.	MINNS F L	Herouvillette, 11
14208129	09/06/44	Pte.	SILVESTER W J	Herouvillette, 15
5671655	09/06/44	Pte.	STARR J F	Herouvillette, 13
5385887	09/06/44	Pte.	SYMONDS W C R	Hermanville, 1-F-6
5388112	10/06/44	WOII(CSM)	WILLIAMS E E	Forest Row, England, 1464
5388025	10/06/44	Pte.	BROOKS B	Hermanville, 1-H-8
5391618	10/06/44	Pte.	COTTLE D T	Ranville, IA-F-12
74981	10/06/44	Captain	MARRIOTT J	Herouvillette, 16
5382177	10/06/44	Pte.	MILLS D N	Herouvillette, 18
5381191	11/06/44	L/Sgt.	LANGHOR J	Ranville, IA-J-12
5441727	13/06/44	Pte.	TRESIDDER W E P	Ranville, IA-D-19
214607	13/06/44	Lieut.	VAN KLAVEREN G V	Ranville, IA-D-20
5385898	13/06/44	Pte.	WALKER F W	Ranville, I-F-19
5385916	13/06/44	Cpl.	WREN L M	Ranville, IA-E-19
5385921	13/06/44	L/Cpl.	YOUNG H G	Ranville, IA-K-20
5381155	14/06/44	Pte.	CANTWELL H E	Ranville, IA-G-19
5389247	14/06/44	Lieut.	DREW A C	Ranville, VA-N-1
278361	14/06/44	Pte.	PANKHURST J A	Ranville, IA-J-21
5682894	15/06/44	Pte.	ROBERTS L H G	Ranville, IA-K-21
5392827	15/06/44	Pte.	WILRYCX D A	Ranville, IA-K-19
5341014	16/06/44	Pte.	BLAIR R G	Ranville, IA-B-15
5377988	16/06/44	WOII(CSM)	FLEXEN R G	Ranville, IA-C-15
5955181	16/06/44	Captain	MORLEY G	Northwood, England, G-115
109536	19/06/44	WOII(CSM)	BRABNER M J	Ranville, IA-F-15
5381345	19/06/44	Major	CREW J W	M.I.A. Bayeux, P.16C.1
5574092	19/06/44	Lt(QM)	DANIELLS R C	Ranville, IA-L-15
75263	19/06/44	Cpl.	FAVELL E V M	Ranville, IA-D-15
205030	19/06/44	L/Cpl.	JAMES J	M.I.A. Bayeux, P.16C.1
5388004	19/06/44	Pte.	PONTIN D A	Ranville, IA-E-15
5388477	20/06/44	Cpl.	FULLER C H	Ranville, IIA-F-2
5391705	20/06/44	Pte.	PARSONS W C	Herouvillette, 23
5379209	25/06/44	Cpl.	GEORGE E T	Herouvillette, 24
5388986	25/06/44	Pte.	NICHOLLS J D	Herouvillette, 25
5438704	25/06/44	Cpl.	PHILLIPS C	Herouvillette, 26
5380669	25/06/44	Pte.	REYNOLDS W	Ranville, IIA-K-2
5382901	27/06/44	Cpl.	LANGBRIDGE E H	
6032087	30/06/44	Pte.	PEER T G	Manor Park, England, 77-505
5729642	02/07/44	L/Sgt.	EARL C E	Ranville, IIIA-K-7
5382145	04/07/44	Pte.	RUSSELL P J N	Ranville, IVA-M-11
5393683	05/07/44	Pte.	GILMORE T A	M.I.A. Bayeux, P.16C.1
5682623	15/07/44	Pte.	PEPPERALL D	Ranville, IVA-E-15
5382332	19/07/44	Lieut.	SMYTH P B	Ranville, IVA-L-7
189415	23/07/44	Lieut.	REVNELL G I	M.I.A. Bayeux, P.16C.1
5389343	25/07/44	Pte.	YOUNG K E	Oxford(Rose Hill), England, G-3-128
14657447	29/07/44	Pte.	WHITE H W	Deptford(Brockley), England, J-123
5886602	07/08/44	Pte.	DRAGE C E	Wellingborough, England, 1105
5344307	10/08/44	Pte.	CLARIDGE R A	Ranville, IA-M-10
5388147	13/08/44	Cpl.	READER C A	Banneville La Campagne, VIII-E-1
5390850	17/08/44	Pte.	DREW J R A	Ranville, IA-C-4
5393348	22/08/44	Pte.	CLIFFE W J	Vauville
5570241	22/08/44	Pte.	STACEY J	Tourgeville, 4-G-2
5439868	25/08/44	Pte.	BANNATYNE G	Beuzeville, 3

Date	Number	Rank	Name	Location
26/08/44	184575	Lieut.	BULFORD P G	Beuzeville, 2
27/08/44	5381460	Pte.	CLAPTON M C	Fatouville Grestain
07/12/44	5392995	Pte.	REEVES J W C	High Wycombe, England, J-L439

1st Bn The Royal Ulster Rifles

Date	Number	Rank	Name	Location
06/06/44	14663448	Rfn.	WOODBURN J	M.I.A. Bayeux, P.17C.3
07/06/44	7020645	L/Cpl.	BARRY P E	Ranville, IA-A-7
07/06/44	155053	Lieut.	BOUSTEAD J D A	Ranville, IVA-L-8
07/06/44	7010278	Sgt.	COYLE J	Ranville, IVA-N-8
07/06/44	7020032	Rfn.	GLASS S	Ranville, IA-A-1
07/06/44	7045689	Rfn.	GODSAVE P A	Ranville Church, 31
07/06/44	14409065	Rfn.	HALVEY J P	Bayeux, X-M-7
07/06/44	6409930	Rfn.	HANKEY T	Ranville, IIA-N-6
07/06/44	7013019	Cpl.	JEFFERSON N	Ranville, IIA-C-5
07/06/44	7022700	Rfn.	JOHNS W H	Ranville, IA-L-17
07/06/44	14640325	Rfn.	LOWE L	M.I.A. Bayeux, P.17C.3
07/06/44	7047994	Rfn.	MAGUIRE P	Bayeux, X-M-4
07/06/44	7015140	Cpl.	McCAYNA G	Ranville, IA-J-17
07/06/44	6983599	Rfn.	McFARLAND N	Bayeux, X-M-2
07/06/44	6985348	Rfn.	McQUILLAN R H J	Ranville, III-B-25
07/06/44	6104465	Rfn.	MERRELL W R	Ranville, IA-L-12
07/06/44	14216689	L/Cpl.	MOORE W J	Bayeux, X-M-6
07/06/44	176458	Captain	MORGAN R N	Ranville, IA-L-7
07/06/44	6985185	Rfn.	NELSON J H	M.I.A. Bayeux, P.17C.3
07/06/44	5125850	L/Cpl.	O'BRIEN C	Bayeux, X-M-5
07/06/44	6409738	L/Cpl.	O'CONNOR P J	Ranville, IVA-O-8
07/06/44	7012565	Rfn.	OLIVER J C	Ranville, IA-K-7
07/06/44	7047510	Rfn.	O'REILLY M	Ranville, IVA-J-8
07/06/44	7012816	Rfn.	REILLY J J V	Bayeux, X-M-3
07/06/44	14591203	Rfn.	SHAKESPEARE A	M.I.A. Bayeux, P.17C.3
07/06/44	7019933	Rfn.	STEVENSON R J	Ranville, IA-M-7
07/06/44	14672347	Rfn.	TESTRO L G	Ranville, IIA-D-3
07/06/44	7044822	Rfn.	TURNER W	Ranville, IVA-F-20
07/06/44	4927999	L/Cpl.	WINFIELD W	Ranville Church, 5
07/06/44	4462353	L/Sgt.	WRAY T	Ranville, IVA-E-2
08/06/44	7019670	L/Cpl.	CHARLES A	Ranville, IVA-G-2
08/06/44	6985178	Rfn.	GREER H	Ranville, IVA-D-2
08/06/44	7019652	Rfn.	MULLINS P J	Ranville, IVA-H-2
08/06/44	7016562	Cpl.	PAYNE E D	Ranville, IVA-K-8
08/06/44	7045517	Rfn.	RAYNHAM S R	Ranville, IVA-F-20
09/06/44	7021234	Rfn.	STARR A L	Ranville, IA-D-3
09/06/44	7012990	Rfn.	McILROY J	Ranville, IIA-H-15
09/06/44	14412609	Rfn.	MEARNS H	M.I.A. Bayeux, P.17C.3
09/06/44	7020918	Rfn.	PROSSER R H J	Ranville, V-B-23
10/06/44	7017941	Rfn.	WILLIS N	Belfast City, Northern Ireland, D1-332
10/06/44	7011223	Cpl.	GREER J	Hermanville, 3-B-3
11/06/44	3386927	Rfn.	STOGDALE J	Ranville, IIIA-F-4
12/06/44	14416538	Rfn.	MAGILL N M	Ranville, IA-K-1
13/06/44	6920834	L/Cpl.	SAWER A C J	Ranville, IIIA-L-4
13/06/44	7013649	Rfn.	CHAMBERS T	Hermanville, 1-L-1
13/06/44	14914912	Rfn.	COUSINS C J H	Ranville, IIIA-B-4
13/06/44	7046474	Cpl.	HEGAN W J	Ranville, IIIA-M-4
14/06/44	7013745	Rfn.	McCARTHY T	Ranville, IIIA-E-4
16/06/44	7022592	Rfn.	TURRELL H G	Ranville, IIIA-G-17
16/06/44	7019461	L/Cpl.	CRAWFORD W	Ranville, IVA-D-17
19/06/44	7017133	Lieut.	GUALDI R	Ranville, IVA-F-17
19/06/44	90695	Rfn.	QUINN R	Ranville, VA-Q-2
19/06/44	7018189	Rfn.	JOHNSTON W	Ranville, IVA-E-17
19/06/44	7014137	Rfn.	KEOGH P F B	Ranville, VA-Q-6
19/06/44	7014413	Cpl.	McGUIRE N	Ranville, VA-Q-3
20/06/44	7019287	Rfn.	O'CONNOR T	Ranville, IVA-H-17
23/06/44	7017332	Cpl.	RILEY R	Cambes en Plaine, G-18
25/06/44	7013455	Rfn.	SMITH W H	Hermanville, 1-E-21
06/07/44	7019824	Cpl.	PARROT T A	M.I.A. Bayeux, P.17C.3
07/07/44	105616	Lieut.	ARCHDALE M M L	La Delivrande, VIII-K-4
09/07/44	14411473	Cpl.	O'FLANAGAN P	Hermanville, 2-A-3
10/07/44	7012285	Cpl.	DEMPSTER E D	Ranville, IIIA-J-1
10/07/44	7046106	Rfn.	McBURNEY W A	Ranville, IVA-B-19
10/07/44	7019887	Rfn.	BLYTHE J	Ranville, IVA-B-21
10/07/44	235669	Lieut.	CRANSTON A S	La Delivrande, VI-F-5
12/07/44	7018906	Rfn.	GRAHAM T G	La Delivrande, IV-B-4
13/07/44	5681989	Rfn.	EDMONDS G	Ryes, Bazenville, IV-J-5
18/07/44	7012388	Lieut.	MOFFETT J C	Ranville, IVA-B-13
06/08/44	203952	Rfn.	MAGINNIS G A	La Delivrande, IV-B-10
17/08/44	14403337	Rfn.	DILLON E C	Ranville, IIA-J-2
18/08/44	7017020	Rfn.	TOPPING S	Ranville, IIA-G-14
18/08/44	14685407	Pte.	JARMAIN R E	La Delivrande, I-J-6
20/08/44	7370624	Rfn.	TAYLOR D	La Delivrande, I-C-6
22/08/44	4207893	Major	WALKER G J	Tourgeville, 4-G-4
23/08/44	66181	Rfn.	JOHNSTON E F	Tourgeville, 4-G-4
23/08/44	14216134	Cpl.	SCANLON B J	Tourgeville, 4-G-5
24/08/44	7012844	Rfn.	SOUTHAM E	Tourgeville, 7-G-5
25/08/44	6984231	Rfn.	FEENEY C	Trouville, 23-V-18
11/09/44	14411392	Rfn.	SMYTH J T	Bayeux, III-L-2
13/09/44	7012767	Lieut.	McCONNELL C	Oscott College, England, A-306
04/10/44	258718	Lieut.	EDMONDS D P	Southgate, England, HD-1214
	105619		MacFADDEN J T N	Hanover, Germany, 15-F-6

The cross erected to the Airborne troops on Ranville cemetery. The Glider-chains are hooked to compressed air bottle into gliders. (Memorial Pegasus.)